MANAGING THE EXTERNAL ENVIRONMENT

The Open Business School

The Open Business School offers a three-tier ladder of opportunity for managers at different stages of their careers: the Professional Certificate in Management; the Professional Diploma in Management; and the MBA. If you would like to receive information on these open learning programmes, please write to the Open Business School, The Open University, Milton Keynes MK7 6AA, England.

This volume is a Course Reader for the Open University Course B885, *The Challenge of the External Environment*.

MANAGING THE EXTERNAL ENVIRONMENT

A Strategic Perspective

edited by

David Mercer

with

Rod Barratt
Gordon Burt
Harold Carter
Norman Fox
Edith Thorne
Alan Warde

The Open University

Published in association
with The Open University

SAGE Publications
London • Newbury Park • New Delhi

SAGE Publications Ltd
6 Bonhill Street
London EC2A 4PU

SAGE Publications Inc
2455 Teller Road
Newbury Park, California 91320

SAGE Publications India Pvt Ltd
32, M-Block Market
Greater Kailash – I
New Delhi 110 048

British Library Cataloguing in Publication Data
   Managing the external environment: A strategic
perspective.
   I. Mercer, David
   658.4

   ISBN 0–8039–8628–9
   ISBN 0–8039–8629–7 pbk

Library of Congress catalog card number 91-050650

Typeset by Mayhew Typesetting, Rhayader, Powys
Printed in Great Britain by Billing and Sons Ltd, Worcester

Contents

Acknowledgements

The chapters in this book were selected, by the team of academics credited on the title page, to be the basic reader for the Open University School of Management course 'The Challenge of the External Environment'. Particular responsibilities for the choice of chapters in relation to domains of environmental analysis were as follows: Edith Thorne, Economics; Harold Carter, Politics; Alan Warde, the Social Environment; and Rod Barratt and Norman Fox, the Technological Environment.

In the creation of this book we were supported by other Open University academics who were members of the course team, including Gordon Dyer and Robin Mason, as well as its external members, including Jim Attridge of ICI Pharmaceuticals, Graham Galer of Shell International, Denis Loveridge of Pilkingtons, David Skyrme of Digital Equipment Corporation, and Bob Tyrell of the Henley Centre for Forecasting.

Our thanks are also due to our secretary, Angela Rippin, for her invaluable assistance; but especially to the course manager, Val Page, who more than anyone else managed the impossible administrative task of bringing together these few papers from the many hundreds available.

Finally, we would also like to thank Sue Jones, our editor at Sage Publications, for her contribution to the linking editorial commentary, and for actually bringing the book into existence.

The editors and publishers wish to thank the following for permission to use copyright material: American Economic Association for Oliver E. Williamson, 'The Modern Corporation: Origins, Evolution Attributes', *Journal of Economic Literature*, Vol. XIX, Dec. 1981; Ampex Corporation for photograph, 'First Commercial Videotape Recorder'; Basil Blackwell Ltd for Bernice Martin, 'The Expressive Revolution' in *A Sociology of Contemporary Cultural Change*, 1981; Harvard Business Review for Philip Kotler, 'Megamarketing', *Harvard Business Review*, March/April 1986. Copyright © 1986 by the President and Fellows of Harvard College; Sir Adrian Cadbury, 'Ethical managers make their own rules', *Harvard Business Review*, Sept./Oct. 1987. Copyright © 1987 by the President and Fellows of Harvard College; Pierre Wack, 'Scenarios: shooting the rapids', *Harvard Business Review*, Nov./Dec. 1985. Copyright © 1985 by the President and Fellows of Harvard College; and George Stalk, Jr., 'Time – The Next Source of Competitive Advantage', *Harvard Business Review*, July/Aug. 1988. Copyright © 1988 by the President and Fellows of Barvard College; Hodder and Stoughton Ltd for R.E. Pahl, 'Some remarks on informal work, social polarization and the social structure', *International Journal of Urban and Regional Research*, Vol.12, No.2, June 1988, Edward Arnold; Jossey-Bass Inc. Publishers for G. Morgan, 'Proactive Management' in *Riding the Cutting Edge of Change: Developing Managerial Competencies for a Turbulent World*, 1988; Lawrence & Wishart Ltd for Dick Hebdige, 'After the Masses' in *New Times: The Changing Face of Politics in the 1990s*, eds Stuart Hall and Martin Jaques, 1989; Pergamon Press PLC for Bernard Taylor, 'Strategic Planning – Which Style do you Need?', *Long Range Planning*, Vol.17, No.3, 1984; Arion N. Pattakos, 'Growing Activist Groups: How Can Business Cope?', *Long Range Planning*, Vol.22, No.3, 1989; Alan I.H. Pink, 'Strategic Leadership through Corporate Planning at ITC', *Long Range Planning*, Vol.21, No.1, 1988; Carol Kennedy, 'The Transformation of AT&T, *Long Range Planning*, Vol.22, No.3, 1989; Spyros Makridakis, 'Management in the 21st Century', *Long Range Planning*, Vol.22, No.2, 1989; and Herman Daems, 'The Strategic Implications of Europe 1992', *Long Range Planning*, Vol.23, No.3, 1990; Pictor International Ltd for photograph, 'New York Stock Exchange'; Routledge for extracts from W.G. Runciman, 'Relative Deprivation and the Concept of Reference Groups' in *Relative Deprivation and Social Justice*, Routledge and Kegan Paul, 1966; Sage Publications Ltd for Mike Featherstone, 'Lifestyle and Consumer Culture', *Theory, Culture & Society: Explorations in Critical Social Science*, Vol.4, No.1, Feb. 1987; Scientific American, Inc. for S. Berger, M.L. Dertouzos, R.K. Lester, R.M. Solow and L.C. Thurow, 'Toward a New Industrial America', *Scientific American*, Vol.260, No.6, June 1989. Copyright © 1989 by Scientific American, Inc.; John Wiley & Sons for Michel Godot, 'From Forecasting to 'La Prospective' – A New Way of Looking at Futures', *Journal of Forecasting*, Vol.1 1982. Every effort has been made to trace all the copyright holders, but if any have been inadvertently overlooked the publishers will be pleased to make the necessary arrangement at the first opportunity.

This book is dedicated to the memory of
Norman Fox

Introduction

The theme of this book is the strategic management of an organization's relationship with its external environment. In particular, the book focuses on the need to identify and understand the key forces likely to shape that environment in the future, and the role of strategic planning in both anticipating change and proactively *creating* a desired future.

Of course, the notion of 'environmental analysis' in order to anticipate potential threats and opportunities has been part of the concept of strategic planning for a long time. Yet frequently the environmental analysis undertaken by managers has only addressed events and relationships in the organization's near or day-to-day environment – for example, customers and competitors. It is still relatively unusual for the themes of this book – such as fundamental changes in the sociocultural environment, the likely future impact of major technological change, even the role of activist pressure groups – to be integral to an organization's strategic-planning process.

One possible reason for this is the focus by managers on time-scales. Thus research for the Open Business School amongst senior management from approximately 100 of the 500 Fortune companies found that these senior managers tended to consider time horizons rather than environmental domains. Specifically they saw the topics of this book as relating to a period five to ten years ahead and not so relevant to decision-making for the nearer five-year future. Understandable as this may be, it is nevertheless regrettable, for the factors currently shaping future developments in the 'wider' environment may well determine the long-term success or failure of the organization.

The first section of the book sets a context by considering the process of 'contemplating the future'. Section two then moves to address four key domains of environmental analysis: Economic; Political; Social; Technological.

This traditional framework is a somewhat artificial one, for many activities and issues do not fit entirely comfortably within such groupings and others spread across several domains. Nevertheless the categories have some recognizable and practical utility, not least of which is that most of the literature from which the book has been drawn reflects them.

The chapters included in this second section represent a mix of those written specifically for a management audience and those drawn from the wider social sciences. This mix has been a deliberate choice. While the immediate implications for management may not always be explicitly drawn, ideas from such fields as economics, political science and sociology, fields long concerned with these domains, offer important 'food for thought' for management. Indeed one of the functions of the book is to provide a bridge between management thinking and pertinent analyses from the other social sciences.

The final section explores how the themes of the earlier sections can be related to processes of strategic planning and implementation.

A last word in this introduction, about the concept of the 'external environment'. There has been much debate within management literature about whether it is appropriate to talk of an environment external to the organization. Two issues in particular have been important in this debate. First, it has been argued that the boundaries between an organization and its 'environment' are often difficult to define (see also Chapter 6 in this book, by Williamson). Second, a perspective concerned with 'anticipating and adapting to the challenges of the environment' has been criticized as offering a somewhat deterministic and reactive model of the organization. Our own position would also reject a view of organizations as passive reactors to environmental change. Indeed much of the first section of the book is concerned with the importance of proactive participation in the *creation* of desirable futures. Nevertheless there is, again, some pragmatic utility in talking of broader social, political and economic environments within which various forces and actors operate to affect an organization in potentially highly significant ways.

SECTION 1

EXPLORING THE FUTURE

This first section of the book explores a number of themes relating to 'understanding and managing the future'. For as we have already argued, the value for managers of analysing the external environment comes from contemplating its future, and considering how an understanding of the present and the past can usefully contribute to this activity.

The first chapter, by Spyros Makridakis from his book, *Management in the Twenty-first Century*, outlines Makridakis' predictions about the types of business firms and managers most likely to emerge in the twenty-first century. It is also about the process of forecasting, and how an analysis of trends in the near and even distant past can be used as the basis for forward projection.

One might disagree with some of Makridakis' conclusions – the evidence that growing economies of scale will lead to less consumer choice is, for example, questionable in the light of recent evidence to the contrary. Nevertheless, as an example of one approach to how management might review the long-term future through trend analysis and extrapolation, it offers a fascinating – if idealist – model.

The next chapter by Gareth Morgan, extracted from his book, *Riding the Waves of Change*, presents a somewhat different perspective. Morgan also argues for the need for organizations to 'tune into the future' and to undertake the intelligence and information-gathering activities that this involves. In addition, he focuses on the need to proactively *engage* with the future. This requires the capacity to undertake 'transformational' activities, in order to minimise the impact of the fractures caused by unanticipated environmental change, together with the development of proactive, opportunity-seeking mindsets on the part of managers.

Chapter 3, 'Megamarketing', by Philip Kotler, takes a narrower view. Kotler looks specifically at the analysis of markets and their potential futures. However, he adds two important 'Ps' to the four (Product, Place, Price, Promotion) that are generally accepted as a framework for that discipline. These additional 'Ps', Power and Public Relations, are indeed highly relevant for dealing with the external environment.

Kotler's is the most conservative approach, only expanding the near (market) environment by these two extra factors. It does illustrate, though, the minimum which needs to be addressed by management.

Overall these three different perspectives (Makridakis, Morgan and Kotler) are complementary. Each approaches the task of analysing the external environment from a different direction and each adds another angle of vision.

We have already mentioned forecasting in the context of Makridakis' chapter. The fourth chapter in this section, 'From forecasting to "la prospective"', by Michel Godet, is specifically about the forecasting process. It is included partly because it highlights some of the problems associated with conventional forecasting principles and methods. More significantly, however, it discusses the use of *scenarios* to explore a *range* of possible alternative futures. Godet underlines that, to quote from the chapter, 'the future is not written: it has still to be built'. In contrast to traditional forecasting methods which tend to emphasize deterministic prediction and downplay the role of human action, the perspective presented here is of 'futures' which are multiple, uncertain and the outcome of the actions of various actors who, nonetheless, wield unequal power to influence events. From this standpoint, a key activity of futures planning is to explore ways of participating in the *creation* of a desirable future.

Finally in this section, 'Groupthink', by Irving L. Janis, is a salutary reminder of the pitfalls that may await decision-makers involved in futures planning. Janis examines the ways in which a senior decision-making group, particularly under crisis pressure, can become locked in self-reinforcing conformity or 'concurrence-seeking' – the groupthink of the title – leading to blinkered analysis and appraisal. This can include a tendency to ignore the ethical or moral consequences of the group's decision. The author also outlines a range of practices that can be adopted to prevent groupthink.

1

Management in the twenty-first century

Spyros Makridakis

Consider that you were a businessman 500 years ago. Your market was local. Most of what you sold was produced regionally and it was practically the same as that sold by your father and grandfather. Shipping took a long time and communications outside your own town were tardy. In your world change was extremely slow and you did not have to worry about forecasting the future environment or what you sold.

Today we live in a global village. Products can be shipped world-wide in a matter of days. Communications are instant. The life cycle of products is short and competition is high since there are few barriers to entry. Our world witnesses an incredible amount of change by all historical standards, even those of 50 years ago. The fast pace of change has created what Toffler (1970) calls a 'future shock' for those unable to adapt to such change.

This chapter is intended for business executives. It describes major, forthcoming changes in the business environment, businesses themselves, as well as the managers who would be required to run them. Understanding and acting on such changes has become imperative today. First, the fast changing world does not allow us to wait for a change to come, evaluate its impact, and then react. Instead, executives have to anticipate forthcoming changes, get prepared before they arrive and proact. Second, managers have a social responsibility (Drucker, 1987) as governments are less involved (e.g. through privatizations) with directing a nation towards desired goals. For these reasons a clear idea of the future and what it holds is becoming a necessity, so that the future environment can be moulded into desired directions and business firms become capable of adapting as smoothly as possible to the changes that are bound to arrive. Thus, questions such as those listed in the next paragraph become of critical importance.

What will business firms look like in the twenty-first century? What type of managers will be needed to operate them? Will the trend towards larger firms continue? How will the information (computer) revolution affect the organizational structure and mode of operation of the business

Extracted by permission of Pergamon Press PLC from *Long Range Planning*, 22(2) 1989: 37–53.

firms of the next century? Where will the new opportunities be found?
What are the dangers lying ahead? What type of strategies will be needed
to survive and prosper in the twenty-first century? These are important
questions. Can they be answered, however, with any degree of confidence?

Many people have become wary of any form of forecasting, in particular concerning long-term predictions. They view forecasting as nothing
more than crystal-balling with little, or no, scientific or rational basis.
Such a view has been reinforced by prominent errors in forecasting events
that did not materialize (e.g. the forthcoming widespread use of nuclear
energy) *as well as* failures in predicting events of far-reaching consequences (e.g. the appearance and impact of computers and the Information Revolution) that have already occurred. It is therefore, important to
persuade the reader that the approach used in this chapter (what I call
metaforecasting) has nothing to do with crystal-balling. Instead it is based
on rational principles that allow us to arrive at predictions about the
future which are scientifically sound.

Long-term patterns in human history

Table 1 on page 8 lists the major innovations or breakthroughs since the
dawn of civilization. A study of such innovations/breakthroughs reveals
that the following conclusions are of importance for long-term forecasting:

1 The manual work performed by human beings has been supplemented
   (e.g. through the use of tools to better perform certain tasks),
   substituted (e.g. using tractors in land cultivation), or amplified (e.g.
   employing levers or cranes to lift heavy weights) by a variety of means.
2 Mental work has been also supplemented, substituted, or amplified by
   a variety of means although this occurred much later than is the case
   with corresponding manual tasks.
3 There are clusters of innovations/breakthroughs that occur concur-
   rently or within a relatively short time-span.
4 The rate of innovations/breakthroughs has increased considerably
   during the last 200 years. The reason for this increased rate is the invention of machines that use mechanical energy, to supplement, substitute
   or amplify manual work. This has given rise to what is now known as
   the Industrial Revolution.
5 The late 1940s marked the beginning of another revolution, the information or computer revolution. This has also supplemented, substituted
   or amplified work, but this time, mental, and not manual labour. The
   Information Revolution has, so far, produced similar results to those of
   the Industrial Revolution, and has further accelerated the rate of
   technological change.
6 There are considerable spin-offs of the Industrial and Information
   Revolutions to all areas of our personal and family lives, as well as to
   entertainment, transportation and medicine.

7 The importance of technology has increased over time. Consider for instance, the role of technology in the discovery of America by Christopher Columbus vs its role in the Neil Armstrong moon landing. Furthermore, even in areas such as medicine, or in the harnessing of nature's resources or capabilities, innovations and/or breakthroughs depend to a greater extent on technology now than ever before.

The business firm of the twenty-first century

Manufacturing firms appeared and prospered during the Industrial Revolution. Their *raison d'être* was to master human and capital resources and use them to apply the machine technology required to produce large quantities of goods. They could, therefore, enjoy large economies of scale, although once these reached a certain size, increased complexity and settled-in bureaucracy minimized the benefits to be gained from them, or even resulted in diseconomies.

As the Industrial Revolution progressed, technology became more complicated. Specialized firms, to build the machines and tools needed by the manufacturing companies, appeared, making technology available to anyone who could afford to pay for it. The competitive advantages of using better machines specially built for a single manufacturer disappeared. As a matter of fact, new entrants were often at an advantage because their machinery was more modern than that of their established competitors. Competitive advantages (in addition to economies of scale) in production were, therefore, restricted to using the most modern technology bought from the specialized engineering firms producing and selling such technology. Attention was then shifted to marketing the goods produced and to introducing new or better products.

Manufacturing technology proliferated in many areas, including transportation, weapons, agriculture, housing, domestic comforts and home entertainment. In addition, a host of service industries appeared (e.g. banking, insurance, travel, entertainment) to satisfy the needs of the growing (both in size and numbers) business firms and those of the affluent consumers whose income exceeded their requirements for necessities and durable goods. In addition to the manufacture of goods, chemical production was a growing area during the Industrial Revolution. A wide variety of chemicals were discovered and used to improve agricultural production (e.g. fertilizers), replace raw materials (e.g. synthetic rubber and fibres), to produce consumer or industrial goods, and come up with new medicines. The trend towards plentiful and inexpensive goods covering all consumer needs was established.

The strong parallels between the Industrial and Information Revolutions can be used to predict the type of firm that will exist in the twenty-first century. The manufacturing firm of the twenty-first century will be in a position similar to that of the agricultural firm of today. This means

Table 1 *Major innovations/breakthroughs that changed established trends in human history and/or prevailing attitudes*

Epoch	Approximate time (years from 1988)	Innovation/Breakthrough	Consequence/Reason
		I. TECHNOLOGY	
A	1,750,000	Primitive tools	● Extending human capabilities
B	100,000	Making and using gear for hunting	
	40,000	Making and using weapons	
D	5500	The wheel	● Reducing and/or making manual work easier
	4000	Bronze and other metals	
	3500	Boats and sailboats	
	800	The clock, compass and other measurement instruments	● Facilitating and/or making mental work easier
E	600	Gunpowder	
	500	The printed book	
	350	Mechanical calculators	
F	210	Engines	● Improving comfort and/or speed of transportation
	180	Railroads	
	150	Electricity	
	130	Image and sound reproduction	
G	90	Telecommunications	● Increasing speed and/or availability of telecommunications
	85	Aeroplanes	
	70	Automobiles and roads	
	60	Mass-produced chemical products	
	45	Nuclear weapons	● Improving quality of arts and entertainment
	40	Computers	
	35	Mass-produced home appliances	
H	35	The transistor	● Improving material quality of life
	30	Extensive use of fertilizers	
	30	Artificial satellites	
	25	Lasers	
	20	Microtechnology (microchips, biochemistry and genetic engineering)	
	20	The moon landing	

Epoch	Approximate time (years from 1988)	Innovation/Breakthrough	Consequence/Reason
		II. EXPLOITING NATURE'S RESOURCES/CAPABILITIES	
A	400,000	Hunting	
	300,000	Harnessing of fire	● Decreasing dependence on the environment
	150,000	Shelter	
C	20,000	Permanent settlements	● Exploiting nature's capabilities
	20,000	Domestication of animals	
	15,000	Agriculture	
	10,000	Using animals for transportation and labour	
D	3500	Irrigation systems	● Using nature's resources
	3000	Harnessing wind power	
	2000	Using horses for transportation and labour	
E	800	Using the energy of falling water	
F	180	Using coal and oil for energy	● Adapting to changes in the environment
H	45	Nuclear energy	
		III. SOCIAL AND INTELLECTUAL HUMAN ACHIEVEMENTS	
A	1,500,000	Social organization to care for children	● Better mastery of environment
	500,000	Language	
	400,000	Immigration	
C	20,000	Religion	● Need for socialization
	7000	First cities	
	5500	Alphabet	
	5000	Abacus	
D	3500	Money for transactions	● Need for knowledge
	3000	Number system	
	2500	Arts, philosophy, sciences	
	2500	Democracy	● Drive towards equality
E	500	Scientific experimentation	
	500	The discovery of the new worlds	
	475	*The Prince* by Machiavelli is written	
	400	Large-scale commerce	● Desire for achievement
	300	Scientific astronomy	
	300	Mathematical reasoning	

continued

Table 1 *contd.*

Epoch	Approximate time (years from 1988)	Innovation/Breakthrough	Consequence/Reason
F	210	Discovery of oxygen (beginning of chemistry)	
	200	French and American revolutions	
	150	Babbage's failed computer	
	150	Political ideologies (communism, capitalism)	• Appreciation of arts
	120	Foundations of genetics	
G	100	Financial, banking, and insurance institutions	
	80	The theory of relativity	• Desire to reduce future uncertainty
	50	The concept of the computer is demonstrated mathematically	
		IV. MEDICINE	
D	2500	The doctor as a healer	• Curing disease
E	500	Therapy based on sound medical reasoning	• Prolonging life expectancy
	300	Drugs with real medical value	
H	90	X-ray	• Providing better diagnostics
	55	Antibiotics	
	30	Oral contraceptives	• Preventing unwanted pregnancies
	20	Tissues and organ transplants	
	10	The CT (CAT or body) scan	

A = The emergence of human domination; B = The first hand-made tools to extend human capabilities; C = The beginning of human civilization; D = The foundation of modern civilization; E = The foundations of modern science and society; F = The start of the Industrial Revolution; G = The Industrial Revolution; H = Spin-offs of the Industrial Revolution, the start of the Information Revolution.

that the percentage of people employed in manufacturing will drop substantially (the percentage of people employed in agriculture amounted to about 70 per cent of the population before the Industrial Revolution, while it is less than 2 per cent in the United States today) to a percentage similar to that of agriculture today. Similarly, manufactured products will be in plentiful supply and competition among the firms producing them will be as fierce as it is among agricultural firms today. Competitive advantages among the various manufacturers will be few, as the same high-level technology will be available to all. Differences in the quality of products will be slight or non-existent, as several/many firms will be producing the same goods using the same technologies. Furthermore, since material needs are finite, they will eventually be satisfied. This would result in a slowdown of the growth in demand, bringing over-capacity similar to that existing today in agricultural production.

Economies of scale will become the single most important factor in gaining competitive advantages in manufacturing. This is particularly true for information products because once developed, they can be reproduced and shipped at almost zero cost. Thus, the larger the production the smaller the unit cost and the faster the recovery of the developmental, sunk costs. Firms would, therefore, be motivated to produce as much as possible, to license or sell their production technology, to achieve the maximum number of distribution channels and, in general, to reach production and distribution levels which are as high as possible. Thus, the trend towards larger firms will continue in the twenty-first century, resulting in some super-giant manufacturing organizations.

Where are the limits to growth? Will increased complexity and reduced efficiency slow down the benefits gained from economies of scale? Similarly, will the reduced motivation of employees working for super-giant companies put the brakes on size? If the organization of firms does not change considerably from that of today, there is no doubt that a plateau in growth will be reached. However, decentralized, semi-autonomous firms and/or new forms of organizations (e.g. manufacturing/distribution organizations similar to the fastfood chains of McDonald's or Burger King, manufacturing/dealer symbiosis where the dealer is a part-owner of the firm) are likely to emerge. Furthermore, better telecommunications, fewer people working in manufacturing firms, and improvements in computerized management systems are likely to extend the limits of growth in size before diseconomies of scale result.

At present, the largest organization is the Catholic Church, whose structure and management has not fundamentally changed for almost twenty centuries. There is no compelling reason why, if needed, business firms using creative forms of organization and new tools cannot and will not achieve or surpass the size of the Catholic Church. Unless, of course, their size is restricted by governments, or other international bodies.

The above discussion does not imply that the only type of manufacturing firms in the twenty-first century will be giant and super-giant ones.

Obviously, peripheral firms supplying or serving the giants will also exist. In addition, specialized manufacturers geared towards specific markets will also operate alongside the super-giants. However, the dominant firms of the twenty-first century will inevitably be giant multinational corporations capable of fully exploiting economies of scale in research, manufacturing and marketing.

Together with economies of scale, competitive advantages will be gained by developing/introducing new products (mostly by combining hardware and software technologies) and/or creating new needs. Thus, identifying new markets, creating new wants, and introducing new fads and fashions will become imperative if one is to avoid product saturation and to achieve competitive advantages. In turn, these activities would require huge R & D budgets, and/or enormous advertising/marketing expenditures, further fuelling the need for super-giant firms capable of mastering the required resources and willing to take the risks necessary to develop and commercialize new products/ideas.

Biochemistry and genetic engineering will play roles that are similar or more crucial than those played by chemistry and genetics during the Industrial Revolution. Their growth and importance will increase as the biochemical and genetic engineering technologies are being linked to computers, lasers and computer-driven production. Improved or new products for both consumer *and* industrial uses will appear, and new, improved industrial processes will emerge. As with manufacturing firms, R & D costs for biochemistry and genetic engineering will be enormous, necessitating the creation of large firms capable of harnessing economies of scale. As the synergy among biochemical/genetic engineering firms, information technology companies, and the traditional manufacturing corporations becomes more critical, joint firms covering all three areas will eventually emerge. The integrating factor of such firms will be research and development, marketing/distribution capabilities, as well as the capital and human resources required to conceive, develop, manufacture and distribute/market the new products/processes.

The Industrial Revolution has increased the personal disposable income of a large segment of the population. At the same time it has created a class of rich and super-rich whose expectations and needs differ from those of the 'average' consumer. Product positioning to reach the high-income segment has been a successful practice of firms that distinguish themselves and/or their products from those which are mass produced. The Information Revolution will further increase spending income and create even more rich and super-rich. Marketing skills in segmentation and positioning one's product will, therefore, become critical ingredients in the battle to satisfy the needs of the affluent. The size of the firms in this category could range from the very small, geared to a particular segment, to the super-giants that apply a mixture of high-tech and individualized production to create and/or satisfy the needs of specific segments. Thus, a form of mass-produced, customized products aimed at specific segments (this is possible using computer-driven manufacturing systems) could become possible.

The service sector will grow substantially more than manufacturing, in particular once the Information Revolution has reached a plateau similar to that the Industrial Revolution has entered into today. The growth in services will increase employment and will compensate for decreases in manufacturing workers. However, as service companies will also automate their operations, overall employment will, eventually, stagnate or decrease, necessitating fewer hours of daily work, fewer workdays per week, or considerably longer yearly vacations.

Changes in the service sector will be substantial and are also more difficult to predict. New forms of services and new types of service firms will probably emerge. Furthermore, service and marketing practices will most likely change in the twenty-first century. Services industries, as well as the types of services they offer, will be greatly affected by the Information Revolution, as service differentiation and customer loyalty is usually weak in this sector. Small changes in the conception of the service being offered or its perceived utility, or of the by-products of such services, can drastically affect sales and market shares. Service firms will, therefore, have to be constantly re-thinking their business, innovating and/or keeping up with their competitors. The marketing of services will, thus, become the crucial factor determining successful service firms. Furthermore, since barriers to entry would be weak, competition will be keen, necessitating that service firms be flexible and that they constantly monitor the environment for changes that might affect them.

The size of service firms need not be large. Family operations and small firms can operate alongside super-giant multinationals. Economies of scale, although important for advertising purposes, are not critical for providing specialized services which might even be thought to be of greater value if individualized and customized. For instance, high-quality restaurants, small high-priced hotels, first-rate universities, high-power research centres and similar services cannot be mass produced or mass marketed. Their value lies in their uniqueness and the limit to the number of customers they can serve. Thus, segmentation and positioning will leave room for small service firms (in particular as there will be a lot of wealthy people willing to spend their money on individualized services if these can identify and appropriately serve the right segment).

Although specific developments are difficult to predict, general trends point towards significant growth in entertainment, education and re-education, travelling, vacationing, medical care, marketing and research/consulting. These can be considered to be the emerging growth services of the twenty-first century that will compensate for decreases in manufacturing and stagnation in other service sectors.

The manager of the twenty-first century

The architects of the Industrial Revolution were engineers. Using their ingenuity, they transformed manual skills (which took many years of apprenticeship and numerous years of practice to acquire) into a machine design that could replicate them and, in so doing, produce similar goods at a fraction of the cost, and at a higher speed. Moreover, their ability to produce such machines economically and repair them when they did not work properly, enabled entrepreneurs to use machines for production purposes.

Initially, a single engineer was capable of mastering the technology required and both creating and repairing the new machines, or variations of existing ones. As technology became more complex, however, specialized engineers (mechanical, civil, chemical, electrical, etc.) were needed. As engineering expertise cannot be instantly acquired, schools specializing in teaching engineering knowledge and skills became essential. As the Industrial Revolution progressed, so did the demand for engineers who were paid high salaries and were often promoted to managerial positions and the top jobs within the firm. This privileged role, high salaries, and the heavy demand for engineers, however, reached a plateau in the 1960s when the focus shifted to MBA education and business graduates. Today, there are still many well-paid engineers, although they are diminishing in number, but their pay is usually less than that earned by MBAs, and their tasks are fundamentally different from those performed by engineers before the peak of the Industrial Revolution.

In machine engineering, for instance, the major task of today's engineers is to develop (design, construct and test) new machines and production processes, or to improve the efficiency of existing ones. Their task is aided by standardized parts which can be purchased from specialized firms that design, construct and produce such parts. Engineers are not obliged, therefore, to start from scratch. Their designs are based on readily available 'building boxes'. Moreover, few engineers today are involved in machine repair. First, machines do not break down as often as before, but should they, it suffices to identify the problem and change the defective part (an important principle in designing machines today is that they can be easily repaired by substituting the part(s) that frequently cause problems). In other cases, it might even be more economical to replace the inoperative machine by a new one. Engineers, however, are not needed in either case. The repair side of the engineering job has been simplified and standardized in such a way that it can now be delegated to maintenance personnel, who can do the job using appropriate tools and procedures that were also developed by engineers. The end result is a new type of engineer, whose task is to perform creative work, or to solve new, important problems. All other functions that were previously part of engineering jobs have been delegated. In my opinion, the job of managers has followed, and will continue to follow, stages similar to those of engineers.

First, there was a single manager, usually the owner, who managed the entire firm. Then came specialized functional managers (finance, production, marketing managers) whose job, in addition to dealing with people, was mostly to perform repetitive tasks required for the day-to-day operation of the business. Today we are at the point in the Information Revolution when many repetitive managerial tasks could be standardized and performed by the computer, or be simplified and made part of an expert system. Computer programmes and expert systems would, in turn, permit the delegation of all repetitive managerial tasks to clerical personnel who could perform them aided by the appropriate software programme. This raises the question of who the new manager will be and what qualities will be required to manage the firm of the twenty-first century.

The large majority of manual tasks have or will be substituted, supplemented, or amplified by combinations of hardware and/or software technologies. Even a highly skilled task performed by a brain surgeon will be greatly supplemented and amplified by computers, electronic microscopes, TV scans, computer-guided lasers, and a host of other technologies (Makridakis, 1987). The neurosurgeon would be required to be a first-class technician. The judgement of such a neurosurgeon would be restricted to interpreting the information provided and intervening should problems arise. Moreover, experience would become less important, or even disadvantageous, as new doctors, right out of school, would be better masters of the new, fast-changing technology. In the final analysis, the only tasks that cannot be substituted by computers and expert systems will be new, important problem-solving situations as well as functions/tasks that require creative thought processes.

Dealing with people will always remain a critical management task. However, its nature will also change. First, there will not be so many people to manage (in particular in manufacturing firms). Second, people will no longer perform routine boring tasks; this will increase motivation and decrease the amount of supervision required. Third, employees will perform well-defined tasks facilitating the evaluation of their performance. Fourth, a great deal of work will be creative (conceiving new products/services, research, strategy, advertising, etc.) requiring new types of imaginative managers capable of maximizing the output of such creative people.

Thus, in addition to his or her own creativity, a critical management skill in the twenty-first century will be the capacity to supervise the creativity of others, since creative thinking would be one of the few remaining factors that could not be supplemented, or substituted by computers and which, if properly used, could bring competitive advantages.

Top managers, and their qualities, are more difficult to predict. In my opinion, they will be rare and paradoxical: creative and practical, visionary and pragmatic, flexible and persistent, easygoing and demanding, risk-taking and conservative, in addition to being excellent politicians, superb deal-makers, as well as visible and effective public statesmen. And, once found, they will be paid extremely well.

Can people with creative potential be identified? Can creativity be taught? At present, advertising agencies and R & D departments are some of the few places directly concerned with the management of creativity. But no firm conclusions regarding creativity can be reached. Although creativity can be encouraged, it is not easy to identify creative people beforehand. Moreover, although some organizations (e.g. Bell Laboratories, 3M) seem to have produced more creative output than others it does not seem that rules encouraging organizational creativity can be found and applied across the board. Finally, it does not seem that special education or background increases creativity. On the other hand, we are still in the early stages. Once the importance of creativity becomes clear, resources and talent will concentrate their efforts on finding new 'creative' solutions. In my opinion, this is the new challenge of management education if business schools are not to become obsolete.

Conclusions

In this chapter, I have predicted the type of business firms and managers most likely to exist in the twenty-first century. In making my predictions, I have attempted to avoid the mistakes made by forecasters of the past, when making long-term predictions. By analysing established patterns in human history (see Table 1), a trend showing that technology has been playing an increasingly important role became obvious. Furthermore, such a trend does not seem likely to change, but, instead, it will probably accelerate through the influence of the Information Revolution. The critical assumption of the predictions made in this chapter has been that there is an analogy between the Industrial and Information Revolutions. If the reader does not accept this assumption, he or she should not accept my predictions. Another important assumption is that, at present, we are at the same time-period on the time-scale as the Industrial Revolution was in the mid-1930s. This assumption is not as critical, since the reader can decide on another time-period. Such a modification will only affect the rate of change expected to result from the Information Revolution in the coming years. Finally, the reader might not agree with some of my reasoning. This is not critical either as different viewpoints and alternative conclusions about the future are inevitable. My objective has been based on an endeavour to provide a consistent rationale showing major trends rather than on the belief that I can predict specific events or the exact time of their appearance. The reader may accept only part of my reasoning and modify the forecasts provided accordingly.

It is necessary to understand and accept that *all* forecasts about the future are uncertain and must always be considered as such. On the other hand, uncertainty must not become an excuse to avoid making decisions and taking actions to prepare oneself to better face up to the future. Such decisions are necessary in order to reduce the impact of future surprises. To this end, major trends must be identified and predictions based on such trends made.

Forecasting presents a paradox. To be accurate, forecasts must be general in terms of the event(s) being predicted and vague in terms of the time the event(s) could occur. However, to be useful, forecasts must be specific and precise. This paradox can only be resolved on a case-to-case basis through individual (or company-wise) thinking. The job of a forecaster is to present a wide range of alternatives which can neither be specific nor precise, in order to avoid inaccuracies. Individuals and companies must consequently evaluate these forecasts and translate them to specific predictions and then decide how they might affect their future existence. In so doing, they must inevitably take certain risks. A list of general and vague (in terms of time) predictions are presented in Table 2. Individuals and companies need to evaluate them to determine which will affect them and how, and what actions and strategies are needed to succeed.

Another mistake forecasters often make is to underestimate the rate and degree of technological change. Table 3 develops further the watch/ aeroplane analogy. Although the implications might sound like science fiction, they might not be too far from future reality. Business executives should, therefore, consider the consequences involved and the type of decisions and actions they will need to take at present, in the face of what Toffler (1970) calls, the future shock.

Finally, the question is often asked, 'What will happen after the Information Revolution?' The answer is 'Not much'. People perform manual and/or mental tasks. Once such tasks have been replaced to the maximum by machines and/or computers, there will be nothing left. The next stage will come when computers can imitate and/or surpass the highest of the human intellectual abilities, that is problem-solving, learning and creativity. However, such computers are not likely to appear soon. When and if they do, it will be interesting to see if the prediction that, at that time, humans will be to computers what pets are today to humans, will actualize. In the meantime, humans will continue to hold a huge competitive advantage over computers by the fact that they are superb problem-solvers, they can learn, if given adequate feedback, and that they can be creative. These talents, which must be cultivated as far as possible, will become the critical skills of the twenty-first century.

Table 2   *Possible future innovations/breakthroughs that would probably change established trends and/or prevailing attitudes*

Estimate in years from now widespread applications			Innovation/Breakthrough	Consequence/Reason
Low	Likely	High		
			I. HARDWARE-BASED TECHNOLOGY	
5	10	20	Mass global telecommunications (message/data, sound, image)	● Continued substitution of unskilled and semi-skilled labour by machines
5	15	35	Super automation (in office and factory)	● Large shifts in employment patterns
5	20	40	Applications of superconductivity	
10	20	40	Mass use of lasers	● Fewer hours of work
15	25	35	Mass use of lightweight super-strength materials (ceramic, plastic, synthetic metals)	● Cheaper and more plentiful products
20	40	150	Super miniaturization	
30	50	150	Super efficient engines	● Faster transportation and speedier and less costly telecommunications
30	60	200	Hypersonic transport (air, train, other)	
			II. SOFTWARE-BASED TECHNOLOGY	
5	15	35	Super automation (in office and factory)	● Heavy substitution of office and/or service personnel by 'computer'-based technology
5	15	50	Widely used expert systems	
20	50	100	General purpose robots	● Large shifts in employment patterns
25	50	150	Intelligent products (cars, home appliances, etc.)	
25	100	400	Real artificial intelligence	
50	200	600	Intelligent computers	
75	400	800	Intelligent robots	● 'Automation' of homes and offices
100	600	1000	Super smart specific-purpose robots	
500	5000	20,000	Computers and robots that can imitate or surpass human intelligence, and/or creativity	● Large changes in the way professional work is done

Table 2 *contd*

Estimate in years from now widespread applications			Innovation/Breakthrough	Consequence/Reason
Low	Likely	High		
			III. BIOCHEMICAL AND RELATED TECHNOLOGIES	
5	15	30	Improved agricultural production	● New and improved products
10	20	50	Eradicating pollution	
10	25	60	Improved production from animals	● Cheaper and more plentiful products
10	30	70	Mass-produced biochemical compounds	
25	40	80	Widely used biochemical processes	● Clean air and water
15	30	100	New bio and/or genetically engineered products	
30	50	200	Altering gene structure	
50	300	800	New, powerful energy sources	● New and vast sources of energy
20	1000	5000	New forms of life	
			IV. EXPANDING HUMAN PRESENCE	
15	40	80	Full-scale space stations	● Opening new frontiers to expand human presence
20	50	150	Marine life	
30	200	400	Colonizing the moon	
100	400	1000	Colonizing planets of our solar system	
10	500	Never	Communicating with extraterrestrials	
1000	5000	100,000	Colonizing planets beyond our solar system	
			V. MEDICINE	
10	30	50	Preventative medicine	● Towards eradicating disease
15	40	60	General purpose drugs	
15	40	60	General purpose vaccines	● Substantially prolonging life expectancy
15	25	50	Expert systems for medical diagnosis	
30	50	100	Mass-produced artificial organs	● Improving diagnostics

Table 2 *contd.*

\multicolumn{3}{c}{Estimate in years from now widespread applications}			Innovation/Breakthrough	Consequence/Reason
Low	Likely	High		
40	60	120	Preventive organ transplants	
60	100	400	Cures and preventions before birth	
150	300	2000	Growing limbs naturally	• Replacing the doctor with expert systems
			VI. HOME LIFE, LEISURE TIME, EDUCATION	
33	6	10	Super-powerful, affordable home computers	• Reducing and facilitating work at home
3	6	10	Electronic post, on-line messages, ordering of goods, reservations, transfer of money and similar transactions through home computers	• Improving quality and expanding entertainment coverage at home
4	8	15	Super-high fidelity sound and image systems	
5	10	20	The fully integrated home communication centre (sound, image, telephone and computers)	• Performing a host of tasks by home computer
5	10	20	Telecopying (buying or renting) and storing music, videos, films, books, newspapers, magazines in home computers	
5	10	25	Vacation supermarkets	
5	15	25	Super automation at home	• Super-automated homes
10	20	30	The home entertainment centre (receiving programmed and live events from around the world in large colour stereophonic TV-type sets)	
10	20	30	Home appliances programmed by computers	• New forms of education and research
15	25	35	Lifelike computer games and realistic simulations	
15	25	40	Specialized research universities	
15	30	50	Specially tailored computer education	
15	30	60	Flexible workplace in widespread use	
30	50	100	Robots as home servants	

Table 3   *Making watches 200 years ago and aeroplanes 50 years from now*

	Fabricating a watch 200 years ago	Implications	Making a mass-produced watch today
Method	The 250, or so, parts needed to make a watch were made separately using the crude hand-tools that existed at that time	Imagine a watchmaker (or any other person) 200 years ago. Could he, in his wildest dreams, have conceived that a watch could be produced in 10 minutes, or that digital watches showing time in hundredths of seconds, the day of the week, the year, including multiple alarms, calculators and a place for storing telephone numbers and appointments could exist? Could the watchmaker have imagined his skills becoming obsolete?	Digital watches are made automatically using specially designed microchips. Analogue watches are assembled semi-automatically using ready-made parts produced automatically elsewhere.
Time to complete task	About 1 month.	The month has become minutes. A time reduction of between 1200 and 12,000 times.	Less than 1 minute for digital. About 10 minutes for analogue.
Cost in current (1988) US dollars	The equivalent of today's wages (of workers at a similar level of skill) for a master watchmaker, an assistant, and three apprentices, plus equipment overheads, etc. Estimated cost of about $10,000.	A cost reduction by between 2000 and 10,000 times.	Less than $1 for digital. About $5 for analogue.

Table 3 *contd.*

	Constructing a jumbo jet today	Implications	Making a mass-produced aeroplane 50 years from now
Method	The various pre-made parts are assembled together by skilled workers and the body is built using an assembly-line approach.	Imagine a technology that could produce a small passenger aeroplane in less than 1 hour, at a cost of about $10,000 (based on conservative estimates). Consider the implications: will there be air-traffic jams similar to those on today's highways? Will people live in the Caribbean and work in Atlanta? Will people spend their weekends skiing in the Alps (in the winter) or the Andes (in the summer)? Will houses have two aeroplane-garages? What about vehicles (combining helicopter design with that of an aeroplane) that can take off and land on roofs, or in backyards? Even if the estimates are off by a factor of 10, the basic analogy and trends hold. Alternatively, consider the predictions which will be made, not 50, but 100 or 150 years from now.	Giant machines, guided by computers and robots, construct a conventional aeroplane. A new type of aeroplane (using a completely brand-new technology) is made by a single machine.
Time to complete task	About 2 months.		Less than 2 minutes for aeroplanes using the new technology. About 20 minutes for aeroplanes using the old technology.
Cost in current (1988) US dollars	About $75,000,000.		Less than $7000 for aeroplanes using the new technology. About $40,000 for aeroplanes using the old technology.

References

Drucker, P. F. (1987) 'Social innovation – management's new dimension', *Long Range Planning*, 20 (6): 29–34.

Makridakis, S. (1987) 'The emerging long term: appraising new technologies and their implications for management', in S. Makridakis and S. Wheelwright (eds), *The Handbook of Forecasting*, 2nd edn. New York: John Wiley.

Toffler, A. (1970) *Future Shock*. Geneva: Orbit Publishing.

2

Proactive management

Gareth Morgan

Let's face it . . . most people, when they look at something, tend to see the obstacles. The trick is to turn around and say . . . What is actionable about this? What is the opportunity in this? How can we *make* an opportunity out of it? There is a small percentage of the population who will look at any important matter, however negative, and see the opportunity in it. . . . That's what we've go to encourage.

Turbulence and change in the socioeconomic environment creates many problems and opportunities. To deal with these successfully, organizations and their managers will need to approach them in a positive, opportunity-seeking way. And as the executive quoted above suggests, this depends on an ability to see the positive lines of development in a situation, however negative it might seem.

This proactive, entrepreneurial approach to management was viewed by many executives as a key competence. And numerous ideas were offered on how it can be developed in practice. They are explored in this chapter in terms of three interrelated themes:

1 the development of *proactive mindsets*;
2 an ability to *manage from the outside in*; and
3 the development of *positioning and repositioning skills*.

Together, they provide the profile of an emergent style of management that is likely to become increasingly prominent in the years ahead.

Developing proactive mindsets

To what extent are our organizations still operating in a catch-up mode, down-sizing and down-scaling in response to yesterday's challenge, without really coming up with tomorrow's response? . . . Many organizations are talking tomorrow, but operating in catch-up mode. . . . How do we separate catch-up from leap-ahead, and jump on the latter?

As the above quotation suggests, many organizations are approaching

Reprinted from G. Morgan, *Riding the Cutting Edge of Change*. (San Francisco: Jossey-Bass, 1988), pp. 36–53.

the future while locked in the past. They are busy trying to adapt to changes that have already happened, overlooking the fact that by the time appropriate adjustments have been made, the future will have moved on. To ride the cutting-edge of change one must do more than react. One must anticipate possible change and position oneself to deal with opportunities and challenges in a proactive rather than reactive way.

Executives involved in discussing this issue recognized that while the situation can vary from one sector of the economy to another, this ability to be proactive will become an increasingly important competence. Four aspects of this proactive orientation attracted particular attention during the course of discussion:

1 'looking ahead' and 'driving in forward mode';
2 adopting an opportunity-seeking attitude;
3 turning negatives into positives; and
4 being a leader rather than a follower.

Driving in 'forward mode'

The ability to get out of a 'react-mode' so that one is 'in the driving seat', shaping rather than being shaped by change, was seen as being particularly important. As one chief executive expressed the problem:

> We need to keep looking ahead. . . . We need to drive in forward mode, to get out of react mode. We need to look at the future on a regular basis. . . . In my organization we've been in a react mode for years – not wanting to face the realities out there. . . . CEO's in particular need an ability to take off the blinkers, to look ahead, to step outside, and to be consistently monitoring what's coming down the pipe; they need an ability to anticipate.

Operationally this means that organizations must be able to 'tune into the future' by developing and using 'intelligence' and information-gathering functions, keeping abreast of emerging trends in a way that will allow one to take appropriate initiatives. In particular, senior executives need to adopt a 'change can come from anywhere' philosophy, and to understand the context in which they are operating as broadly and deeply as possible.

> How can I zero in on the 'discontinuities', 'break-points', 'sheers', 'rival scenarios' or 'fracture-lines' (different executives characterize the discontinuities in different ways) that are going to change the shape and future of my organization and my industry?
>
> How can I begin to understand these forces in a way that will allow my organization to take advantage of the changes and dislocations that are likely to arise?

These are the kind of questions that can help keep an understanding of one's context actionable and focused. By attempting to identify the critical fractures or break-points shaping one's environment, managers have a means of identifying those 'seven or eight issues' that are crucial for the future of their organization. The very attempt to identify these issues can itself make an enormous contribution to an organization's understanding of its environment. And systematic efforts to unfold their consequences can do much to create a future-oriented view that is able to take account of a wide range of possible outcomes. So often, organizations are in search of 'one budget' and 'one plan' rather than being sensitive to the idea that any one of several scenarios are equally possible. By using some form of fracture analysis to explore the future in a focused yet relatively open way, one can bring the implications of these possible futures into the present, and consider their likely impacts. All this helps an organization understand its existing strengths and weaknesses much more clearly, and identifies the directions in which it can move.

An 'opportunity-seeking' attitude

We need to invent more opportunities and to enlarge our horizons. . . . Increasingly we need people who can perceive opportunities, and not just come up with new ideas. It's a kind of entrepreneurship, but the word is much abused. . . . With a proactive mindset you identify opportunities in a very active way. You don't just gather information on what's there: you *create*! . . . Everyone from the CEO down needs to find ways of enlarging opportunities. . . . If we don't, then our competitors are going to put us out of business. . . . We are facing broad challenges, and we need to search for opportunities on a macro basis. . . . We will need to develop this skill in the future. In the past we've been mainly concerned with optimizing the use of scarce resources, never much more. Now we have to go beyond (this kind of) stewardship. In the new environment we have to invent demand (for products and services), and new skills and attitudes are necessary.

Astute managers are responsible for creation . . . they look for fracture points . . . they recognize that opportunity comes with change, and that change creates the opportunity to do the right things . . . There must be a way of sensitizing people to break-points, and of showing them how to handle them.

This ability to develop and seize opportunities was emphasized in many aspects of executive discussion. It was prominent in discussions suggesting that organizations should actively search their environments for potential fracture points to identify new entrepreneurial initiatives. And it was prominent in discussions on problem-solving. For example, it was suggested that even the blackest clouds could be made to have silver linings, and that an optimistic 'there must be a way of dealing with this' attitude is crucial for developing a proactive approach.

The process of opportunity-seeking leads one to emphasize one's creative potential in shaping relationships with the environment. It recognizes that success or failure is not something that just 'happens' to an organization, but is something which is the product of the way an organization chooses to deal with the threats with which it is faced, and the opportunities which it can make. The proactive approach is best fuelled when members of an organization always approach problems and issues with a view to enlarging their set of opportunities. The approach fine-tunes an organization's ability to deal with change. And, as one chief executive put it, it can actually lead one to create change as a means of developing a competitive advantage:

> If there is a highly stable market area in my industry, then I will take a close look and try to find a way of creating some change. We create change to keep at the front edge.

The opportunity-seeking attitude is crucial for establishing a leading-edge position, whether for organizations moving from innovation to innovation, or for those that wish to sustain a well-established niche by developing operational competencies that are better than those of anyone else. Opportunity-seeking keeps an organization alive and vibrant – enthused rather than overwhelmed by the challenge of change. And, as noted by many of the executives involved in this project, it is a quality that needs to be widely spread throughout an organization.

Turning negatives into positives

In discussing this opportunity-seeking attitude, much was made of the need to use the negative aspects of situations as reference points for creating new opportunities. A number of chief executives expressed this sentiment in the following terms:

> You have to turn the negatives into positives.

> Competitive forces force *me* to become more competitive.

> Sometimes, from those dark holes, you tend to look and say, well 'What's available?', and you start to produce.

> By identifying all the negatives out there you can identify really nice profitable opportunities. But you have got to list them; you have to identify them and look around. It is now part of our (corporate) culture that we really get those negatives on the table. We call them major factors, but they always tend to be negative. We identify them, and ask 'How are we going to drive a strategy around them?'

The approach is well illustrated in the philosophy of an organization that has extensive relations with government and other public organizations, and has to deal with a tangle of regulations and interest groups in securing contracts. Rather than fight against the regulations, opinions and differing viewpoints, managers see these influences as a series of constraints which must be tackled in a creative way. Their approach is to identify all the negative factors relating to the project as early as they possibly can, for example, the factors that are likely to add to costs, or create delays, and then forge a creative design that will either eliminate the basic concerns and problems, or meet them in a direct and satisfactory manner. The potential problems result in special features that help to sell the project and make it a success.

Being a 'leader rather than a follower'

> You have to be ready to move very quickly. . . . If you can get to the point where you are ahead, and everybody else reacts to you, and keep that rolling, you will be very successful and get a lot of benefits.

> In our business the difference between ourselves and one of our competitors (which is going to move from a $70 million profit to a $10 million loss in just two years) is the difference between who was first and who was second. The difference, the biggest variable, and our research shows it, was innovation . . . We were first in terms of an across the board set of changes.

> Being number one. Whether it is in implementing a production process or recognizing a trend, that is where the action is these days – recognizing things ahead of other people; being aware of what is coming down. We can get hung-up sometimes on words and phrases out of books and studies and all the rest of it, but the facts are: if there is something out there that is going to happen, you had better recognize it, and you had better be doing the things now which will help you through that situation.

These quotations speak for themselves and reinforce a point made above: it is usually much better to be leading initiatives rather than responding to those of others. The essence of the proactive mindset rests in this kind of positive, energetic approach to the management of internal and external relations. Building on the idea that in a changing world one usually has to change or be changed, it favors action rather than reaction. Sometimes this will mean 'going with the flow' of anticipated events, and at other times it will mean trying to alter the nature and direction of the flow, especially through action with others. Proactive management may lead to various kinds of joint action in relation to shared concerns, that can transform the environment in very significant ways.

Managing from the 'outside in'

A proactive relationship with one's environment implies that it is important to keep close contact with that environment. But, there is a vast difference in doing this from the 'inside out' as opposed to the 'outside in'.

Many organizations are preoccupied with 'inside out' management. They approach, understand, and act in relation to their environment in terms that make sense from *internal* divisions and perspectives, or in terms of what powerful members *want* to do. As a result, they often end up acting in fragmented and inappropriate ways.

Some organizations, on the other hand, try to build from the 'outside in', in the sense that they try and 'embrace' the environment holistically, and shape internal structures and processes with this wider picture in mind. They use the views and needs of customers and other key stakeholders as a mirror through which they can see and understand their own strengths and weaknesses. And they use these insights to re-shape their activities and relations with the environment. This 'outside in' approach to management provides the focus of an important managerial competence that can be developed in various ways. Executive discussions identified three specific ways of promoting the approach, summarized here under the following headings:

1 Sustaining a transformative market orientation;
2 Choosing appropriate frontiers for development; and
3 Understanding oneself through the eyes of key stakeholders, especially one's competitors.

Sustaining a transformative market orientation

When managers talk about sustaining a market orientation it usually means 'doing good market research', 'listening to customers', and 'trying to find rewarding niches'.

But in the view of some executives, there is another interpretation that embraces the above, but goes far beyond. It involves realizing that it is possible to use a focus on potential transformations in one's market as a means of identifying early warnings of the need for potential transformations in one's organization. This approach requires that we change the definition of market away from the idea that it represents a collection of buyers in the here and now, towards the idea that it represents a *domain* of operation which may change in dramatic ways, and in the process, turn an organization on a new course.

The significance of this orientation is illustrated in the following example, raised in a group discussion addressing this issue:

> I'm the director of a small printing company, and we print a lot of bank cheques. Well, what is technology going to do? Is there going to be a market for bank cheques? You and I, who use cheques, can't tell. (To find out) we have to go to the technology guys and say 'ten years down the road, how are people going to be making payments? Are they going to be using little pieces of paper, . . . using plastic debit cards, or what? And if (the latter) is the defining market, how do we handle that? Will (the market for printed cheques) disappear completely, or is there going to be a sort of residual that is going to be there?' . . . (The approach) has got to be market-driven, but it sure doesn't depend on the immediate purchaser of the product to tell you what the market is going to be like. He doesn't know. It's the technology boys in town (that know).

The printing firm is faced with a dilemma as to how to stay in business: by securing a niche that will keep it in the paper-printing trade, or by moving in new directions that will involve new technologies, and perhaps move it outside the printing trade as traditionally conceived.

The dilemma is shared by many other firms in a wide variety of fields. For example, many firms in the financial services industry are having to re-think their products and identity as traditionally separate services such as banking, consumer credit, real estate, and insurance become integrated under the umbrella of 'one stop' financial centers. These services are now being built from a *customer standpoint*, rather than from an internal *production or supplier standpoint*, the premise on which the separate services have been developed. The general trend is widespread. For example, many consumer goods manufacturers are now moving to a customer- rather than production-oriented view of their products – e.g. integrated stereo, TV and other audio-visual systems, rather than separate televisions, radios, record players, telephones, and computers. The trend will challenge and change the identity, and in many cases, the very existence of firms operating in these various industries.

The transformative forces that a market-oriented firm needs to monitor are wide-ranging, and involve a sensitivity for the changing needs of one's existing customers, an awareness of emerging technological possibilities, the activities of competitors and potential competitors, the emergence of the internationalized global economy, and other broad contextual trends. As one executive expressed it:

> The degree of complexity you've got to exhibit is increasingly complex. You've got to be sensitive to so many damn things . . . having your antennae twitching in all these directions at once, and still be able to make sense of it, and to be able to say 'Okay, this is what I do now. But I'm positioning myself now so that I will be ready for the things that I think are going to happen in five or ten years time, and I will be able to stand up to things that appear over the horizon that I have never even thought about.' It's a very, very demanding position for senior executives.

Choosing appropriate frontiers for development

An 'outside in' perspective requires managers to distance themselves from current operations, and to ask very fundamental questions about the basic identity of their organization. For as one executive put it:

> If we see ourselves (as being) defined by the tasks we are performing right now, we might turn out to be less able to see what else we might be doing. Our product influences our description of ourselves . . .

What business are we really in?; Are we a product? Or, are we a technology?; Are we a distribution system?; Are we just a 'market niche'? As is well known, questions such as these can do much to help an organization focus on appropriate frontiers for development. For example, as the executive quoted above went on to suggest:

> Typically, integrated oil companies are providers of oil products to the consumer. . . . (But) you see the most shrewd ones becoming (more) like traders of products. . . . They have changed their emphasis (towards that) of a trading company. . . . There are other industries that are (moving in the same direction). . . . For example, there are organizations that are shifting out of manufacturing . . . into the business of providing products to consumers (e.g. by putting their label on products produced by others). That is their job. And that restructures the nature of (their business).

Executives discussing this issue of frontier development made much of the need to develop competencies that will encourage the kind of questioning reflected in the following examples:

> Are we a printing firm producing bank cheques, or a firm meeting the evolving requirements relating to the documentation of financial transactions? Are we in the paper-printing trade? Or are we a firm that will seek to operate with a variety of technologies?

> Are we an insurance company, or in the financial services industry? Are we going to specialize in selling a range of separate financial packages, or in selling investment services concerned with financial planning, etc?

> Are we in the motorcycle business or in the distribution of leisure products?

> Are we an integrated oil company moving resources from the ground to an end consumer, or are we a commodity trading company?

> Are we in mining or refining?

> Are we a producer of electronic hardware, or in the information management business?

> Are we manufacturers; should we be distributors who subcontract the manufacturing?

> We're in metal-stamping; should we be in plastics?

> We're a software firm; as more and more programming is built onto silicon chips should we become a trouble-shooting firm that specializes in making computer systems work in practice?

These executives also emphasized the importance of being very clear about the kind of distinctive advantages that one's organization is going to pursue, for example, in terms of:

- an emphasis on innovation;
- an emphasis on product differentiation;
- an emphasis on marketing and promotional skills;
- an emphasis on 'service' and continuing customer relations;
- an emphasis on low-cost production;
- an emphasis on distribution;
- an emphasis on the possibility of developing collaborative relations with other actors.

Executives' opinions varied with regard to which of these frontiers of development were of greatest importance, since it was recognized that conditions vary from one sector of the economy to another. For example, some executives perceived the importance of developing continuing capacities for R & D and innovation as being of key significance, while others stressed the importance of focusing on 'adding-value', service to customers, an edge in low-cost quality production, the ability 'to time entry', e.g. into new markets, and in the use of new technologies. The following quotations illustrate the range of opinion:

> I believe that the success of my organization (in the packaged goods industry) has a lot more to do with our laboratory engineering people than it has to do with the fifty or sixty million dollars we spend on advertising. . . . The marketing efforts (of different organizations) neutralize each other. . . . You have to have it, but the market is more sensitive to innovations in your product.

> In my industry (electronics) you have to have good marketing, and you have to have a fast production line, because you need to get the product out of the door before the competitors come.

> In my industry (electronics/communications) there is a recognition that you won't be able to differentiate yourself in the market-place significantly through product advantage or technological advantages. These are very short term. They last a matter of months, and then the competition is there. . . . (So you have to) focus on differentiating in the market-place through response to customer needs or customer satisfaction.

> A focus on adding value at every stage (in software development) would set us out alone (when compared with our competitors).

> If you're a low-cost producer you can always serve your customer. If you're high cost you have less room to maneuver. Quality is not enough. For example, successful quality producers like IBM force the price down and the competition out. . . . If you can make money in bad times, you'll be OK in the good. In inflationary times you can pass on your sins of omission; in deflationary times you can't – it's too competitive.

> We are under attack (by new companies entering the automotive parts market) so we are trying to go with distribution strength. My management team knows that we have got to become more market-driven; we have got to control more distribution; we have to expand our product range, to make us more important to our customers. . . . If we can get the distribution in place we will be able to hold off the competition.

As noted above, it is unwise to make generalizations on which of these frontiers are most important. It all depends on the evolving character of the situation with which one is dealing, e.g. in terms of the structure of competition with which one is faced, the length of product life-cycles, and so on. The important point is that managers should approach the positioning process in a systematic and critical way, choosing appropriate frontiers for development that will keep them in close touch with the demands of the changing environments with which they have to deal.

Understanding oneself through the eyes of key stakeholders, especially one's competitors

An 'outside in' approach to management can also be fostered by focusing on key stakeholders in the environment. For example, an organization can learn much about itself by asking senior executives to define the main corporate competitors. The choice of a competitor implies a choice about the frontiers within which an organization sees itself conducting business.

Who are our competitors now?

How are they competing with us?

What does this tell us about the critical frontiers within which *we* are conducting business?

How can we change these frontiers to be more effective?

If we change, who will our new competitors be?

How can we be effective in relation to these new competitors?

Where will our competition be coming from in five years' time? In ten years' time? In twenty years' time?

What does this tell us about the future frontiers on which *we* will have to do business?

What new competencies will we need to develop?

What transitions will we have to make?

This line of questioning can be enormously constructive. For it encourages an 'outside in' approach to the identification and choice of frontiers for development, especially when an organization recognizes that its main competition may be coming from outside its immediate business domain. As one executive put it:

> When the competition seems to be coming from outside rather than from inside your industry, you need a new understanding of the business you're in.

The point has relevance for many industries and organizations: for courier firms and the Post Office, confronting competition in the form of national and international electronic mail; for schools, universities and business schools facing increasing competition from 'market-oriented' educational programs launched in the corporate sector; for Western manufacturing firms that must confront the reality of competition in the Third World; for copper producers facing the challenge of fibre optics and plastic pipes; for unions facing the problem that they cannot unionize robots and microprocessors; and so on.

When one thinks about one's competition in such broad terms, it is difficult to avoid re-thinking the nature of one's business and the strategies being pursued. Further, when the standpoint of potential competitors is used to identify the specific strengths and weaknesses of one's existing organization, many detailed operational insights of relevance to the here and now emerge.

For example, one of the executives involved in this project described how the planning process in his organization is energized by producing 'competitor plans'. Regular task-forces are established with the mandate of adopting the perspective of a primary competitor, and of producing a plan that will give that competitor an advantage over the parent firm. This view from the outside, free from the constraints of how the parent is doing business at present, and free from the internal politics of decision-making that may lead people to favor one strategy over another, provides the basis for a critical evaluation of the parent's position, and what it should do to take account of the strengths and weaknesses of the competitor plan. The approach allows the organization to see and challenge itself in an open and constructive way through a process that is only bounded by the imagination and ingenuity of the task-force producing the competitor plan. There is great potential for making this kind of critical review from the outside a part of an organization's ongoing management process.

Developing positioning and re-positioning skills

> Perhaps the most important investment an organization can make is to ensure that it has the capacity to adjust to the fractures and other changes occurring in its environment.

> If the jolts are coming with increasing rapidity, and greater impact, then . . . you've got to have a response capacity built in.

The kind of proactive, 'outside in' management described in previous sections demands much in terms of an organization's 'response capacities', and general ability to rise to the opportunities and challenges of a changing environment. Executives involved in this project were pretty well unanimous on the importance of developing such capacities, for all too often, it is in the implementation phase that potentially great projects begin to flounder.

But there are a number of specific points relating to problems often encountered in the positioning and re-positioning process that will demand special attention in the development of future competencies. They will be discussed here under four headings:

1 Risk-taking, 'sticking to the knitting', and the 'bottom line';
2 The problem of 'packaging': incrementalism versus grand designs;
3 Balancing creativity and discipline; and
4 The importance of timing.

Risk-taking, 'sticking to the knitting', and the 'bottom line'

The positioning process raises a major paradox for many organizations, because there is often a tension between trying to achieve significant shifts in direction, and maintaining healthy financial performance in the here and now. Major new projects can call for long- or short-term investments that may put an enormous strain on the financial viability of an organization, fueling a financial conservatism that can often block or get in the way of desirable change. The problems of handling this tension, and of finding creative ways of launching new investments, point towards important new managerial competencies in the financial sphere.

In addition, there are important social and cultural aspects to this tension, for the risk-taking and changes involved in any significant re-positioning can often run against widely held corporate values. For example, the very act of seeking to reposition an organization may itself open an executive to criticism. As one executive expressed it:

> The process (of re-positioning) contradicts a very strong value that has been found to be very, very responsible behavior in business . . . stick to your knitting and do what you do best.

And, as another put it:

> You are more easily punished for the risk that goes wrong than the risk that you didn't take, or the mistakes you didn't make.

The point is that in terms of corporate values, there may be important pressures favoring conservative actions rather than those with an above average degree of risk. The development of appropriate response capacities in an organization thus requires that close attention be devoted to these aspects of corporate culture.

Attention also needs to be paid to the problem of reconciling the demands for effective operation in the 'here and now' with the transitions and demands required for effective re-positioning. The problem can create much division in the organization, for as one executive put it:

> As I see it, you have to build a schizophrenic organization, one aspect of which . . . deals with the here and now: . . . since to make a profit this year, we've got to ship the goods out of the door, and we've got to satisfy the customers today . . . and another aspect of which builds for the long-term future, by building a structure that is competitive with the main business. I mean, its purpose eventually – I know we don't articulate it this way – but its purpose is to put the here and now aspect out of business. And over a period of time it will do that. Now, that creates a tension in that organization that we don't know how to manage.

Here again there is an important area for the development of managerial competence. Whether we are talking about the 'schizophrenic' potential described above, or the problems of overcoming technical or departmental divisions, effective re-positioning demands an ability to rally the energies of employees so that they help rather than block the required changes.

The problem of 'packaging': incrementalism versus grand designs

Many of the problems discussed above can be partly resolved in the way change is introduced and handled. For example, there are many ways of minimizing risk and exposure by moving in an incremental way. Some of the key issues were expressed by one executive in the following terms:

> In the management of organizations we tend to think in terms of packages. We need an ability to take opportunities and structure them into packages of

incremental decisions, to avoid putting oneself totally at risk. We have to expand our horizons to take new opportunities without endangering everything. The approach needed is *not* a total systems engineering approach (where everything is laid out from beginning to end), but one which is much more incremental. It's more than experimenting, and real skills are needed. . . . (Perhaps) we can develop clear ideas about packaging.

When the strategists, and systems designers get involved many blocks arise, because they can't see the end point. For example, (in a large corporation) it is often possible to get one's foot in the water by seeing whether an experiment can succeed: spending $10 million to see whether you want to spend $500 million. But many corporate thinkers say 'What's the point, unless you can move to the $500 million straight away?' They are only interested in the big projects. But by spending $5 or $10 million in a number of places you may be able to get to the one that will require $500 million.

The idea that incremental, experiment-oriented approaches to change can provide an effective way of approaching the re-positioning process occurred in many guises throughout executive discussions. To adopt this kind of incrementalism does not mean that an organization commits itself to aimless trial and error. For the experimental approach can be implemented within the context of a clear sense of corporate mission, and of what the organization is ultimately trying to do. Indeed, one of the most important skills required of top executives is that of being able to translate an overall sense of direction into 'actionable packages', thus making a vision a reality. This important leadership skill is crucial in developing the general capacities required for effective re-positioning.

Balancing creativity and discipline

The re-positioning process requires a creative, opportunity-seeking approach. But it also requires great discipline. For opportunities, once found, must usually be followed and explored in a systematic way. The 'schizophrenic' properties evident in the tensions created between present and future discussed above, are also found in the tensions between creativity and discipline. For many creative people who thrive on the challenge, excitement and openness of the idea-generating process, often shun the rigor required to make their ideas a success. It is thus important to strike some balance and integration here. For some organizations it will be found, to use the words of one chief executive:

> In cycles of searching for opportunities followed by working through their effects . . . periods in entrepreneurial mode, followed by consolidation, then breaking again into a more entrepreneurial view.

In other organizations, especially where innovation and change are the main driving force, creativity and discipline have to be integrated in an ongoing way. In both cases, important managerial skills are required to ensure that creativity and discipline are sustained on a continuous basis, and ride in tandem.

The importance of timing

Finally, there is the issue of making the right move at the right time. For example, as two executives expressed the problem:

> With product life-cycles as short as eighteen months, and products sometimes taking years to develop, a product can be obsolete before it gets to market. Timing is crucial.

> You go through a technological change (e.g. fast production lines to minimize cost). Then, a couple of years later you are going in reverse (e.g. slower lines with smarter machines that can make greater adjustments to accommodate changing product designs, and hence consumer preferences). . . . This is one of the great problems in manufacturing and other fields. You say: 'Hey, there is a direction', and you go with it, and you invest for a three or four year return, and then the market-place does a turnabout on you, and you have got a problem. You are sitting there with obsolete or unused equipment. I think this area, for managers, is a very critical one. I am faced with precisely this issue right now. Do I go a particular route or another one? I have got a ten million dollar proposal in front of me. And I am looking at it and saying, 'I don't know'.

An organization can read the environment in an appropriate way, and make all the right decisions. But if the timing is incorrect, or the 'windows of opportunity' are different from those anticipated, the best laid plans can flounder. There are no obvious recipes for improving managerial judgments on these difficult issues. But they will undoubtedly play an important part in the competencies of managers in the years ahead, and the general effectiveness of the kind of proactive management discussed in this chapter.

3

Megamarketing

Philip Kotler

Megamarketing impinges on the responsibilities of some non-marketing executives and argues that marketers should feel comfortable using power to accomplish their purposes.

Successful marketing is increasingly becoming a political exercise, as two recent episodes – one international and the other domestic – illustrate:

- Pepsi-Cola outwitted its arch rival Coca-Cola, by striking a deal to gain entry into India's huge consumer market of 730 million people. Coca-Cola had dominated the Indian soft drink market until it abruptly withdrew from India in 1978 in protest over Indian government policies. Coca-Cola, along with Seven-Up, tried to reenter, but hard work and effective political marketing gave Pepsi the prize.

  Pepsi worked with an Indian group to form a joint venture with terms designed to win government approval over the opposition of both domestic soft drink companies and anti-MNC legislators. Pepsi offered to help India export its agro-based products in a volume that would more than cover the cost of importing soft drink concentrate. Furthermore, Pepsi promised to focus considerable selling effort on rural areas as well as major urban markets. Pepsi also offered to bring new food-processing, packaging, and water treatment technology to India. Clearly, Pepsi-Cola orchestrated a set of benefits that would win over various interest groups in India.

- Citicorp, the US banking giant, had been trying for years to start full-service banking in Maryland. It had only credit card and small service operations in the state. Under Maryland law, out-of-state banks could provide only certain services and were barred from advertising, setting up branches, and other types of marketing efforts.

  In March 1985, Citicorp offered to build a major credit card center in Maryland that would create 1000 white-collar jobs and further offered the state $1 million in cash for the property where it would locate. By imaginatively designing a proposal to benefit Maryland, Citicorp will become the first out-of-state bank to provide full banking services there.

Reprinted from *Harvard Business Review*, March/April 1986: 117–24. Copyright © 1986 by the President and Fellows of Harvard College.

These two instances demonstrate the growing need for companies that want to operate in certain markets to master the art of supplying benefits to parties other than target consumers. This need extends beyond the requirements to serve and satisfy normal intermediaries like agents, distributors, and dealers. I am talking about third parties – governments, labor unions, and other interest groups – that, singly or collectively, can block profitable entry into a market. These groups act as gatekeepers, and they are growing in importance.

Markets characterized by high entry barriers can be called *blocked* or *protected* markets. In addition to the four Ps of marketing strategy – product, price, place, and promotion – executives must add two more – power and public relations. I call such strategic thinking *megamarketing*.

Marketing is the task of arranging need-satisfying and profitable offers to target buyers. Sometimes, however, it is necessary to create additional incentives and pressures at the right times and in the right amounts for non-customers. Megamarketing thus takes an enlarged view of the skills and resources needed to enter and operate in certain markets. In addition to preparing attractive offers for customers, megamarketers may use inducements and sanctions to gain the desired responses from gatekeepers. I define megamarketing as the strategically coordinated application of economic, psychological, political, and public relations skills to gain the cooperation of a number of parties in order to enter and/or operate in a given market. Megamarketing challenges are found in both domestic and international situations.

This chapter describes marketing situations that call for megamarketing strategies and shows how companies can organize their power and public relations resources to achieve entry and operating success in blocked markets.

Strategies for entry

As they mature, markets acquire a fixed set of suppliers, competitors, distributors, and customers. These players develop a vested interest in preserving the market's closed system and seek to protect it against intruders. They are often supported by government regulatory agencies, labor unions, banks, and other institutions. They may erect visible and invisible barriers to entry: taxes, tariffs, quotas, and compliance requirements.

Examples of such closed markets abound. A long-standing complaint against Japan concerns the visible and invisible barriers that protect many of its markets. Besides facing high tariffs, foreign companies encounter difficulty in signing up good Japanese distributors and dealers, even when the non-Japanese companies offer superior products and better margins. Motorola, for example, fought for years to sell its telecommunications equipment in Japan. It succeeded only by influencing Washington to apply pressure on Japan and by redesigning its equipment to comply with Japan's tough and sometimes arbitrary standards.

Other countries as well are erecting barriers to the free entry of foreign competitors to protect their manufacturers, suppliers, distributors, and dealers. France, for example, has adopted a number of official and un-official measures to limit the number of Japanese cars and consumer elec-tronics products entering its market. France for a time routed Japanese video-cassette recorders into Poitier, a medium-sized inland town, for record-keeping and inspection purposes; only two inspectors were assigned to handle the mounting volume of Japanese goods. The goods sat in customs for so long that Japan's market share and profits were severely restricted.

The British and French developers of the Concorde airplane encountered obstacles in their efforts to obtain landing rights to serve a number of cities; most prominent among the opposition were entrenched airlines and protesters against noise. The Concorde group, which needed to sell sixty-four planes to break even, sold only sixteen; the result was the costliest new product failure in history.

Of course, companies that have trouble breaking into new markets are not always victims of blocked markets. The problem may be inferior products, overpricing, financing difficulties, unwillingness to pay taxes or tariffs that other companies pay, or protection of the market by a legitimate patent. By blocked markets, I mean markets in which the established participants or approvers have made it difficult for companies with similar or even better marketing offers to enter or operate. The barriers may include discriminatory legal requirements, political favoritism, cartel agreements, social or cultural biases, unfriendly distribution channels, and refusals to cooperate. These create the challenge that megamarketing has to overcome.

How can companies break into blocked markets? There is usually an easy way and a hard way. The easy way is to offer many concessions, thus making it almost unprofitable to enter the market. Japan recently won a coveted contract in Turkey to build a 3576-foot suspension bridge spanning the Bosporus Strait. Its bid was so low that both the competitors and the Turks were startled; the rivals were left grumbling about unfair competi-tion. Complained the manager of Cleveland Bridge & Engineering, 'It would be cheaper [for Japan] to go to the Turks and say, "We'll give you the bridge".'

The hard way is to formulate a strategy for entry, a task calling for skills never acquired by most marketers through normal training and experience. Marketers are trained primarily in the use of the four Ps: product, price, place, and promotion. They know how to create a cost-effective marketing mix that appeals to customers and end-users. But customers and end-users are not always the main problem. When a huge gate blocks the company's path into the market, it needs to blast the gate open or at least find the key so that its goods can be offered to potential customers.

To further complicate matters, not one but several gates must be opened for the company to reach its goal of selling in the blocked market. The company must identify each gatekeeper and convert it by applying influence or power.

Moreover, the strategic marketing effort does not end with successful entry into the protected market. The company must know how to stay in as well as break in. Indian government regulations forced Coca-Cola and IBM to leave the country after many years of operating there. Today, IBM in France is doing its best to withstand French protectionist sentiment; its program includes political and public opinion strategies.

Megamarketing skills

The following two examples help illustrate megamarketing problems and the skills needed to cope successfully.

Freshtaste and the Japanese market

Freshtaste, a US manufacturer of milk-sterilizing equipment, wants to introduce its equipment into Japan but has encountered numerous problems (Cateora and Hess, 1979). Sterilized milk is a recent innovation that offers two main advantages over fresh milk: it can be stored at room temperature for up to three months and has twice the refrigerated shelf-life of ordinary milk after the package is opened. Freshtaste has developed superior equipment for sterilizing milk that avoids the unpleasant side effects of sterilization – a cooked and slightly burnt taste and a filminess that lingers in the mouth after the milk is swallowed.

In searching for new markets for its equipment, the company sees Japan as a good candidate. Japan has a large population, a low but growing rate of per capita milk consumption, and a limited availability of fresh milk. As Freshtaste sets out to sell its equipment to large Japanese dairies, it encounters the following obstacles:

1 It has to develop an advertising campaign to change Japanese milk consumption habits and convince Japanese consumers of the advantages of buying and drinking sterilized milk.
2 The Consumers' Union of Japan opposes the product because of concerns about sterilized milk's safety.
3 Dairy farmers located near large cities oppose the distribution of sterilized milk. They fear competition from faraway dairies, since sterilized milk has a long inventory life and can be shipped long distances.
4 Several large retailers say they will not carry sterilized milk because of interest-group pressure. Milk speciality stores, which thrive on home deliveries, also oppose the introduction of sterilized milk.
5 The Health and Welfare Ministry and the Ministry of Agriculture and

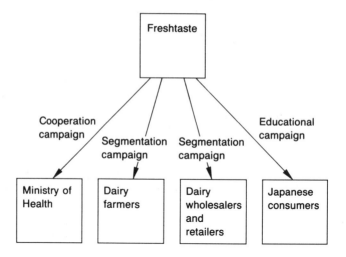

Figure 1   *Freshtaste's megamarketing challenge*

Forestry have indicated they will wait and gauge consumer acceptance of sterilized milk before taking action to approve or disapprove general distribution.

Freshtaste must thus undertake campaigns tailored to each barrier, as shown in Figure 1. It must seek cooperation from the Ministry of Health; attract support from favorable segments of dairy farmers, wholesalers, and retailers; and educate Japanese consumers. The company faces a formidable megamarketing problem calling for adroit political and public relations skills as well as normal commercial ones. It must be sure that the Japanese market is large enough, and the probability of successful entry high enough, to justify the cost and time involved in trying to enter this market.

Japanese consumer electronics in India

Japanese companies have coped with blocked markets in ingenious ways. India, for example, banned the import of luxury consumer electronics products in a drive to conserve its foreign hard currency and protect its fledgling home consumer electronics industry. Yet Japanese companies like Sony, Panasonic and Toshiba have taken steps to pry open the Indian market, however slightly, to its brands of televisions, video-cassette recorders, and stereos (Rajan Varadarajan, 1984).

Although many Japanese consumer electronics products are not officially available in India, several Japanese companies advertise their products in Indian newspapers and magazines in order to build preference for them should they become available at a later date. In the meantime, this advertising influences the selection of Japanese products by Indian tourists in Sri Lanka, Singapore, and other free markets as well as by

Table 1 *Marketing and megamarketing contrasted*

	Marketing	Megamarketing
Marketing objective	To satisfy consumer demand	To gain market access in order to satisfy consumer demand or to create or alter consumer demand
Parties involved	Consumers, distributors, dealers, suppliers, marketing firms, banks	Normal parties plus legislators, government agencies, labor unions, reform groups, general public
Marketing tools	Market research, product development, pricing, distribution planning, promotion	Normal tools plus the use of power and public relations
Type of inducement	Positive and official inducements	Positive inducements (official and unofficial) and negative inducements (threats)
Time frame	Short	Much longer
Investment cost	Low	Much higher
Personnel involved	Marketers	Marketers plus company officers, lawyers, public relations and public affairs staff

Indian workers laboring in other countries. Furthermore, some Japanese products enter the Indian market unofficially and are immediately purchased by consumers.

In addition, the Japanese government supports Japanese companies by lobbying the Indian government for a relaxation of the ban or for its transformation into quotas or normal tariffs. In return, Japan offers to buy more Indian goods and services.

Thus, although the Japanese businesses cannot export certain products to India, they have pursued megamarketing actions on several fronts to gain access to this vast and fertile market.

Megamarketing vs marketing

Although companies face a growing number of blocked markets, they are rarely organized to develop or execute megamarketing strategies. By comparing megamarketing with marketing, Table 1 suggests why. The comparison means reviewing elementary aspects of marketing, but the review is necessary to evaluate megamarketing effectively.

Marketing objectives In normal marketing situations, a market already exists for a given product category. Consumers understand that category and simply choose among a set of brands and suppliers. A company entering the market will define a target need or customer group, design the appropriate product, set up distribution, and establish a marketing communications program. On the other hand, megamarketers face the problem of first gaining market access. If the product is quite new, they must also be skilled in creating or altering demand. This requires more skill and time than simply meeting existing demand.

Parties involved   Marketers routinely deal with several parties: customers, suppliers, distributors, advertising agencies, market research firms, and others. Megamarketing situations involve even more parties: legislators, government agencies, political parties, public-interest groups, unions, and churches, among others. Each party has an interest in the company's activity and must be sold on supporting, or at least not blocking, the company. Megamarketing is thus a greater multiparty marketing problem than marketing.

Marketing tools   Megamarketing involves the normal tools of marketing (the four Ps) plus two others: power and public relations.

Power. The megamarketer must often win the support of influential industry officials, legislators, and government bureaucrats to enter and operate in the target market. A pharmaceutical company, for example, that is trying to introduce a new birth control pill into a country will have to obtain the approval of the country's ministry of health. Thus the megamarketer needs political skills and a political strategy.

The company must identify the people with the power to open the gate. It must determine the right mix of incentives to offer. Under what circumstances will the gatekeepers acquiesce? Is legislator X primarily seeking fame, fortune, or power? How can the company induce this legislator to cooperate? In some countries, the answer may be with a cash payoff (a hidden P). Elsewhere, a payoff in entertainment, travel, or campaign contributions may work. Essentially, the megamarketer must have sophisticated lobbying and negotiating skills in order to achieve the desired response from the other party without giving away the house.

Public relations. Whereas power is a push strategy, public relations is a pull strategy. Public opinion takes longer to cultivate, but when energized, it can help pull the company into the market.

Indeed, power alone may not get a company into a market or keep it there. In the late 1960s, for example, Japanese chemical companies received permission to open chemical factories in Korea by exploiting Korea's desperate need to expand its heavy industry. They played the power game with the Korean government by offering technological assistance, new jobs, and side payments to government officials. In the early 1970s, however, the Korean media accused Japanese factories of exposing young female workers to toxic chemicals; most of them became infertile. The Japanese companies tried to pay government officials to quiet the media but they could not silence public opinion. They should have paid more attention to establishing responsible production methods and cultivating the public's goodwill.

Before entering a market, companies must understand the community's beliefs, attitudes, and values. After entering, they need to play the role of good citizen by contributing to public causes, sponsoring civic and cultural events, and working effectively with the media. Olivetti, for example, has won a good name in many markets by making large contributions to worthwhile causes in host countries. It has shown skill in the strategic management of its corporate public image.

Type of inducement Marketers are trained primarily in the art of using positive inducements to persuade other parties to cooperate. They believe in the voluntary exchange principle: each party should offer sufficient benefits to the other to motivate voluntary exchanges.

Megamarketers, however, often find that conventional inducements are insufficient. The other party either wants more than is reasonable or refuses to accept any positive inducement at all. Thus the company may have to add unofficial payments to speed the approval process. Or it may threaten to withdraw support or mobilize opposition to the other party. The relationships of auto manufacturers with their franchised dealers and of drugstore chains with some pharmaceutical manufacturers demonstrate how companies use raw power from time to time to gain their ends (Ridgway, 1957, Palamountain, 1955).

Although companies occasionally use negative as well as positive inducements, most experts believe that positive inducements are better in the long run (Skinner, 1971). Negative inducements are ethically questionable and may produce resentment that can backfire on the marketer.

Time frame Most product introductions take only a few years. Megamarketing challenges, on the other hand, usually require much more time. Numerous gates have to be opened, and if the product is new to the public, much work has to be done to educate the target market.

Investment cost Because the effort must be sustained over a long period and may entail side payments to secure the cooperation of various parties, megamarketing involves higher costs as well as more time.

Personnel involved Marketing problems are normally handled by a product manager, who draws on the services of advertising specialists, market researchers, and other professionals. Megamarketing problems require additional skilled personnel, both inside and outside the company: top managers, lawyers, public relations and public affairs professionals. Megamarketing planning and implementation teams are large and require much coordination. For example, when KLM, the Dutch airline, sought landing rights in Taiwan, the company's president participated, its international department exploited its contacts with Taiwan officials, its public relations department put out favorable news stories and arranged news conferences, and its lawyers participated in the negotiations to make sure the contracts were sound.

Although new skills are required to enter blocked markets, marketing professionals need not be specially trained in the additional skills. Rather, they need to broaden their view of what it takes to enter these markets and to coordinate various specialists to achieve the desired goals.

Marketers as political strategists

Few marketers are trained in the art of politics and are thus unaccustomed to using power to achieve favorable transactions. Most marketers think that value, not power, wins in the marketplace.

The growth of protected markets, however, requires marketers to incorporate the notion of power into their strategies. Marketing is increasingly becoming the art of managing power. What do they need to know about power? They need to know that power is the ability of one party (A) to get another party (B) to do what it might not otherwise have done. It is A's ability to increase the probability of B's taking an action. A can draw on at least five bases of power to influence B (French and Raven, 1959).

Rewards   A offers to reward B for engaging in the desired behavior. The reward might be recognition, entertainment, gifts, or payments. Marketers are expert in the use of rewards.

Coercion   A threatens to harm B in the absence of compliant behavior. A may threaten physical, social, or financial harm. Marketers have been loath to use coercive power because of its doubtful ethical status, because it does not square with the marketing concept, and because it can create hostility that can backfire on the marketer.

Expertise or information   A offers B special expertise, such as technical assistance or access to special information, in exchange for B's compliance.

Legitimacy   A is seen to have a legitimate right to make certain requests of B. An example would be the Japanese premier asking Nippon Electric Company to put Motorola on its approved supplier list.

Prestige   A has prestige in B's mind and draws on this to request B's compliance. An example would be Chrysler president Lee Iacocca requesting a meeting with officials in a foreign country to present arguments for opening a Chrysler plant in that country.

Power is key to megamarketers. Companies that find themselves blocked from a market must undertake a three-step process for creating an entry strategy: mapping the power structure, forging a grand strategy, and developing a tactical implementation plan.

Mapping the power structure

Executives must first understand how power is distributed in the particular target community (city, state, nation). Political scientists identify three types of power structures (Mitchell and Lowry, 1973). The first type is a pyramidal power structure in which power is invested in a ruling elite, which may be an individual, a family, a company, an industry, or a clique. The elite carries out its wishes through a layer of lieutenants, who in turn manage a layer of doers. The marketing strategist who wants to operate in such a community can get in only if the ruling elite approves or is neutral.

The second type is a factional power structure in which two or more factions (power blocs, pressure groups, special-interest groups) compete for power in the community. Political parties are an example. The competing parties represent different constituencies – labor, business, ethnic minorities, or farmers. Here the company's strategists must decide with which factions they want to work. In allying with certain factions, the company usually loses the goodwill of others.

The third type is a coalition power structure in which influential parties from various power blocs form temporary coalitions. When power is in the hands of a coalition, however temporarily, the company has to work through the coalition to secure its objectives. Or the company can form a countercoalition to support its cause.

Identifying the power structure as pyramidal, factional, or coalitional is only the first step of the analysis. Executives next have to assess the relative power of various parties. A's power over B is directly related to B's dependence on A. B's dependence on A is directly proportional to B's interest in goals controlled by A and inversely proportional to B's chance of achieving the goals without A. In other words, A has power over B to the extent that A can directly affect B's goal attainment and B has few alternatives (Emerson, 1962).

Forging a grand strategy

In planning entry into a blocked market, the company must identify opponents, allies, and neutral groups. Its aim is to overcome the opposition, and it can choose from three broad strategies:

1 Neutralize opponents by offering to compensate them for any losses. The theory of welfare economics holds that a proposed action will generally be supported if everyone benefits or if those who benefit can satisfactorily compensate those who are hurt. Compensation costs should be included as part of the total cost when determining whether it pays to go forward with the project.

2 Organize allies into a coalition. The company's potential supporters may be scattered in the community, and their individual power is less than their potential collective power. Thus the company can further its cause by creating a coalition of allies.
3 Turn neutral groups into allies. Most groups in a community will be unaffected by the company's entry and thus indifferent. The company can use influence and rewards to convert these groups into supporters.

A growing number of companies are forming strategic alliances – licensing arrangements, joint ventures, management contracts, and consortia – to overcome blocked markets. Examples of strategic partnering in the automobile industry include General Motors–Toyota, Ford–Mazda, and Renault–AMC. In other industries, we have such examples as Honeywell–Ericsson in communications, Sharp–Olivetti in office automation equipment, and Philips–Siemens in voice-synthesis technology (Conrads, 1983). Intercompany networking offers a superior means for securing entry and operating clout in otherwise blocked markets.

Still another approach is to harness the power of one's government to aid in opening another country's market. This calls for effective 'at home' lobbying of the sort Motorola did in getting the US government to pressure Japan into opening its telecommunications market. Similarly, American computer companies lobbied in Washington to get President Reagan to threaten banning various Brazilian exports to the United States if Brazil did not rescind its bill banning the sale of foreign-made computers in Brazil.

Developing a tactical implementation plan

Once a company has chosen a broad strategy, it must create an implementation plan that spells out who does what, when, where, and how. Activities can be sequenced in two broad ways: in linear or multilinear fashion (Figure 2). Adopting a linear approach, Freshtaste (described earlier) can try first to win the approval of Japan's Minister of Health to market its product because, without that approval, the company cannot succeed. If it gets the approval, Freshtaste might then try to convince one or more large retailers to carry sterilized milk. Again, if it cannot accomplish this, it will withdraw. In this way, Freshtaste accumulates successive commitments before entering the market.

Multilinear sequencing will shorten the time required for accomplishing the project. Freshtaste executives could contact the minister and the supermarket chains simultaneously. If some supermarket chains sign up, Freshtaste can then contact some dairies and start a consumer education campaign. If, however, some crucial commitment is not forthcoming, Freshtaste will withdraw. This approach may lose more money but settle the issues earlier.

Linear
sequencing
approach

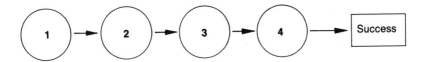

Multilinear
sequencing
approach

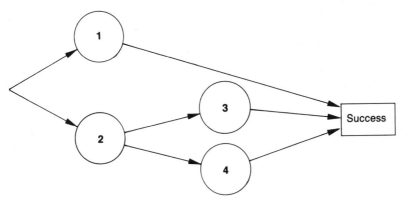

1 Contact Minister of Health and Welfare; 2 Contact a few large supermarket chains;
3 Contact some key dairies; 4 Run an educational campaign for consumers.

Figure 2   *Two ways to implement a tactical plan*

Implications of megamarketing

Megamarketing broadens the thinking of marketers in three ways:

1 Enlarging the multiparty marketing concept. Marketers spend much
  time analyzing how to create preference and satisfaction in target
  buyers. Because other parties – governments, labor unions, banks,
  reform groups – can block the path to the target buyers, marketers
  must also study the obstacles these parties create and develop strategies
  for attracting their support or at least neutralizing their opposition.
2 Blurring the distinction between environmental and controllable
  variables. Marketers have traditionally defined the environment as
  those outside forces that cannot be controlled by the business. But
  megamarketing argues that some environmental forces can be changed
  through lobbying, legal action, negotiation, issue advertising, public

relations, and strategic partnering (Zeithaml and Zeithaml, 1984).

3 Broadening the understanding of how markets work. Most market thinkers assume that demand creates its own supply. Ideally, companies discover a market need and rush to satisfy that need. But real markets are often blocked, and the best marketer does not always win. We have seen that foreign competitors with offers comparable or superior to those of local companies cannot always enter the market. The result is a lower level of consumer satisfaction and producer innovation than would otherwise result.

Some may oppose the enlarged view of marketing proposed here. After all, megamarketing impinges on the responsibilities of some non-marketing executives and argues that marketers should feel comfortable using power to accomplish their purposes. Marketers normally deal with other parties in the most courteous manner; many will suffer image shock in adopting the megamarketing approach. Yet this innocence has led companies to fail in both international and home markets where trans-actions are marked by tough bargaining, side payments, and various complexities. Megamarketing offers executives an approach to dealing with rising international and domestic competition for large-scale and long-term sales.

Note

The author would like to thank Professor Nikhilesh Dholakia of the University of Rhode Island, Professor David Ford of the University of Bath, England, Clive Porter of Marketing Science International of Australia, and Professor Hans Thorelli of Indiana University for their helpful comments.

References

Cateora, Philip R. and Hess, John M. (1979) *International Marketing*. Homewood, IL: Richard D. Irwin. p. 234.

Conrads, Robert J. (1983) 'Strategic partnering: a new formula to crack new markets in the 80s', *Electronic Business Management*, March: 23.

Emerson, Richard M. (1962) 'Power-dependence relations', *American Sociological Review*, February: 31.

French, John R. P., Jr and Raven, Bertram (1959) 'The bases of social power', in Dorwin Cartwright (ed.), *Studies in Social Power*. Ann Arbor, MI: Institute for Social Research. p. 118.

Mitchell, John B. and Lowry, Sheldon G. (1973) *Power Structure, Community Leadership and Social Action*. Columbus: Ohio State University Cooperative Extension Service.

Palamountain, Joseph C. (1955) *The Politics of Distribution*. Cambridge, MA: Harvard University Press.

Rajan Varadarajan, P. (1984) 'A strategy for penetrating Third World markets with high entry barriers: an exposition of the Japanese approach'. Unpublished paper, Texas A&M University.

Ridgway, Valentine F. (1957) 'Administration of manufacturer-dealer systems', *Administrative Science Quarterly*, March: 464.

Skinner, B. F. (1971) *Beyond Freedom and Dignity*. New York: Alfred A. Knopf.

Zeithaml, Carl P. and Zeithaml, Valarie A. (1984) 'Environmental management: revising the marketing perspective', *Journal of Marketing*, spring: 47.

4

From forecasting to 'la prospective' – a new way of looking at futures

Michel Godet

Classical forecasting and its errors

The economic history of industrial society has been marked by repeated forecasting errors. What is serious is not so much the existence of errors, as the systematic ignoring of past errors when new forecasts are made.

In 1972, before what came to be known as the energy crisis, forecasts of energy consumption reckoned on the continuance of a declining trend in relative oil prices until 1980–5. The present economic crisis is partly due to the forecasts that cheap energy would continue to be available. The enormity of the errors highlights the ridiculous precision with which the forecasts are presented. In a period of a few years, forecasts of energy prices increased more than fourfold.

The need for an overall view

Most of the forecasting models include a few explanatory variables, most of which can be easily quantified. They do not taken into account the development of new relationships and the possible changes in trends. A major failure in forecasting arises from the fact that the economy is regarded as autonomous. Economic forecasting is therefore divorced from social and political forecasting and is itself fragmented into technological, demographic and other forecasts.

On the other hand, there is a strong need to study an entire system in which everything is more and more interdependent and in which the whole, as distinct from the sum of the parts, is reflected in each part. Since the parts are interdependent, reasoning based on the assumption of 'everything else being held constant' cannot explain the evolution of social economic phenomena where everything moves simultaneously. An understanding of the whole is necessary, therefore, to deal with the individual parts of a system, and not the other way round, as is advocated by 'classical' long-term forecasting approaches.

Reprinted from *Journal of Forecasting* 1 (1982): 293–301. Reproduced by permission from John Wiley & Sons Ltd.

The limits of quantification and models

The impossibility of forecasting the future as a function solely of past data explains the weakness of econometric modelling which does not integrate qualitative and non-quantifiable parameters such as the wishes and behaviour of relevant actors. It should be emphasized that the dangers of false quantification – quantifying involves giving priority to what is quantifiable at the expense of what is not – should not lead to the total rejection of numbers. But we should use them with extreme caution, especially since statistics are flawed by errors. As Morgenstern (1972) emphasizes, national income and consumers purchasing figures include errors of the magnitude of plus or minus 10–15 per cent. Thus input data are incomplete and contain errors; furthermore, the choice of model is not neutral, but conditions the result. The model embodies a theory whose value is limited by the fact that, although there is a single set of data used, there can be a multiplicity of models and interpretations. Model users, on the other hand, believe unduly in the objectivity of their models.

In addition, models are deterministic, but the future depends largely on human actions based on the exercise of free will, which makes them unrealistic. Furthermore, 'classical' forecasting models are not only deterministic, but also assume structural stability, which is another source of forecasting error, since changes are always possible.

Finally, quantitative models tend to reassure. Their mathematics has become more and more sophisticated, and in relying on them, it is easy to forget that the hypothesis and choice of model determine the results achieved. 'The use of mathematics does not in itself solve the problem, even if it allows the problem to be posed more rigorously. For instance, a system of false concepts remains a system of false concepts even when a whole body of theorems is rigorously deduced. The formulation of equations does not in itself confer scientific quality' (Amin, 1971).

The absence of neutrality of information and forecasts

Information about the future, as that of the present or the past, is rarely neutral: usually it serves specific interests. How many studies and analyses are lying hidden in drawers because they are politically undesirable; how many pertinent reports are emptied of their substance by careful selection of words; how many realities are ignored because they do not fit preconceived ideas. Information is manipulated simply because it is a major source of power. As Crozier and Friedberg (1977: 107, 181) have pointed out 'information is a rare commodity, and its communication and exchange are not neutral and free processes. To inform someone, to give him information which he does not possess, is to divest oneself, to relinquish those trump cards which could be sold, to make oneself vulnerable in the face of takeover attempts. . . . Total communication is impossible.

To enter into a relationship with another, to seek to open up to him is at the same time to hide and to protect oneself behind fortifications and to oppose him. Briefly any relation with another is strategic and contains a power component, however repressed or sublimated it may be.'

The past and the present are irreversible, unique and certain, but the knowledge we have of them is incomplete; even if the facts of the past are certain, they are only a tiny part of the unknown number of phenomena that make up reality. In consequence, history is only a bet on one of many interpretations (the facts are unique, their interpretations are multiple). It is in this sense that we can say that there are several pasts, or rather several approximations to the same past which one never totally knows.

By the same token, any forecasting requires choices within a system of values, and an ideology, implicit or explicit. Forecasting is, therefore, only valid insofar as this system and ideology is itself acceptable to the reader or the user.

The publication of forecasts themselves influences the future as people inevitably react to forecasts. Thus, a forecast that there will be a scarcity of sugar can become a self-fulfilling prophecy when large numbers of people believe it and rush to buy sugar, thus creating a real scarcity.

To 'la prospective' as an approach to dealing with the future

The inadequacy of 'classical' forecasting techniques can be explained by their down playing, or outright ignoring, of the role played by creative human actions in determining the future. This creative attitude is recognized by the 'prospective' approach, which reflects awareness of a future that is both deterministic and free, both passively suffered and actively willed.

'Prospective', first used by Berger (1964) has become widespread in expressing this new attitude to the future. The word 'forecasting' remains too strongly charged with its classical meaning of prediction and is used mainly in the sense of quantified calculations.

The future is not written: it has still to be built

To understand the future, one must first start with the past; what we regret about the past is usually the future ahead of us. Thus, the past is a dead future. The only determinism we grant the past consists of the varying degrees of freedom that past actions have left us to act in the present so as to realize some future plan. What happens in the future results from our past actions, while our desire explains present actions. From this viewpoint, there is no determinism except in the sense that a given evolution of the past presents one particular range of possible futures and not another. Man, insofar as he has not committed or

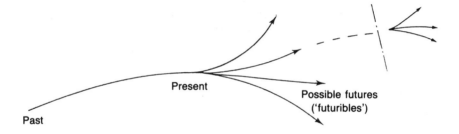

Figure 1   *A multiple and uncertain future*

mortgaged his future, retains many degrees of freedom from which he can profit. He can, then, promote one or another alternative future(s) depending upon what he regards as more desirable in relation to his own objectives.

The future should not be envisaged in a unique and predetermined mode, or as a continuation of the past: the future is multiple and uncertain. The plurality of the future and the degrees of freedom for human action go hand in hand; the future is not written; it remains to be built. This is an advantage since man has control over what might come; on the other hand, the ability of man to influence the future is a major source of uncertainty as far as forecasting is concerned. There are constraints in terms of how much the future can be influenced. Nevertheless, in a world which is unequal and confrontational, the future is the result of the interaction of unequal human forces, shaped by human actions, trends, and constraints. Finally, the future does not belong to everyone in the same way and the same degree: some actors exercise a greater influence than others.

To accept that the future is multiple, and that there is no unique model describing its evolution, is also implicitly to acknowledge that the horizons of 'prospective' are to be viewed in the plural (see Figure 1). Structural changes, resistances, and discontinuities are part of the future. Furthermore, the acceleration of change, coupled with the variety of systems studied, leads to accepting a range of different time-scales. From this point of view, the concepts of short, medium and long term are not important except as a function of the problem being studied. For instance, 'long-term' is when many things may have changed.

The future is the raison d'être of the present

Societies are most frequently in a state of transition when the old equilibrium of forces has disappeared. But when the old equilibrium is not yet born or stable, it is necessary to look at the future to clarify the present, so that 'the future is the *raison d'être* of the present'. 'Prospective' is an anticipated retrospective.

We are well familiar with the forces of the past, but to explain the present, we must also ask ourselves about the future. To understand more fully today the events that occurred in 1960 or to understand what is happening today, we must place ourselves in 1990 or beyond. With regard to the essentially subjective nature of reflection about the future, it is primarily the idea we form of the future that explains the present. For example, in basing an individual's consumption at a given moment on expected future income (theory of continuous income), Milton Friedman places importance on psychological factors. To say that production in a given year depends on prices in previous years explains nothing in itself. What is important for the entrepreneur is his idea of the price in future years, whether or not it is relative to that of past years. This determines his production and investment plans. The image of the future thus imprints itself on the present.

On that basis, and if several futures are possible, the one which will in fact be produced is born as much from the confrontations of the projections of the various actors as from the continuation of existing trends. The various actors present in a system often have contradictory ideas and preferences about possible futures. The future must be considered as the result of these different forces. In order to identify the most probable results, it is necessary to understand fully the projects and intentions of the actors, their methods of action on one another, coupled with the constraints imposed on them.

The image of the future is not solely speculative; it is, in particular, normative and results as much from actions as from constraints. The purpose of the prospective approach is to prepare the way (both desirable and feasible) for the future. Its aim is to guide our present actions so as to expand the field of the feasible. It should, in particular, lead to the careful consideration of decisions that could irreversibly determine the future, or deprive us of freedom of movement. A prospective decision, therefore, is less concerned with maximizing short-term advantage. Its major consideration is to keep as many choices open as possible.

Central to the approach advocated in this chapter is that the future is emerging, but its details are unknown. Despite these unknowns, it is necessary to take decisions today which will commit us in the future. Often our ability to predict future events is limited, and in the lack of precise information, we might find it necessary to gamble. This must be done, however, without mortgaging the future. We need freedom of action. The future is unpredictable, increasingly changing, and uncertain.

A key to understanding crises

In our view, the future is mainly the result of conflicts between unequal actors in a system of variable constraints. The future possibilities are multiple and undetermined – to be an actor implies freedom and, consequently, uncertainty. By looking at desires or wishes as a productive force of the future it is possible to understand better why political, economic and social structures break down when constraints increase beyond a certain level. Problems inevitably arise when the gap between reality and aspirations becomes too wide. This is why it is important to deal with these problems by understanding the gap between wishes and aspirations.

Crisis reflects a change in the rules of the game and the functioning (relationships) of a system. This change is desired by certain actors and rejected by others. There is a crisis when, as a result of the changing balance of power, the gap between reality and aspirations becomes too great and requires new rules. The crisis takes place when the change is sufficiently powerful to disturb the former rules of the game, but not powerful enough to impose new rules. As long as the old is dying, but the new is not yet born, the system will be unregulated and in a state of crisis.

The monetary, economic and energy crises which we have experienced since the beginning of the 1970s confirms this analysis. The monetary crisis reflects the relative political and economic decline of the United States as compared with the other Western nations. In the new relationships, the dollar is not sufficiently powerful to play its former role as a regulator, but is still too powerful to be ignored. The crisis will last until another rule is found and accepted by the participants of the monetary game.

The energy crisis is of similar type – the quadrupling of oil prices does not result from a sudden change in the quantities available or required but only from a change in the conditions of the supply, that is to say in the balance of power between producers and consumers.

The old price fixing rules have disappeared, new rules were established for which we were not prepared and which we refused to accept. There was gap between the new reality and the former aspirations. Current and future increases in oil prices can only confirm or nullify the authority of the new rules of the game. The physical shortages which are predicted are only the logical consequences of our refusal to clearly see the new reality facing us and take necessary measures (capital investments, exploration, energy-savings).

Crises, on the other hand, develop because we refuse to adapt our behaviour and our structures to the new rules of the game. Crises can be visualized as the difference between existing rules, which we have already learnt, and those which still have to be learnt. It must be accepted that crises will last as long as our period of learning. We cannot expect to end crises other than by changing our behaviour and possibly our lifestyles (for more details, see Godet, 1980).

Comparing 'classical' forecasting and 'la prospective'

Partial viewpoints, quantitative variables, the perception of relationships as static, the explanation of the future by the past, the search for a unique and predetermined future with the help of deterministic models, are

Table 1 *Characteristics of classical forecasting compared with those of the prospective approach*

	Classical forecasting	Prospective approach
Viewpoint	Piecemeal 'Everything else being equal'	Overall approach 'Nothing else being equal'
Variables	Quantitative, objective and known	Qualitative, not necessarily quantitative, subjective, known or hidden
Relationships	Static, fixed structures	Dynamic, evolving structures
Explanation	The past explains the future	The future is the *raison d'être* of the present
Future	Single and certain	Multiple and uncertain
Method	Deterministic and quantitative models (econometric, mathematical)	Intentional analysis Qualitative (structural analysis) and stochastic (cross-impacts) models
Attitude to the future	Passive or adaptive (future *comes* about)	Active and creative (future *brought* about)

embodied in 'classical' forecasting. The result of such attitudes towards forecasting can be huge forecasting errors. Most important however, is that actions and wishes, the things that cannot be expressed by equations, have no place in 'classical' forecasting.

The 'prospective' approach actively participates in the creation of the future. Its characteristics are radically different from those of 'classical' forecasting. Numerous forecasting errors and, in fact, the crisis in forecasting as a whole could be avoided by using the prospective approach. Table 1 shows seven characteristics of the 'prospective' approach and distinguishes them from those of 'classical' forecasting.

The scenario method, widely used in 'prospective', is a powerful tool for constructing alternative futures. It is from these futures that decision-makers can choose the one which best fits their objectives and which can be attained given existing constraints.

The method of scenarios as used by 'la prospective'

'La prospective' accepts that the future is multiple, the outcome of various actors and their actions. The scenarios method, as used in the 'prospective' approach, is concerned with deriving these multiple futures and with exploring the pathways leading to them. Literary scenarios, however, although they may represent a stimulating exercise for the imagination, suffer from a lack of credibility. It is impossible to verify the validity and plausibility of the hypotheses advanced. This is why an alternative way has been developed by the 'prospective' approach whose objectives are:

1 To identify which points should be studied as a matter of priority (key variables), by confronting the variables relating to the phenomenon being studied and the variables describing the environment, using an overall explanatory analysis as exhaustive as possible. Structural analysis makes it possible to take this overall view. In particular, the MICMAC 1 (Cross Impact Matrices-Multiplication Applied to Classification) method, which analyses the direct relationships and feedback effects between variables makes it easier to understand the dynamics of the system being studied (Godet, 1979).
2 To determine the interrelationships among the key variables, the relative power of the fundamental actors, their strategies, the resources which they have at their disposal, their objectives, and the constraints which they must overcome. This is the specific object of the retrospective and the present situation analysis.

When a scenario has been chosen, some 'classical' forecasting techniques can be used, within the framework defined by the scenario, to translate this scenario into quantitative terms.

The method of scenarios has been applied in many cases during the last few years. It consists of three major phases (see Figure 2):

(a) The construction of the base, where the problem posed is situated in its broadest environment and where the existing state of the system is studied so as to understand the mechanisms and to identify the development prospects.
(b) The elaboration of the scenarios, where, using the results of the previous phase, the probabilities of realization of the various possible final images are obtained, with the use of cross impact matrix methods (Duperin and Godet, 1975). This makes it possible to select from among the most probable scenarios a reference scenario, which is then supplemented by the study of contrasted scenarios (optimistic and pessimistic scenarios). Each of these qualitative scenarios is translated in quantitative terms through appropriate forecasting techniques.
(c) The selection of the strategic actions to be taken so that the organization may attain its objectives, taking into account the possibilities of change in the system in which it is involved.

Conclusions – complementarity between 'la prospective' and forecasting

To criticize is not to reject. Although quantification at any price may seem dangerous, the numerical results of 'classical' forecasting models (time series econometric) do provide stimulating indicators and valuable reference points for a consideration of the future. We believe that there is a certain complementarity between the 'prospective' and 'classical'

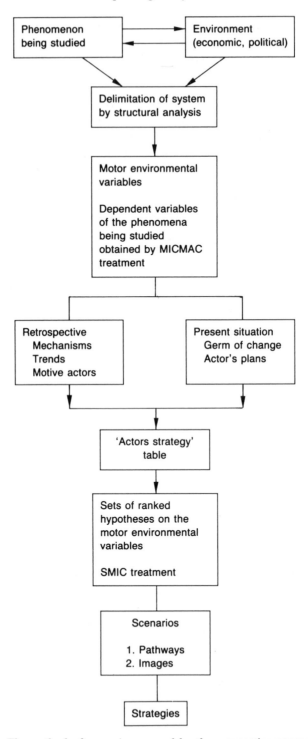

Figure 2   *The method of scenarios as used by the prospective approach*

What will TC look like in the future.

↳ the manual work performed by human beings has been supplemented?

↳ "long term patterns in human history"

(7)

HOW LIFE WOULD BE BETTER:

- Sickness Absense
- Stress & conflict
- Efficiency, morale, profitability increased

Real work story

Managing

forecasting. A forecasting model is valuable only by virtue of its hypotheses (econometric, political, . . .) whereas the objective of the 'prospective' approach is to discuss and validate the hypotheses that will make the model consistent and realistic.

Naturally, this complementarity does not hold in a uniform manner. In the long term, when everything or almost everything may have changed, the 'prospective' approach places almost no reliance on 'classical' forecasting methods since structural changes are the rule. On the other hand, as the forecasting horizon becomes progressively shorter, 'classical' forecasting methods play an increasingly important role insofar as the existence of structural stability can be assumed not to be violated. Furthermore, trends identified in the past can be extrapolated into the future. The chances of structural changes are considerably less as the forecasting horizon becomes shorter.

The prospective approach is not a substitute for making prophecies about the future. However, by its use of scenarios and by explicitly accepting that the objectives and wishes of the various actors involved do affect the future, provides the field of forecasting with an alternative approach to studying the future.

Bibliography

Amin, S. (1971) *L'accumulation à l'Echelle Mondiale*, 2nd edn. Paris: Anthropos.

Berger, G. (1964) *Phénoménologie du Temps et Prospective*. Paris: Presses Universitaires de France.

Berger, G. (1967) *Etapes de la Prospective*. Paris: Presses Universitaires de France.

Cournand, A. and Levy, M. (1973) *Shaping the Future: Gaston Berger and the Concept of Prospective*. New York: Gordon and Breach Science Publishers.

Crozier, M. and Friedberg, E. (1977) *L'Acteur et le Système*. Paris: Le Seuil.

Duperin, J. C. and Godet, M. (1975) 'SMIC 74: a new cross impact method', *Futures*, 7 (4): 302–12.

Godet, M. (1976) 'Scenarios of air transport development to 1990 by SMIC 74 a new cross impact method', *Technological forecasting and social change*, 9: 279–88.

Godet, M. (1979) *The Crisis in Forecasting and the Emergence of the Prospective Approach*. New York: Pergamon.

Godet, M. (1980) *Demain les Crises: de la Résignation à l'Antifatalité*. Paris: Hachette.

Jouvenel, B. (1964) *L'Art de la Conjecture*. Monaco: Du Rocher.

Lesourne, J. (1979) *Interfutures: Facing the Future, Mastering the Probable and Managing the Unpredictable*. Paris: OECD.

Lesourne, J. (1982) *Les Mille Sentiers de l'Avenir*. Paris: Seghers.

Morgenstern, O. (1972) *Précision et Incertitudes des Données Economiques*. Paris: Dunod.

Saint-Paul, R. and Teniere-Buchot, P. F. (1974) *Innovation et Évaluation Technologique*. Paris: Entreprise Moderne d'Edition.

5

Groupthink

Irving L. Janis

'How could we have been so stupid?' President John F. Kennedy asked after he and a close group of advisers had blundered into the Bay of Pigs invasion. For the last two years I have been studying that question, as it applies not only to the Bay of Pigs decision-makers but also to those who led the United States into such other major fiascos as the failure to be prepared for the attack on Pearl Harbor, the Korean War stalemate and the escalation of the Vietnam War.

Stupidity certainly is not the explanation. The men who participated in making the Bay of Pigs decision, for instance, comprised one of the greatest arrays of intellectual talent in the history of American Government – Dean Rusk, Robert McNamara, Douglas Dillon, Robert Kennedy, McGeorge Bundy, Arthur Schlesinger Jr, Allen Dulles and others.

It also seemed to me that explanations were incomplete if they concentrated only on disturbances in the behavior of each individual within a decision-making body: temporary emotional states of elation, fear, or anger that reduce a man's mental efficiency, for example, or chronic blind spots arising from a man's social prejudices or idiosyncratic biases.

I preferred to broaden the picture by looking at the fiascos from the standpoint of group dynamics as it has been explored over the past three decades, first by the great social psychologist Kurt Lewin and later in many experimental situations by myself and other behavioral scientists. My conclusion after poring over hundreds of relevant documents – historical reports about formal group meetings and informal conversations among the members – is that groups that committed the fiascos were victims of what I call 'groupthink'.

'Groupy'

In each case study, I was surprised to discover the extent to which each group displayed the typical phenomena of social conformity that are regularly encountered in studies of group dynamics among ordinary citizens. For example, some of the phenomena appear to be completely in line with findings from social-psychological experiments showing that

Reprinted from *Psychology Today* (US), Nov. 1971. pp. 43–5; 74–7.

powerful social pressures are brought to bear by the members of a cohesive group whenever a dissident begins to voice his objections to a group consensus. Other phenomena are reminiscent of the shared illusions observed in encounter groups and friendship cliques when the members simultaneously reach a peak of 'groupy' feelings.

Above all, there are numerous indications pointing to the development of group norms that bolster morale at the expense of critical thinking. One of the most common norms appears to be that of remaining loyal to the group by sticking with the policies to which the group has already committed itself, even when those policies are obviously working out badly and have unintended consequences that disturb the conscience of each member. This is one of the key characteristics of groupthink.

1984

I use the term groupthink as a quick and easy way to refer to the mode of thinking that persons engage in when *concurrence-seeking* becomes so dominant in a cohesive ingroup that it tends to override realistic appraisal of alternative courses of action. Groupthink is a term of the same order as the words in the newspeak vocabulary George Orwell used in his dismaying world of *1984*. In that context, groupthink takes on an invidious connotation. Exactly such a connotation is intended, since the term refers to a deterioration in mental efficiency, reality testing and moral judgments as a result of group pressures.

The symptoms of groupthink arise when the members of decision-making groups become motivated to avoid being too harsh in their judgments of their leaders' or their colleagues' ideas. They adopt a soft line of criticism, even in their own thinking. At their meetings, all the members are amiable and seek complete concurrence on every important issue, with no bickering or conflict to spoil the cozy, 'we-feeling' atmosphere.

Kill

Paradoxically, soft-headed groups are often hard-hearted when it comes to dealing with outgroups or enemies. They find it relatively easy to resort to dehumanizing solutions – they will readily authorize bombing attacks that kill large numbers of civilians in the name of the noble cause of persuading an unfriendly government to negotiate at the peace table. They are unlikely to pursue the more difficult and controversial issues that arise when alternatives to a harsh military solution come up for discussion. Nor are they inclined to raise ethical issues that carry the implication that *this fine group of ours, with its humanitarianism and its high-minded principles, might be capable of adopting a course of action that is inhumane and immoral.*

Norms

There is evidence from a number of social-psychological studies that as the members of a group feel more accepted by the others, which is a central feature of increased group cohesiveness, they display less overt conformity to group norms. Thus we would expect that the more cohesive a group becomes the less the members will feel constrained to censor what they say out of fear of being socially punished for antagonizing the leader or any of their fellow members.

In contrast, the groupthink type of conformity tends to increase as group cohesiveness increases. Groupthink involves non-deliberate suppression of critical thoughts as a result of internalization of the group's norms, which is quite different from deliberate suppression on the basis of external threats of social punishment. The more cohesive the group, the greater the inner compulsion on the part of each member to avoid creating disunity, which inclines him to believe in the soundness of whatever proposals are promoted by the leader or by a majority of the group's members.

In a cohesive group, the danger is not so much that each individual will fail to reveal his objections to what the others propose but that he will think the proposal is a good one, without attempting to carry out a careful, critical scrutiny of the pros and cons of the alternatives. When groupthink becomes dominant, there also is considerable suppression of deviant thoughts, but it takes the form of each person's deciding that his misgivings are not relevant and should be set aside, that the benefit of the doubt regarding any lingering uncertainties should be given to the group consensus.

Stress

I do not mean to imply that all cohesive groups necessarily suffer from groupthink. All ingroups may have a mild tendency toward groupthink, displaying one or another of the symptoms from time to time, but it need not be so dominant as to influence the quality of the group's final decision. Neither do I mean to imply that there is anything necessarily inefficient or harmful about group decisions in general. On the contrary, a group whose members have properly defined roles, with traditions concerning the procedures to follow in pursuing a critical inquiry, probably is capable of making better decisions than any individual group member working alone.

The problem is that the advantages of having decisions made by groups are often lost because of powerful psychological pressures that arise when the members work closely together, share the same set of values and, above all, face a crisis situation that puts everyone under intense stress.

The main principle of groupthink, which I offer in the spirit of

Parkinson's Law is this: *the more amiability and* esprit de corps *there is among the members of a policy-making ingroup, the greater the danger that independent critical thinking will be replaced by groupthink, which is likely to result in irrational and dehumanizing actions directed against outgroups.*

Symptoms

In my studies of high-level governmental decision-makers, both civilian and military, I have found eight main symptoms of groupthink.

Invulnerability

Most or all of the members of the ingroup share an *illusion* of invulnerability that provides for them some degree of reassurance about obvious dangers and leads them to become overoptimistic and willing to take extraordinary risks. It also causes them to fail to respond to clear warnings of danger.

The Kennedy ingroup, which uncritically accepted the Central Intelligence Agency's disastrous Bay of Pigs plan, operated on the false assumption that they could keep secret the fact that the United States was responsible for the invasion of Cuba. Even after news of the plan began to leak out, their belief remained unshaken. They failed even to consider the danger that awaited them: a worldwide revulsion against the US.

A similar attitude appeared among the members of President Lyndon B. Johnson's ingroup, the 'Tuesday Cabinet,' which kept escalating the Vietnam War despite repeated setbacks and failures. 'There was a belief', Bill Moyers commented after he resigned, 'that if we indicated a willingness to use our power, they [the North Vietnamese] would get the message and back away from an all-out confrontation. . . . There was a confidence – it was never bragged about, it was just there – that when the chips were really down, the other people would fold.'

A most poignant example of an illusion of invulnerability involves the ingroup around Admiral H. E. Kimmel, which failed to prepare for the possibility of a Japanese attack on Pearl Harbor despite repeated warnings. Informed by his intelligence chief that radio contact with Japanese aircraft carriers had been lost, Kimmel joked about it: 'What, you don't know where the carriers are? Do you mean to say that they could be rounding Diamond Head (at Honolulu) and you wouldn't know it?' The carriers were in fact moving full-steam towards Kimmel's command post at the time. Laughing together about a danger signal, which labels it as a purely laughing matter, is a characteristic manifestation of groupthink.

Rationale

As we see, victims of groupthink ignore warnings; they also collectively construct rationalizations in order to discount warnings and other forms of negative feedback that, taken seriously, might lead the group members to reconsider their assumptions each time they recommit themselves to past decisions. Why did the Johnson ingroup avoid reconsidering its escalation policy when time and again the expectations on which they based their decisions turned out to be wrong? James C. Thomson Jr, a Harvard historian who spent five years as an observing participant in both the State Department and the White House, tells us that the policy-makers avoided critical discussion of their prior decisions and continually invented new rationalizations so that they could sincerely recommit themselves to defeating the North Vietnamese.

In the fall of 1964, before the bombing of North Vietnam began, some of the policy-makers predicted that six weeks of air strikes would induce the North Vietnamese to seek peace talks. When someone asked, 'What if they don't?' the answer was that another four weeks certainly would do the trick.

Later, after each setback, the ingroup agreed that by investing just a bit more effort (by stepping up the bomb tonnage a bit, for instance), their course of action would prove to be right. *The Pentagon Papers* bear out these observations.

In *The Limits of Intervention*, Townsend Hoopes, who was acting Secretary of the Air Force under Johnson, says that Walt W. Rostow in particular showed a remarkable capacity for what has been called 'instant rationalization.' According to Hoopes, Rostow buttressed the group's optimism about being on the road to victory by culling selected scraps of evidence from news reports or, if necessary, by inventing 'plausible' forecasts that had no basis in evidence at all.

Admiral Kimmel's group rationalized away their warnings, too. Right up to 7 December 1941, they convinced themselves that the Japanese would never dare attempt a full-scale surprise assault against Hawaii because Japan's leaders would realize that it would precipitate an all-out war which the United States would surely win. They made no attempt to look at the situation through the eyes of the Japanese leaders – another manifestation of groupthink.

Morality

Victims of groupthink believe unquestioningly in the inherent morality of their ingroup; this belief inclines the members to ignore the ethical or moral consequences of their decisions.

Evidence that this symptom is at work usually is of a negative kind – the things that are left unsaid in group meetings. At least two influential persons had doubts about the morality of the Bay of Pigs adventure. One of them, Arthur Schlesinger Jr, presented his strong objections in a memorandum to President Kennedy and Secretary of State Rusk but suppressed them when he attended meetings of the Kennedy team. The other, Senator J. William Fulbright, was not a member of the group, but the President invited him to express his misgivings in a speech to the policy-makers. However, when Fulbright finished speaking the President moved on to other agenda items without asking for reactions of the group.

David Kraslow and Stuart H. Loory, in *The Secret Search for Peace in Vietnam*, report that during 1966 President Johnson's ingroup was concerned primarily with selecting bomb targets in North Vietnam. They based their selections on four factors – the military advantage, the risk to American aircraft and pilots, the danger of forcing other countries into the fighting, and the danger of heavy civilian casualties. At their regular Tuesday luncheons, they weighed these factors the way school teachers grade examination papers, averaging them out. Though evidence on this point is scant, I suspect that the group's realistic adherence to a standardized procedure induced the members to feel morally justified in their destructive way of dealing with the Vietnamese people – after all, the danger of heavy civilian casualties from US air strikes was taken into account on their checklists.

Stereotypes

Victims of groupthink hold stereotyped views of the leaders of enemy groups: they are so evil that genuine attempts at negotiating differences with them are unwarranted, or they are too weak or too stupid to deal effectively with whatever attempts the ingroup makes to defeat their purposes, no matter how risky the attempts are.

Kennedy's groupthinkers believed that Premier Fidel Castro's air force was so ineffectual that obsolete B-26s could knock it out completely in a surprise attack before the invasion began. They also believed that Castro's army was so weak that a small Cuban-exile brigade could establish a well-protected beach-head at the Bay of Pigs. In addition, they believed that Castro was not smart enough to put down any possible internal uprisings in support of the exiles. They were wrong on all three assumptions. Though much of the blame was attributable to faulty intelligence, the point is that none of Kennedy's advisers even questioned the CIA planners about these assumptions.

The Johnson advisers' sloganistic thinking about 'the Communist apparatus' that was 'working all around the world' (as Dean Rusk put it) led them to overlook the powerful nationalistic strivings of the North Vietnamese government and its efforts to ward off Chinese domination. The crudest of all stereotypes used by Johnson's inner circle to justify their policies was the domino theory ('If we don't stop the Reds in South Vietnam, tomorrow they will be in Hawaii and next week they will be in San Francisco,' Johnson once said.) The group so firmly accepted this stereotype that it became almost impossible for any adviser to introduce a more sophisticated viewpoint.

In documents on Pearl Harbor, it is clear to see that the Navy commanders stationed in Hawaii had a naive image of Japan as a midget that would not dare to strike a blow against a powerful giant.

Pressure

Victims of groupthink apply direct pressure to any individual who momentarily expresses doubts about any of the group's shared illusions or who questions the validity of the arguments supporting a policy alternative favored by the majority. This gambit reinforces the concurrence-seeking norm that loyal members are expected to maintain.

President Kennedy probably was more active than anyone else in raising skeptical questions during the Bay of Pigs meetings, and yet he seems to have encouraged the group's docile, uncritical acceptance of defective arguments in favor of the CIA's plan. At every meeting, he allowed the CIA representatives to dominate the discussion. He permitted them to give their immediate refutations in response to each tentative doubt that one of the others expressed, instead of asking whether anyone shared the doubt or wanted to pursue the implications of the new worrisome issue that had just been raised. And at the most crucial meeting, when he was calling on each member to give his vote for or against the plan, he did not call on Arthur Schlesinger, the one man there who was known by the President to have serious misgivings.

Historian Thomson informs us that whenever a member of Johnson's ingroup began to express doubts, the group used subtle social pressures to 'domesticate' him. To start with, the dissenter was made to feel at home, provided that he lived up to two restrictions: (a) that he did not voice his doubts to outsiders, which would play into the hands of the opposition; and (b) that he kept his criticisms within the bounds of acceptable deviation, which meant not challenging any of the fundamental assumptions that went into the group's prior commitments. One such 'domesticated dissenter' was Bill Moyers. When Moyers arrived at a meeting, Thomson tells us, the President greeted him with, 'Well, here comes Mr Stop-the-Bombing.'

Self-censorship

Victims of groupthink avoid deviating from what appears to be group consensus; they keep silent about their misgivings and even minimize to themselves the importance of their doubts.

As we have seen, Schlesinger was not at all hesitant about presenting his strong objections to the Bay of Pigs plan in a memorandum to the President and the Secretary of State. But he became keenly aware of his tendency to suppress objections at the White House meetings. 'In the months after the Bay of Pigs I bitterly reproached myself for having kept so silent during those crucial discussions in the cabinet room,' Schlesinger writes in *A Thousand Days*. 'I can only explain my failure to do more than raise a few timid questions by reporting that one's impulse to blow the whistle on this nonsense was simply undone by the circumstances of the discussion.'

Unanimity

Victims of groupthink share an *illusion* of unanimity within the group concerning almost all judgments expressed by members who speak in favor of the majority view. This symptom results partly from the preceding one, whose effects are augmented by the false assumption that any individual who remains silent during any part of the discussion is in full accord with what the others are saying.

When a group of persons who respect each other's opinions arrives at a unanimous view, each member is likely to feel that the belief must be true. This reliance on consensual validation within the group tends to replace individual critical thinking and reality testing, unless there are clear-cut disagreements among the members. In contemplating a course of action such as the invasion of Cuba, it is painful for the members to confront disagreements within their group, particularly if it becomes apparent that there are widely divergent views about whether the preferred course of action is too risky to undertake at all. Such disagreements are likely to arouse anxieties about making a serious error. Once the sense of unanimity is shattered, the members no longer can feel complacently confident about the decision they are inclined to make. Each man must then face the annoying realization that there are troublesome uncertainties and he must diligently seek out the best information he can get in order to decide for himself exactly how serious the risks might be. This is one of the unpleasant consequences of being in a group of hardheaded, critical thinkers.

To avoid such an unpleasant state, the members often become inclined, without quite realizing it, to prevent latent disagreements from surfacing when they are about to initiate a risky course of action. The group leader and the members support each other in playing up the areas of convergence in their thinking, at the expense of fully exploring divergencies that might reveal unsettled issues.

'Our meetings took place in a curious atmosphere of assumed consensus,' Schlesinger writes. His additional comments clearly show that, curiously, the consensus was an illusion – an illusion that could be maintained only because the major participants did not reveal their own reasoning or discuss their idiosyncratic assumptions and vague reservations. Evidence from several sources makes it clear that even the three principals – President Kennedy, Rusk and McNamara – had widely differing assumptions about the invasion plan.

Mindguards

Victims of groupthink sometimes appoint themselves as mindguards to protect the leader and fellow members from adverse information that might break the complacency they shared about the effectiveness and morality of past decisions. At a large birthday party for his wife, Attorney General Robert F. Kennedy, who had been constantly informed about the Cuban invasion plan, took Schlesinger aside and asked him why he was opposed. Kennedy listened coldly and said, 'You may be right or you may be wrong, but the President has made his mind up. Don't push it any further. Now is the time for everyone to help him all they can.'

Rusk also functioned as a highly effective mindguard by failing to transmit to the group the strong objections of three 'outsiders' who had learned of the invasion plan – Undersecretary of State Chester Bowles, USIA Director Edward R. Murrow, and Rusk's intelligence chief, Roger Hilsman. Had Rusk done so, their warnings might have reinforced Schlesinger's memorandum and jolted some of Kennedy's ingroup, if not the President himself, into reconsidering the decision.

Products

When a group of executives frequently displays most or all of these inter-related symptoms, a detailed study of their deliberations is likely to reveal a number of immediate consequences. These consequences are, in effect, products of poor decision-making practices because they lead to inadequate solutions to the problems under discussion.

First, the group limits its discussions to a few alternative courses of action (often only two) without an initial survey of all the alternatives that might be worthy of consideration.

Second, the group fails to reexamine the course of action initially preferred by the majority after they learn of risks and drawbacks they had not considered originally.

Third, the members spend little or no time discussing whether there are non-obvious gains they may have overlooked or ways of reducing the seemingly prohibitive costs that made rejected alternatives appear undesirable to them.

Fourth, members make little or no attempt to obtain information from experts within their own organizations who might be able to supply more precise estimates of potential losses and gains.

Fifth, members show positive interest in facts and opinions that support their preferred policy; they tend to ignore facts and opinions that do not.

Sixth, members spend little time deliberating about how the chosen policy might be hindered by bureaucratic inertia, sabotaged by political opponents, or temporarily derailed by common accidents. Consequently, they fail to work out contingency plans to cope with foreseeable setbacks that could endanger the overall success of their chosen course.

Support

The search for an explanation of why groupthink occurs has led me through a quagmire of complicated theoretical issues in the murky area of human motivation. My belief, based on recent social psychological research, is that we can best understand the various symptoms of group-think as a mutual effort among the group members to maintain self-esteem and emotional equanimity by providing social support to each other, especially at times when they share responsibility for making vital decisions.

Even when no important decision is pending, the typical administrator will begin to doubt the wisdom and morality of his past decisions each time he receives information about setbacks, particularly if the information is accompanied by negative feedback from prominent men who originally had been his supporters. It should not be surprising, therefore, to find that individual members strive to develop unanimity and *esprit de corps* that will help bolster each other's morale, to create an optimistic outlook about the success of pending decisions, and to reaffirm the positive value of past policies to which all of them are committed.

Pride

Shared illusions of invulnerability, for example, can reduce anxiety about taking risks. Rationalizations help members believe that the risks are really not so bad after all. The assumption of inherent morality helps the members to avoid feelings of shame or guilt. Negative stereotypes function as stress-reducing devices to enhance a sense of moral righteousness as well as pride in a lofty mission.

The mutual enhancement of self-esteem and morale may have functional value in enabling the members to maintain their capacity to take action, but it has maladaptive consequences insofar as concurrence-seeking tendencies interfere with critical, rational capacities and lead to serious errors of judgment.

While I have limited my study to decision-making bodies in Government, groupthink symptoms appear in business, industry and any other field where small, cohesive groups make the decisions. It is vital, then, for all sorts of people – and especially group leaders – to know what steps they can take to prevent groupthink.

Remedies

To counterpoint my case studies of the major fiascos, I have also investigated two highly successful group enterprises, the formulation of the Marshall Plan in the Truman Administration and the handling of the Cuban missile crisis by President Kennedy and his advisers. I have found it instructive to examine the steps Kennedy took to change his group's decision-making processes. These changes ensured that the mistakes made by his Bay of Pigs ingroup were not repeated by the missile-crisis ingroup, even though the membership of both groups was essentially the same.

The following recommendations for preventing groupthink incorporate many of the good practices I discovered to be characteristic of the Marshall Plan and missile-crisis groups:

1 The leader of a policy-forming group should assign the role of critical evaluation to each member, encouraging the group to give high priority to open airing of objections and doubts. This practice needs to be reinforced by the leader's acceptance of criticism of his own judgments in order to discourage members from soft-peddling their disagreements and from allowing their striving for concurrence to inhibit critical thinking.

2 When the key members of a hierarchy assign a policy-planning mission to any group within their organization, they should adopt an impartial stance instead of stating preferences and expectations at the beginning. This will encourage open inquiry and impartial probing of a wide range of policy alternatives.

3 The organization routinely should set up several outside policy-planning and evaluation groups to work on the same policy question, each deliberating under a different leader. This can prevent the insulation of an ingroup.

4 At intervals before the group reaches a final consensus, the leader should require each member to discuss the group's deliberations with associates in his own unit of the organization – assuming that those associates can be trusted to adhere to the same security regulations that govern the policy-makers – and then report back their reactions to the group.

5 The group should invite one or more outside experts to each meeting on a staggered basis and encourage the experts to challenge the views of the core members.

6 At every general meeting of the group, whenever the agenda calls for an evaluation of policy alternatives, at least one member should play devil's advocate, functioning as a good lawyer in challenging the testimony of those who advocate the majority position.

7 Whenever the policy issue involves relations with a rival nation or organization, the group should devote a sizable block of time, perhaps and entire session, to a survey of all warning signals from the rivals and should write alternative scenarios on the rivals' intentions.

8 When the group is surveying policy alternatives for feasibility and effectiveness, it should from time to time divide into two or more subgroups to meet separately, under different chairmen, and then come back together to hammer out differences.

9 After reaching a preliminary consensus about what seems to be the best

policy, the group should hold a 'second-chance' meeting at which every member expresses as vividly as he can all his residual doubts, and rethinks the entire issue before making a definitive choice.

How

These recommendations have their disadvantages. To encourage the open airing of objections, for instance, might lead to prolonged and costly debates when a rapidly growing crisis requires immediate solution. It also could cause rejection, depression and anger. A leader's failure to set a norm might create cleavage between leader and members that could develop into a disruptive power struggle if the leader looks on the emerging consensus as anathema. Setting up outside evaluation groups might increase the risk of security leakage. Still, inventive executives who know their way around the organizational maze probably can figure out how to apply one or another of the prescriptions successfully, without harmful side effects.

They also could benefit from the advice of outside experts in the administrative and behavioral sciences. Though these experts have much to offer, they have had few chances to work on policy-making machinery within large organizations. As matters now stand, executives innovate only when they need new procedures to avoid repeating serious errors that have deflated their self-images.

In this era of atomic warheads, urban disorganization and ecocatastrophes, it seems to me that policy-makers should collaborate with behavioral scientists and give top priority to preventing groupthink and its attendant fiascos.

SECTION 2

ENVIRONMENTAL ANALYSIS

The economic environment

Most managers are well aware of the significance of the economic environment. There are a wide range of economic/political events that directly impinge on an organization's survival and success, from inflation levels, interest rates, credit measures, currency movements to, more generally, periods of national or global recession. An attempt to anticipate and prepare for, wherever possible, at least broad economic changes is clearly important, and there are indeed a large number of sources of economic analyses for managers to draw upon, including various economic forecasts, fallible as these may be.

The focus of the one chapter in this section is not economic forecasting and analysis. Written by Oliver E. Williamson, a major figure in the field, it is included because it provides an important insight into the realm of economic theory as it relates to the modern organization.

Modern economics has followed a range of paths, from macro-economic theories such as those presented, from opposite poles, by Keynes and Friedman, through to micro-economic analyses in demand economics which take their lead from the marketing theory familiar to many managers. The chapter by Williamson explores the economic role of the organization and, in particular, transaction-cost analysis. Transaction-cost analysis is currently one of the most popular and active areas of research and theorizing in the whole field of economics. As part of the arguments presented, Williamson also undertakes a comprehensive review of other related work within the economic field.

In these ways this single chapter offers a useful insight for management into the character of modern economic theory.

6

The modern corporation: origins, evolution, attributes

Oliver E. Williamson

There is virtual unanimity with the proposition that the modern corporation is a complex and important economic institution. There is much less agreement on what its attributes are and on how and why it has successively evolved to take on its current configuration. While I recognize that there have been numerous contributing factors, I submit that the modern corporation is mainly to be understood as the product of a series of organizational innovations that have had the purpose and effect of economizing on transaction costs.

Note that I do not argue that the modern corporation is to be understood exclusively in these terms. Other important factors include the quest for monopoly gains and the imperatives of technology. These mainly have a bearing on market shares and on the absolute size of specific technological units; but decisions to make or buy, which determine the distribution of economic activity, as between firms and markets, and the internal organization (including both the shape and the aggregate size) of the firm are not explained, except perhaps in trivial ways, in these terms. Inasmuch as these are core issues, a theory of the modern corporation that does not address them is, at best, seriously incomplete.

Specifically, the study of the modern corporation should actively concern itself with and provide consistent explanations for the following features of the organization of economic activity: What are the factors that determine the degree to which firms integrate – in backward, forward, and lateral respects? What economic purposes are served by the widespread adoption of divisionalization? What ramifications, if any, does internal organization have for the long-standing dilemma posed by the separation of ownership from control? Can the 'puzzle' of the conglomerate be unravelled? Do similar considerations apply in assessing multinational enterprise? Can an underlying rationale be provided for the reported association between innovation and direct foreign investment?

It is my contention that transaction-cost economizing figures prominently in explaining these (as well as related) major features of the business environment. Since transaction-cost economizing is socially

Reprinted by permission of the American Economic Association from *Journal of Economic Literature*, 19 (Dec. 1981): 1537–68.

valued, it follows that the modern corporation serves affirmative economic purposes. But complex institutions often serve a variety of purposes – and the corporation can and sometimes is used to pursue antisocial objectives. I submit, however, that (a) objectionable purposes can normally be recognized and dealt with separately; and (b) failure to understand the main purposes of the corporation has been the source of much confusion and ill-conceived public policy.[1] Specifically, antisocial purposes have often been attributed where none existed.

Inasmuch as a sensitivity to transactions and transaction-cost economizing can be traced to the 1930s (Commons, 1951; Coase, 1937), it is somewhat surprising that the importance of the modern corporation as a means of reducing transaction costs has been so long neglected. The main reason is that the origins of transaction costs must often be sought in influences and motives that lie outside the normal domain of economics. Accordingly, a large gap separated an identification of transaction costs, as the main factor to which the study of the organization of economic activity must repair, and efforts to give operational content to that insight.

Some background

General

Assessing the organization of economic activity in an advanced society requires that a bewildering variety of market, hierarchical, and mixed modes be evaluated. Economists, organization theorists, public policy specialists, and historians all have an interest and each have offered interpretations of successive organizational innovations. A coherent view, however, has not emerged.

Partly this is because the principal hierarchical structure to be assessed – the modern corporation – is formidably complex in its great size, diversity, and internal organization. The natural difficulties which thereby resulted would have been overcome sooner, however, had it not been for a number of conceptual barriers to an understanding of this institution. Chief among these are the following:

1 the neoclassical theory of the firm, which is the main referrent to which economists appeal, is devoid of interesting hierarchical features;
2 organization theorists, who are specialists in the study of internal organization and unencumbered by an intellectual commitment to neoclassical economic models, have been preoccupied with hierarchy to the neglect of market modes of organization and the healthy tension that exists between markets and hierarchies;
3 public policy analysts have maintained a deeply suspicious attitude toward non-standard or unfamiliar forms of economic organization; and
4 organizational innovation has been relatively neglected by business and economic historians.

To be sure, this indictment sweeps too broadly. As discussed below, there have been important exceptions. The main features, however, are as I have described. Thus neoclassical theory treats the firm as a production function to which a profit maximization objective has been ascribed. Albeit useful for many purposes, such a construction is unhelpful in attempting to assess the purpose served by hierarchical modes of organization. The firm as production function needs to make way for the view of the *firm as governance structure* if the ramifications of internal organization are to be accurately assessed. Only recently has this latter orientation begun to make headway – and is still in a primitive state of development.

The preoccupation of organization theory specialists with internal organization is a potentially useful corrective. An understanding of the purposes served by internal organization has remained elusive, however, for at least two reasons. First, efficiency analysis plays a relatively minor role in the studies of most organization theory specialists – many of whom are more inclined to emphasize power. The economizing factors that are crucial to an understanding of the modern corporation are thus effectively suppressed. Second, and related, firms and markets are treated separately rather than in active juxtaposition with one another. The propositions that (a) firms and markets are properly regarded as alternative governance structures to which (b) transactions are to be assigned in discriminating (mainly transaction-cost economizing) ways are unfamiliar to most organization theory specialists and alien to some.

Public policy analysts with an interest in the modern corporation might also have been expected to entertain a broader view. If fact, however, many of these likewise adopted a production function orientation – whereby markets were regarded as the 'natural, hence efficient' way by which to mediate transactions between technologically separable entities. This was joined by a pervasive sense that the purposes of competition are invariably served by maintaining many autonomous traders. Even sensitive observers were trapped by this combined technological/atomistic logic. Thus Donald Turner, at a time when he headed the Antitrust Division, expressed skepticism over non-standard business practices by observing that: 'I approach territorial and customer restrictions not hospitably in the common law tradition, but inhospitably in the tradition of antitrust law.'[2] The possibility that efficiency might be served by imposing restraints on autonomous market trading was evidently thought to be slight. This inhospitality tradition also explains ingrained public policy animosity towards vertical integration and conglomerate organization; more generally, industrial organization specialists were encouraged to discover what were often fanciful 'distortions' at the expense of a more basic understanding of the modern corporation in economizing terms.

The neglect of organizational innovations by business and economic historians has been general but by no means complete and shows recent signs of being corrected.[3] Mainly, however, interpretation has played a secondary role to description in most historical studies of organizational change – which, while understandable, contributes to the continuing confusion over the purposes served by the changing organizational features of the corporation.

This chapter attempts to provide a coherent view of the modern corporation by:

1 augmenting the model of the firm as production function to include the concept of the firm as governance structure;
2 studying firms and markets as alternative governance structures in a comparative institutional way;
3 supplanting the presumption that organizational innovations have anticompetitive purposes by the rebuttable presumption that organizational innovations are designed to economize on transaction costs; and
4 interpreting business history from a transaction-cost perspective. Such an approach to the study of the modern corporation (and, more generally, to the study of organizational innovation) owes its origins to antecedent contributions of four kinds.

Antecedents

Theory of firms and markets   The unsatisfactory state of the theory of the firm was recognized by Ronald Coase in his classic 1937 article on 'The Nature of the Firm.' As he observed:

> Outside the firm, price movements direct production, which is coordinated through a series of exchange transactions on the market. Within a firm, these market transactions are eliminated and in place of the complicated market structure with exchange transactions is substituted the entrepreneur-co-ordinator, who directs production. It is clear that these are *alternative means of co-ordinating production*. (Coase, 1952: 333; emphasis added)

Coase went on to observe that firms arose because there were costs of using the price system (1952: 336–8). But internal organization was no cost panacea, since it experienced distinctive costs of its own (1952: 340–2). A balance is struck when the firm has expanded to the point where 'the costs of organizing an extra transaction within the firm become equal to the costs of carrying out the same transaction by means of an exchange in the open market or the costs of organizing in another firm' (1952: 341).

Related insight on the study of firms and markets was offered by Friedrich A. Hayek, who dismissed equilibrium economics with the observation that 'the economic problem of society is mainly one of adaptation to changes in particular circumstances of time and place' (1945: 524), and who held that the 'marvel' of the price system was that it could accomplish this without 'conscious direction' (1945: 527). Setting aside the possibility that Hayek did not make adequate allowance for the limitations of the price system, three things are notable about these observations. First is his emphasis on change and the need to devise adaptive institutional forms. Second, his reference to particular circumstances, as distinguished from statistical aggregates, reflects a sense that economic institutions must be sensitive to dispersed knowledge of a microanalytic kind. And third was his insistence that attention to the details of social processes and economic institutions was made necessary by the 'unavoidable imperfections of man's knowledge' (1945: 530).

The organization of firms and markets has been a subject to which Kenneth Arrow has made repeated contributions. He has addressed himself not only to the economics of the internal organization (Arrow, 1964) but also to an assessment of the powers and limits of markets (Arrow, 1969). Like Coase, he expressly recognizes that firms and markets are alternative modes of organizing economic activity (Arrow, 1974). Moreover, whereas the limits of markets were glossed over by Hayek, Arrow specifically traces these to transaction cost origins: 'market failure is not absolute; it is better to consider a broader category, that of transaction costs, which in general impede and in particular cases block the formation of markets' (1969: 48) – where by transaction costs Arrow has reference to the 'costs of running the economic system' (1969: 48).

Organization theory   Although organization theorists have not in general regarded efficiency as their central concern, there have been notable exceptions. The early works of Chester Barnard (1938) and Herbert Simon (1957b) both qualify.

Barnard was a businessman rather than a social scientist and he addressed internal organizational issues that many would regard as outside the scope of economics. Economizing was nevertheless strongly featured in his approach to the study of organizations. Understanding the employment relation was among the issues that intrigued him. Matters that concerned him in this connection included: the need to align incentives, including non-economic inducements, to achieve enterprise viability; the importance of assent to authority; a description of the authority relation within which hierarchical organizations operate; and the role of 'informal organization' in supporting the working rules upon which formal organization relies. The rationality of internal organization, making due allowance for the attributes of human actors, was a matter of continuous concern to Barnard.

Simon expressly relies on Barnard and carries rationality analysis forward. A more precise vocabulary than Barnard's is developed in the process. Simon traces the problem of organization to the joining of rational purposes with the cognitive limits of human actors: 'it is precisely in the realm where human behavior is *intendedly* rational, but only *limitedly* so, that there is room for a genuine theory of organization and administration' (Simon, 1957a: xxiv). Intended rationality supplies purpose, but meaningful economic and organizational choices arise only in a limited (or bounded) rationality context.

Simon makes repeated reference to the criterion of efficiency (1957a: 14, 39–41, 172–97), but he also cautions that organizational design should be informed by 'a knowledge of those aspects of the social sciences which are relevant to the broader purposes of the organization' (1957a: 246). A sensitivity to subgoal pursuit, wherein individuals identify with and pursue local goals at the possible expense of global goals[4] (Simon, 1957a: 13), and the 'outguessing' or gaming aspects of human behavior (Simon, 1957a: 252) are among these.

Although Simon examines the merits of centralized versus decentralized modes of organization (1957b: 234–40), it is not until his later writing that he expressly addresses the matter of factoring problems according to rational hierarchical principles (Simon, 1962). The issues here are developed more fully in the next main section of this chapter.

Non-strategic purposes   The 'inhospitality tradition' referred to above maintained a presumption of illegality when non-standard or unfamiliar business practices were brought under review. These same practices, when viewed 'through the lens of price theory'[5] by Aaron Director (and his students and colleagues at Chicago), were regarded rather differently. Whereas Turner and others held that anticompetitive purposes were being served, Director and his associates reported instead that tie-ins, resale price maintenance, and the like were promoting more efficient resource allocation.

In fact, non-standard business practices (such as tie-ins) are anomalies when regarded in the full information terms associated with static price theory. Implicitly, however, Chicago was also relying on the existence of transaction costs – which, after all, were the reason why comprehensive price discrimination could not be effected through simple contracts unsupported by restrictive practices from the outset.[6] Be that as it may, Chicago's insistence that economic behavior be assessed with respect to its economizing properties was a healthy antidote and encouraged further scrutiny of these same matters – with the eventual result that an economizing orientation is now much more widely held. Indirectly, these views have spilled over and influenced thinking about the modern corporation as an economizing, rather than mainly a monopolizing entity.[7]

Transaction cost economics

Each of the antecedent literatures just described has a bearing on the transaction-cost approach to the study of economic institutions in general and the modern corporation in particular. Following Commons (1951), the transaction is made the basic unit of analysis. Specifically, attention is focused on the transaction costs of running the economic system (Coase, 1937; Arrow 1969), with emphasis on adaptation to unforeseen, and often unforeseeable, circumstances (Hayek, 1945). The issues of special interest are connected with the changing structure of the corporation over the past 150 years (Chandler, 1962, 1977). Rather than regard these inhospitably, the new approach maintains the rebuttable presumption that the evolving corporate structure has the purpose and effect of economizing on transaction costs. These transaction-cost and business history literatures are linked by appeal to selective parts of the (mainly older) organization theory literature.

As Barnard (1938) emphasized, differences in internal organization often had significant performance consequences and could and should be assessed from a rationality viewpoint. Simon (1957b) extended and refined the argument that internal organization mattered and that the study of internal organization needed to make appropriate allowance for the attributes of human actors – for what Frank Knight has felicitously referred to as 'human nature as we know it' (1965: 270). Then, and only then, does the comparative institutional assessment of alternative organizational forms take on its full economic significance.

Comparative institutional analysis

The costs of running the economic system to which Arrow refers can be usefully thought of in contractual terms. Each feasible mode of conducting relations between technologically separable entities can be examined with respect to the *ex ante* costs of negotiating and writing, as well as the *ex post* costs of executing, policing, and, when disputes arise, remedying the (explicit or implicit) contract that joins them.

A transaction may thus be said to occur when a good or service is transferred across a technologically separable interface. One stage of processing or assembly activity terminates and another begins. A mechanical analogy, while imperfect, may nevertheless be useful. A well-working interface, like a well-working machine, can be thought of as one where these transfers occur smoothly.

In neither case, however, is smoothness desired for its own sake; the benefits must be judged in relation to the cost. Both investment and operating features require attention. Thus extensive prior investment in finely tuned equipment and repeated lubrication and adjustment during operation are both ways of attenuating friction, slippage, or other loss of mechanical energy. Similarly, extensive pre-contract negotiation that covers all relevant contingencies may avoid the need for periodic intervention to realign the interface during execution so that a contract may be brought successfully to completion. Simultaneous attention to both investment (pre-contract costs) and operating expenses (harmonizing costs) is needed if mechanical (contractual) systems are to be designed effectively. The usual study of economizing in a production function framework is thus extended to include an examination of the *comparative costs of planning, adapting, and monitoring task completion under alternative* governance structures – where by governance structure I have reference to the explicit or implicit contractual framework within which a transaction is located (markets, firms, and mixed modes – e.g. franchising – included).

The study of transaction-cost economizing is thus a comparative institutional undertaking which recognizes that there are a variety of distinguishably different transactions on the one hand and a variety of alternative governance structures on the other. The object is to match governance structures to the attributes of transactions in a discriminating way. Microanalytic attention to differences among governance structures and microanalytic definition of transactions are both needed in order for this to be accomplished.

Although more descriptive detail than is associated with neoclassical analysis is needed for this purpose, a relatively crude assessment will often suffice. As Simon has observed, comparative institutional analysis commonly involves an examination of discrete structural alternatives for which marginal analysis is not required: 'In general, much cruder and simpler arguments will suffice to demonstrate an inequality between two quantities than are required to show the conditions under which these quantities are equated at the margin' (Simon, 1978: 6).

Behavioral assumptions

Human nature as we know it is marvelously rich and needs to be reduced to manageable proportions. The two behavioral assumptions on which transaction-cost analysis relies – and without which the study of economic organization is pointless – are bounded rationality and opportunism. As a consequence of these two assumptions, the human agents that populate the firms and markets with which I am concerned differ from economic man (or at least the common caricature thereof) in that they are less competent in calculation and less trustworthy and reliable in action. A condition of bounded rationality is responsible for the computational limits of organization man. A proclivity for (at least some) economic agents to behave opportunistically is responsible for the unreliability.

The term bounded rationality was coined by Simon to reflect the fact that economic actors, who may be presumed to be 'intendedly rational', are not hyperrational. Rather, they experience limits in formulating and solving complex problems and in processing (receiving, storing, retrieving, transmitting) information (Simon, 1957a: 198). Opportunism is related to but is a somewhat more general term than the condition of 'moral hazard' to which Knight referred in his classic statement of economic organization (1965: 251–6).[8] Opportunism effectively extends the usual assumption of self-interest seeking to make allowance for self-interest seeking with guile.

But for the *simultaneous* existence of both bounded rationality and opportunism,[9] all economic contracting problems are trivial and the study of economic institutions is unimportant. Thus, but for bounded rationality, all economic exchange could be effectively organized by contract. Indeed, the economic theory of comprehensive contracting has been fully worked out.[10] Given bounded rationality, however, it is impossible to deal with complexity in all contractually relevant respects (Radner, 1968). As a consequence, incomplete contracting is the best that can be achieved.

Ubiquitous, albeit incomplete, contracting would nevertheless be feasible if economic agents were completely trustworthy. Principals would simply extract promises from agents that they will behave in a stewardship fashion, while agents would reciprocally ask principals to behave in good faith. Such devices will not work, however, if some economic actors (either principals or agents) are dishonest (or, more generally, disguise attributes or preferences, distort data, obfuscate issues and otherwise confuse transactions) and it is very costly to distinguish opportunistic from non-opportunistic types *ex ante*.

Although the dual assumptions of bounded rationality and opportunism complicate the study of economic behavior and may be inessential for some purposes, the study of alternative modes of organization does not qualify as an exception. To the contrary, failure to recognize and make allowance for both is virtually to invite mistaken assessments of alternatives modes.[11] Taking these two behavioral assumptions into account, the following compact statement of the problem of economic organization is suggested: assess alternative governance structures in terms of their capacities to economize on bounded rationality while simultaneously safeguarding transactions against opportunism. This is not inconsistent with the imperative 'maximize profits!', but it focuses attention somewhat differently.

Dimensionalizing

As Coase observed in 1972, his 1937 paper was 'much cited but little used' (1972: 63). The reasons for this are many, including a preoccupation by economists with other matters during the intervening thirty-five years. The main reason, however, is that transaction costs had not been operationalized and it was not obvious how this could be accomplished.

The postwar market failure literature, especially Arrow's insight (1969) that market failures had transaction costs origins, served to focus attention on the troublesome issues. A recognition that market (and internal) failures of all kinds could be ultimately traced to the human factors described above was a second step. The remaining step was to identify the critical dimensions with respect to which transactions differ.

The attributes of transactions that are of special interest to the economics of organization are: (a) the frequency with which transactions recur, (b) the uncertainty to which transactions are subject,[12] and (c) the degree to which transactions are supported by durable, transaction-specific investments (Williamson, 1979a). A considerable amount of explanatory power turns on the last.[13]

Asset specificity can arise in any of three ways: site specificity, as when successive stations are located in cheek-by-jowl relation to each other so as to economize on inventory and transportation expenses; physical asset specificity, as where specialized dies are required to produce a component; and human asset specificity that arises in a learning-by-doing fashion. The reason why asset specificity is critical is that, once the investment has been made, buyer and seller are effectively operating in a bilateral (or at least quasi-bilateral) exchange relation for a considerable period thereafter. Inasmuch as the value of highly specific capital in other uses is, by definition, much smaller than the specialized use for which it has been intended, the supplier is effectively 'locked into' the transaction to a significant degree. This is symmetrical, moreover, in that the buyer cannot turn to alternative sources of supply and obtain the item on favorable terms, since the cost of supply from unspecialized capital is presumably great. The buyer is thus committed to the transaction as well. Accordingly, where asset specificity is great, buyer and seller will make special efforts to design an exchange relation that has good continuity properties. Autonomous contracting gives way to more complex forms of market contracting and sometimes to internal organization for this reason.

Three principles of organizational design

The criterion for organizing commercial transactions is assumed to be the strictly instrumental one of cost economizing. Essentially this takes two parts: economizing on production expense and economizing of transaction costs. In fact, these are not independent and need to be addressed simultaneously. The study of the latter, however, is much less well developed and is emphasized here.

The three principles of organizational design employed here are neither exhaustive nor refined. They nevertheless offer considerable explanatory power in dealing with the main changes in corporate organization reported by Chandler and addressed here. Transaction-cost reasoning supports all three, although only the first, the asset-specificity principle, is tightly linked to dimensionalizing. Bounded rationality and opportunism, however, operate with respect to all three.

The asset-specificity principle turns on the above described transformation of an exchange relation from a large-numbers to a small-numbers condition during the course of contract execution. The second, the externality principle, is often discussed under the heading of 'free rider' effects. The more general phenomenon, however, is that of subgoal pursuit, that is, in the course of executing contracts, agents also pursue private goals which may be in some degree inconsistent with the contract's intended purpose. These two principles influence the choice of contracting form (mainly firm or market). In fact, however, the efficacy of internal organization depends on whether sound principles of internal organizational design are respected, which is to say that the details of internal organization matter. The hierarchical decomposition principle deals with this last.

It will be convenient to assume that transactions will be organized by markets unless market exchange gives rise to serious transaction costs. In the beginning, so to speak, there were markets. Both bureaucratic and production cost considerations favor this presumption. The bureaucratic argument is simply this: market exchange serves to attenuate the bureaucratic distortions to which internal exchange is subject. (Although the reasons for this have been set out elsewhere – Thompson, 1967: 152–4; Williamson, 1975: Chapter 7 – the study of firm and market organization is greatly in need of a more adequate theory of bureaucracy.) The production cost advantages of market procurement are three: static scale economies can be more fully exhausted by buying rather than making if the firm's needs are small in relation to the market; markets can aggregate uncorrelated demands, to thereby realize risk-pooling benefits; and markets may enjoy economies of scope[14] in supplying a related set of activities of which the firm's requirements are only one. Accordingly, transactions will be organized in markets *unless* transaction cost disabilities appear.[15]

Asset specificity principle (all transactions)   Recall that transactions are described in terms of three attributes: frequency, uncertainty, and asset specificity. Although interesting organizational issues are posed when transactions are of only an occasional kind (Williamson, 1979b: 245–54) this chapter deals entirely with the governance of recurring transactions. Also, it will facilitate the analysis to hold uncertainty constant in intermediate degree – which is to say that we are dealing neither with steady state nor highly uncertain events. Accordingly, asset specificity is the transactional dimension of special interest. The first principle of efficient organizational design is this: *the normal presumption that recurring transactions for technologically separable goods and services will be efficiently mediated by autonomous market contracting is progressively weakened as asset specificity increases.*

The production cost advantages of markets decrease and the (comparative) governance costs of markets increase as assets become progressively more specific. Thus as assets become more fully specialized to a single use or user, hence are less transferable to other uses and users, economies of scale can be as fully realized when a firm operates the asset under its own internal direction as when its services are obtained externally by contract. And the market's advantage in pooling risks likewise shrinks. Simultaneously, the transactions in question take on a stronger bilateral character, and the governance costs of markets increase relatively.

The distinction between *ex ante* and *ex post* competition is essential to an understanding of this condition. What may have been (and commonly is) an effective large-numbers-bidding situation at the outset is sometimes *transformed* into a bilateral trading relation thereafter. This obtains if, despite the fact that large numbers of qualified bidders were prepared to enter competitive bids for the initial contract, the winning bidder realizes advantages over non-winners at contract renewal intervals because non-trivial investments in durable specific assets are put in place (or otherwise accrue, say in a learning-by-doing fashion) during contract execution. As set out elsewhere (Williamson, 1979a), the efficient governance of recurring transactions will vary as follows: classical market contracting will be efficacious wherever assets are non-specific to the trading parties; bilateral or obligational market contracting will appear as assets become semi-specific; and internal organization will displace markets as assets take on a highly specific character.[16]

Internal organization enjoys advantages over market contracting for transactions that are supported by highly specific assets at both contract-writing and contract-execution stages. Since highly specific assets cannot be redeployed without sacrificing productivity, both suppliers and purchasers will insist upon contractual safeguards before undertaking such projects. Writing and negotiating such contracts is costly. Additionally, implementation problems need to be faced. The internal direction of firms confers execution advantages over bilateral trading in three respects. First, common ownership reduces the incentives of the trading units to pursue local goals. Second, and related, internal organization is able to invoke fiat to resolve differences whereas costly adjudication is needed when an impasse develops between autonomous traders. Third, internal organization has easier and more complete access to the relevant information when disputes must be settled. The incentive to shift bilateral transactions from markets to firms also increases as uncertainty increases, since the costs of harmonizing a relation among parties vary directly with the need to adjust to changing circumstances.

Externality principle (forward integration)   Whereas the asset-specificity principle refers to transactions that are transformed from large- to small-numbers bidding situations – as buyers, who initially obtained assets or their services in a competitive market, subsequently face suppliers with some degree of monopoly power – the externality principle involves no such market transformation. Also, the asset-specificity principle applies to backward, forward, and lateral integration; by contrast, the externality principle mainly applies to distribution stages.

The externalities of concern are those that arise in conjunction with the unintended debasement of quality for a branded good or service. As discussed below, such debasement is explained by costly metering. The externality is thus a manifestation of the measurement problems to which North refers in his discussion of transaction costs (1978: 972). It appears mainly at the interface between production and distribution. The differential ease of inspecting, and thereby controlling, the quality of components and materials that are purchased from earlier-stage and lateral suppliers as compared with the cost of exercising quality controls over distributors is responsible for this condition.[17]

End-games and fly-by-night distributors aside, the unintended debasement of quality by distributors poses a problem only where the activities of individual distributors affect one another, as when one retailer's poor service in installation or repair injures a product's reputation for performance and limits the sales of other retailers. More generally, if the quality enhancement (debasement) efforts of distributors give rise to positive (negative) externalities, the benefits (costs) of which can be incompletely appropriated by (assigned to) the originators, failure to extend quality controls over distribution will result in suboptimization. Autonomous contracting thus gives way to obligational market contracting (e.g. franchising) if not forward integration into distribution[18] as demand interaction effects become more important. More generally, the second principle of efficient organizational design is this: *the normal presumption that exchange between producers of differentiated goods and distribution stages will be efficiently mediated by autonomous contracting is progressively weakened as demand externalities increase.*

Product differentiation is a necessary but not a sufficient condition for troublesome demand externalities to appear. Manufacturers can sometimes insulate a product against deterioration by special packaging (say by selling the item in hermetic containers with an inert atmosphere and providing replacement guarantees). If, however, such safeguards are very costly, and if follow-on checks and penalties to discourage distributors from debasing the quality image of a product are likewise expensive, autonomous trading will give way to forms of distribution that have superior quality control properties.

Hierarchical decomposition principle (internal organization)[19] Merely to transfer a transaction out of the market into the firm does not, by itself, assure that the activity will be effectively organized thereafter. Not only are bounded rationality and opportunism ubiquitous, but the problems presented by both vary with changes in internal organization. Accordingly, a complete theory of value will recognize that firm structure as well as market structure matters.

Simon makes provision for bounded rationality effects in arguing that the organizational division of decision-making labor is quite as important as the neoclassical division of production labor, where, from 'the information processing point of view, division of labor means factoring the total system of decisions that need to be made into relatively independent subsystems, each one of which can be designed with only minimal concern for its interactions with the others' (Simon, 1973: 270). This applies to both vertical and horizontal aspects of the organization. In both respects the object is to recognize and give effect to conditions of near decomposability.

The vertical slice entails grouping the operating parts into separable entities, the interactions within which are strong and between which are weak. The horizontal slice has temporal ramifications of a strategic versus operating kind. Problems are thus factored in such a way that the higher frequency (or short-run dynamics) are associated with the operating parts while the lower frequency (or long-run dynamics) are associated with the strategic system (Simon, 1962: 477). These operating and strategic distinctions correspond with the lower and higher levels in the organizational hierarchy, respectively. Internal incentives and information flows need, of course, to be aligned, lest distortions be deliberately or inadvertently introduced into the internal information summary and transmittal processes.

The hierarchical decomposition principle can thus be stated as follows: *internal organization should be designed in such a way as to effect quasi-independence between the parts, the high frequency dynamics (operating activities) and low frequency dynamics (strategic planning) should be distinguished, and incentives should be aligned within and between components* so as to promote both local and global effectiveness.

Each of these three principles of organizational design is responsive to considerations of both bounded rationality and opportunism. Thus asset specificity would pose no problems if comprehensive contracting were feasible (which is tantamount to unbounded rationality) or if winning bidders could be relied upon to behave in an utterly reliable and trustworthy fashion (absence of opportunism). The externality principle is mainly a reflection of opportunism (autonomous distributors permit their suppliers' reputations to be degraded because they bear only part of the costs), but, of course, quality control checks would be unneeded if all relevant information could be costlessly displayed and assessed. The hierarchical decomposition principle recognizes the need to divide problems into manageable units and at the same time prevent agents from engaging in dysfunctional pursuit of local goals, which reflect bounded rationality and opportunism concerns, respectively.

A more comprehensive analysis would embed these principles of organization within the larger optimizing framework where demand as well as cost consequences are recognized and where production versus transaction costs tradeoffs are made explicit.[20] For the purposes at hand, however, which take product design as given and focus on distinguishably different rather than close cases, such refinements do not appear to be necessary.

The multidivisional structure

The most significant organizational innovation of the twentieth century was the development in the 1920s of the multidivisional structure. Surprisingly, this development was little noted or widely appreciated as late as 1960. Leading management texts extolled the virtues of 'basic departmentation' and 'line and staff authority relationships', but the special importance of multidivisionalization went unmarked.[21]

Chandler's pathbreaking study of business history, *Strategy and Structure* (1966), simply bypassed this management literature. He advanced the thesis that 'changing developments in business organization presented a challenging area for comparative analysis' and observed that 'the study of [organizational] innovation seemed to furnish the proper focus for such investigation' (1966: 2). Having identified the multidivisional structure as one of the more important of such innovations, he proceeded to trace its origins, identify the factors that gave rise to its appearance, and describe the subsequent diffusion of this organizational form. It was uninformed and untenable to argue that organization form was of no account after the appearance of Chandler's book.

The leading figures in the creation of the multidivisional (or M-form) structure were Pierre S. du Pont and Alfred P. Sloan; the period was the early 1920s; the firms were Du Pont and General Motors; and the organizational strain of trying to cope with economic adversity under the old structure was the occasion to innovate in both. The structures of the two companies, however, were different.

Du Pont was operating under the centralized, functionally departmentalized or unitary (U-form) structure. General Motors, by contrast, had been operated more like a holding company by William Durant – whose genius in perceiving market opportunities in the automobile industry (Livesay, 1979: 232–4) evidently did not extend to organization. Chandler summarizes the defects of the large U-form enterprise in the following way:

> The inherent weakness in the centralized, functionally departmentalized operating company . . . became critical only when the administrative load on the senior executives increased to such an extent that they were unable to handle their entrepreneurial responsibilities efficiently. This situation arose when the operations of the enterprise became too complex and the problems of coordination, appraisal, and policy formulation too intricate for a small number of top officers to handle both long-run, enterpreneurial, and short-run, operational administrative activities. (Chandler, 1966: 382–3)

The ability of the management to handle the volume and complexity of the demands placed upon it became strained and even collapsed. Unable meaningfully to identify with or contribute to the realization of global goals, managers in each of the functional parts attended to what they perceived to be operational subgoals instead (Chandler, 1966: 156). In the language of transaction-cost economics, bounds on rationality were reached as the U-form structure labored under a communication overload while the pursuit of subgoals by the functional parts (sales, engineering, production) was partly a manifestation of opportunism.

The M-form structure fashioned by du Pont and Sloan involved the creation of semi-autonomous operating divisions (mainly profit centers) organized along product, brand, or geographic lines. The operating affairs of each were managed separately. More than a change in decomposition rules was needed, however, for the M-form to be fully effective. Du Pont and Sloan also created a general office 'consisting of a number of powerful general executives and large advisory and financial staffs' (Chandler, 1977: 460) to monitor divisional performance, allocate resources among divisions, and engage in strategic planning. The reasons for the success of the M-form innovation are summarized by Chandler as follows:

> The basic reason for its success was simply that it clearly removed the executives responsible for the destiny of the entire enterprise from the more routine operational activities, and so gave them the time, information, and even psychological commitment for long-term planning and appraisal. . . .
>
> [The] new structure left the broad strategic decisions as to the allocation of existing resources and the acquisition of new ones in the hands of a top team of generalists. Relieved of operating duties and tactical decisions, a general executive was less likely to reflect the position of just one part of the whole. (Chandler, 1966: 382–3)

In contrast with the holding company – which is also a divisionalized form but has little general office capability and hence is little more than a corporate shell – the M-form organization adds (a) a strategic planning and resource allocation capability and (b) monitoring and control apparatus. As a consequence, cash flows are reallocated among divisions to favor high yield uses, and internal incentive and control instruments are exercised in a discriminating way. In short, the M-form corporation takes on many of the properties of (and is usefully regarded as) a miniature capital market,[22] which is a much more ambitious concept of the corporation than the term-holding company contemplates.

Although the structure was imitated very slowly at first, adoption by US firms proceeded rapidly during the period 1945 to 1960. Acceptance of this structure by European firms came later. Lawrence Franko (1972) reports that most large European companies administered their domestic operations through U-form or holding company structures until late in the 1960s, but that rapid reorganization along M-form lines has occurred since. The advent of zero tariffs within the European Economic Community and the postwar penetration of European markets by American multinationals were, in his judgment, important contributing factors.

As W. Ross Ashby (1956: 53) has observed, it is not sufficient to determine the behavior of a whole machine to know the behavior of its parts: 'only when the details of coupling are added does the whole's behavior become determinate'. The M-form structure represented a different solution to the coupling problem than the earlier unitary form structure. It effected decomposability along product or brand lines to which profit center standing could be assigned and it more clearly separated operating from strategic decision-making. It carried Simon's hierarchical decomposition principles to a higher degree of refinement.[23]

As compared with the U-form organization of the same activities, the M-form organization of the large, complex corporation served both to economize on bounded rationality and attenuate opportunism. Specifically:

> Operating decisions were no longer forced to the top but were resolved at the divisional level, which relieved the communication load. Strategic decisions were reserved for the general office, which reduced partisan political input into the resource allocation process. And the internal auditing and control techniques which the general office had access to served to overcome information impactedness conditions and permit fine timing controls to be exercised over the operating parts. (Williamson, 1975: 137–8)

The conglomerate

Chandler's studies of organizational innovation do not include the conglomerate and multinational form of corporate enterprise. These are more recent developments, the appearance of which would not have been feasible but for the prior development of the M-form structure. Inasmuch as transaction-cost economizing is socially valued and has been relatively neglected by prior treatments, my discussion of both of these emphasizes affirmative aspects. But this is intended to redress an imbalance and should not be construed to suggest either that a transaction-cost interpretation is fully adequate or that conglomerates and multinationals pose no troublesome public policy issues.[24] Unrelieved hostility to these two forms of organization, however, is clearly inappropriate. Specifically, conglomerates that have the capacity to allocate resources to high valued uses and multinationals that use the M-form to facilitate technology transfer warrant more sympathetic assessments.

Although diversification as a corporate strategy, certainly predates the 1960s, when general awareness of the conglomerate began to appear, the conglomerate is essentially a post World War II phenomenon. To be sure, General Electric's profit centers number in the hundreds and GE has been referred to as the world's most diversified firm. Until recently, however, General Electric's emphasis has been the manufacture and distribution of electrical appliances and machinery. Similarly, although General Motors was more than an automobile company, it took care to limit its portfolio. Thus Sloan remarked that 'tetraethyl lead was clearly a misfit for GM. It was a chemical product, rather than a mechanical one. And it had to go to market as part of the gasoline and thus required a gasoline distribution system' (Burton and Kuhn, 1979: 6). Accordingly, although GM retained an investment position, the Ethyl Corporation became a free-standing entity rather than an operating division (Sloan, 1965: 224). Similarly, although Durant had acquired Frigidaire, and Frigidaire's market share of refrigerators exceeded 50 per cent in the 1920s, the position was allowed to deteriorate as rivals developed market positions in other major appliances (radios, ranges, washers, etc.) while Frigidaire concentrated on refrigerators. The suggestion that GM get into air conditioners 'did not register on us, and the proposal was not . . . adopted' (Sloan, 1965: 361). As Richard Burton and Arthur Kuhn (1979: 10–11) conclude, GM's 'deep and myopic involvement in the automobile sector of the economy, [prevented] product diversification opportunities in other market areas – even in product lines where GM had already achieved substantial penetration – [from being] recognized'.

The conglomerate form of organization whereby the corporation consciously took on a diversified character and nurtured its various parts, evidently required a conceptual break in the mind-set of Sloan and other prewar business leaders. This occurred gradually, more by evolution than by grand design (Sobel, 1974: 377); and it involved a new group of organizational innovators – of which Royal Little was one (Sobel, 1974). The natural growth of conglomerates, which would occur as the techniques for managing diverse assets were refined, was accelerated as antitrust enforcement against horizontal and vertical mergers became progressively more severe. Conglomerate acquisitions –in terms of numbers, assets acquired, and as a proportion of total acquisitions – grew rapidly with the result that 'pure' conglomerate mergers, which in the period 1948–53 constituted only 3 per cent of the assets acquired by merger, had grown to 49 per cent by 1973–7 (Scherer, 1980: 124).

Morris Adelman's (1961) explanation for the conglomerate is that this form of organization has attractive portfolio diversification properties. But why should the conglomerate appear in the 1960s rather than much earlier? After all, holding companies, which long predated the conglomerate, can accomplish portfolio diversification. And individual stockholders, through mutual funds and otherwise, are able to diversify their own portfolios. At best the portfolio diversification thesis is a very incomplete explanation for the postwar wave of conglomerate mergers.[25]

The Federal Trade Commission also ventured an early assessment of the conglomerate in which organization form features were ignored. The conglomerate was a natural target for the inhospitality tradition. Thus the FTC staff held that the conglomerate had the following properties:

> With the economic power which it secures through its operations in many diverse fields, the giant conglomerate corporation may attain an almost impregnable economic position. Threatened with competition in any one of its various activities, it may sell below cost in that field, offsetting its losses through profits made in its other lines – a practice which is frequently explained as one of meeting competition. The conglomerate corporation is thus in a position to strike out with great force against smaller business in a variety of different industries. (US Federal Trade Commission, 1948: 59)

I submit that some phenomena, of which changing internal organization is one, need to be addressed on their own terms. Adopting this view, the conglomerate is best understood as a logical outgrowth of the M-form mode for organizing complex economic affairs. Thus once the merits of the M-form structure for managing separable, albeit related, lines of business (e.g. a series of automobile or a series of chemical divisions) were recognized and digested, its extension to manage less closely related activities was natural. This is not to say that the management of product variety is without problems of its own. But the basic M-form logic, whereby strategic and operating decisions are distinguished and responsibilities are separated, carried over. The conglomerates in which M-form principles of organization are respected are usefully thought of as internal capital markets whereby cash flows from diverse sources are concentrated and directed to high yield uses.

The conglomerate is noteworthy, however, not merely because it permitted the M-form structure to take this diversification step. Equally interesting are the unanticipated systems consequences which developed as a byproduct. Thus once it was clear that the corporation could manage diverse assets in an effective way, the possibility of takeover by tender offer suggested itself. In principle, incumbent managements could always be displaced by waging a proxy contest. In fact, this is a very expensive and relatively ineffective way to achieve management change (Williamson, 1970: Chapter 6). Moreover, even if the dissident shareholders should succeed, there was still a problem of finding a successor management.

Viewed in contractual terms, the M-form conglomerate can be thought of as substituting an administrative interface between an operating division and the stockholders where a market interface had existed previously. Subject to the condition that the conglomerate does not diversify to excess, in the sense that it cannot competently evaluate and allocate funds among the diverse activities in which it is engaged, the substitution of internal organization can have beneficial effects in goal pursuit, monitoring, staffing, and resource allocation respects. The goal-pursuit advantage is that which accrues to M-form organizations in general: since the general management of an M-form conglomerate is disengaged from operating matters, a presumption that the general office favors profits over functional goals is warranted. Relatedly, the general office can be regarded as an agent of the stockholders whose purpose is to monitor the operations of the constituent parts. Monitoring benefits are realized in the degree to which internal monitors enjoy advantages over external monitors in access to information – which they arguably do (Williamson, 1975: 145–8). The differential ease with which the general office can change managers and reassign duties where performance failures or distortions are detected is responsible for the staffing advantage. Resource-allocation benefits are realized because cash flows no longer return automatically to their origins but instead revert to the center, thereafter to be allocated among competing uses in accordance with prospective yields.[26]

This has a bearing on the problem of separation of ownership from control, noted by Adolph Berle and Gardiner C. Means in 1932. Thus they inquired, 'have we any justification for assuming that those in control of a modern corporation will also choose to operate it in the interests of the stockholders' (Berle and Means, 1932: 121). The answer, then as now, is almost certainly no. Indeed, the evident disparity of interest between managers and stockholders gave rise in the 1960s to what has become known as the managerial discretion literature (Baumol, 1959; Marris, 1964; Williamson, 1964).

There are important differences, however, between the U-form structure, which was the prevailing organization form at the time Berle and Means were writing, and the M-form structure, which in the US was substantially in place by the 1960s. For one thing, as argued above, U-form managers identified more strongly with functional interests and hence were more given to subgoal pursuit. Second, and related, there was a confusion between strategic and operating goals in the U-form structure which the M-form served to rectify – with the result that the general office was more fully concerned with enterprise goals, of which profits is the leading element. Third, the market for corporate control, which remained ineffectual so long as the proxy contest was the only way to challenge incumbent managements, was activated as conglomerates recognized that tender offers could be used to effect corporate takeovers. As a consequence, managements that were otherwise secure and would have permitted managerial preferences to prevail were brought under scrutiny and induced to self-correct against egregious managerial distortions.

To be sure, managerial preferences (for salary and perquisites) and stockholder preferences for profits do not become perfectly consonant as a result of conglomerate organization and the associated activation of the capital market. The continuing tension between management and stockholder interests is evident in the numerous efforts that incumbent managements have taken to protect target firms against takeover (Cary, 1969; Williamson, 1979a; Benston, 1980). Changes in internal organization have nevertheless relieved these concerns. A study of capitalist enterprises which makes no allowance for organization form changes and their capital market ramifications will naturally overlook the possibility that the corporate control dilemma posed by Berle and Means has since been alleviated more by *internal* than it has by regulatory or external organizational reforms.

Not all conglomerates respected M-form principles when they were first organized. The above argument applies only to those where rational decomposition principles were observed and leads to the following testable proposition: conglomerates that were organized along holding company rather than M-form lines (as many were initially) would be less able to cope when adversity appeared, at which time they would be reorganized as M-form firms. Voluntary divestiture is also an interesting conglomerate phenomenon. Such a rationalization of assets is commonly accompanied by internal organizational reforms. Growth maximization theories are mainly at a loss to explain such behavior.

Concluding remarks

There is widespread agreement, among economists and non-economists alike, with the proposition that the modern corporation is an important and complex economic institution. Such agreement is mainly explained by the obtrusive size of the largest firms – running to tens of billions of dollars of assets and sales, with employment numbering in the hundreds of thousands. The economic factors that lie behind the size, shape, and performance of the modern corporation, however, are poorly understood.

This puzzlement is not of recent origin. Edward Mason complained over twenty years ago that 'the functioning of the corporate system has not to date been adequately explained. . . . The man of action may be content with a system that works. But one who reflects on the properties or characteristics of this system cannot help asking why it works and whether it will continue to work' (1960: 4). The predicament to which Mason refers is, I submit, largely the product of two different (but not unrelated) intellectual traditions. The first of these holds that the structural features of the corporation are irrelevant. This is the neoclassical theory of the firm that populates intermediate theory textbooks. Structural differences are suppressed as the firm is described as a production function to which a profit maximization objective has been assigned. The second has public policy roots; this is the inhospitality tradition that I referred to earlier. In this tradition, distinctive structural features of the corporation are believed to be the result of unwanted (anti-competitive) intrusions into market processes.

The transaction-cost approach differs from both. Unlike neoclassical analysis, internal organization is specifically held to be important. Unlike the inhospitality tradition, structural differences are assumed to arise primarily in order to promote economy in transaction costs. The assignment of transactions between firms and markets and the economic ramifications of internal structure both come under scrutiny in these terms. The application of these ideas to the study of transactions in general and of the modern corporation in particular requires that

1 the transaction be made the principal unit of analysis;
2 an elementary appreciation for 'human nature as we know it' supplant the fiction of economic man;
3 transactions be dimensionalized;
4 rudimentary principles of market and hierarchical organization be recognized; and
5 a guiding principle of comparative institutional study be the hypothesis that transactions are assigned to and organized within governance structures in a discriminating (transaction-cost economizing) way.

The view that the corporation is first and foremost an efficiency instrument does not deny that firms also seek to monopolize markets, sometimes by engaging in strategic behavior, or that managers sometimes pursue their own goals to the detriment of system goals. But specific structural preconditions need to be satisfied if strategic behavior is to be feasible[27] – and most firms do not qualify, which is to say that strategic behavior is the exception rather than the rule. Furthermore, most firms will be penalized if efficiency norms are seriously violated for extended periods of time – which serves to curb managerial discretion. The strongest argument favoring transaction-cost economizing, however, is that this is the only hypothesis that is able to provide a discriminating rationale for the succession of organizational innovations that have occurred over the past 150 years and out of which the modern corporation has emerged.

To recapitulate, although railroad mergers between parallel roads can have monopolizing purposes, the joining of end-to-end systems under common management is explained by transaction-cost economics. The hierarchical structures evolved by the railroads were the outcome of internal efforts to effect coordination across interfaces to which common operating responsibilities had been assigned. Older and simpler structures were unable to manage such complex networks, while coordination by end-to-end contracts between successive stations was prohibitively costly.

Forward integration out of manufacturing into distribution was widespread at the turn of the century. More interesting, however, than this general movement is the fact that forward integration was selective – being extensive in some industries (e.g. sewing machines), negligible in others (e.g. dry goods), and mistaken in still others (e.g. sugar). This selective pattern is predicted by and consistent with transaction-cost reasoning – whereas no other hypothesis makes comparably detailed predictions.

The efficiency incentive to shift from the earlier U-form to the M-form structure is partly explained in managerial discretion terms: the older structure was more subject to distortions of a managerial discretion kind – which is to say that opportunism had become a serious problem in the large U-form firm. Equally and probably more important, however, is that the managerial hierarchy in the U-form enterprise was simply over-burdened as the firm became large and complex. The M-form structure represented a more rational decomposition of the affairs of the firm and thereby served to economize on bounded rationality.[28] The subsequent diffusion of this structure was hastened by a combination of product market (pressure on rivals) and capital market (takeover) competition.

The M-form structure, which was originally adopted by firms in relatively specialized lines of commerce was subsequently extended to manage diversified assets (the conglomerate) and foreign direct investments (MNE). A breadth-for-depth tradeoff is involved in the former case, as the firm selectively internalizes functions ordinarily associated with the capital market. MNE activity has also been selective – being concentrated in the more technologically progressive industries where higher rates of R & D are reported and technology transfer arguably poses greater difficulties than is true of technologically less progressive industries. This pattern of foreign direct investment cannot be explained as the pursuit of monopoly but is consistent with transaction-cost reasoning.

The upshot is that a transaction-cost approach to the study of the modern corporation permits a wide variety of significant organizational events to be interpreted in a coherent way.[29] It links up comfortably with the type of business history studies that have been pioneered by Chandler. It has ramifications for the study of regulation (Williamson, 1976; Goldberg, 1976) and for antitrust enforcement. Applications to aspects of labor economics and comparative systems have been made, and others would appear to be fruitful. More generally, while there is room for and need for refinement, a comparative approach to the study of economic institutions in which the economy of transaction costs is the focus of analysis, appears to have considerable promise.

Notes

This chapter has benefitted from the very helpful comments of Moses Abramovitz, Alfred Chandler, Sanford Grossman, Paul Joskow, Scott Masten, Richard Nelson, and Douglass North. Parts of it were given at Rice University as a 1981 Peterkin Lecture, and comments of the faculty and students in attendance were also helpful. For related recent assessments of the modern corporation which, however, emphasizes somewhat different aspects, see Richard Caves (1980), Robin Marris and Dennis Mueller (1980), and Richard Cyert and Charles Hedrick (1972).

1. This argument is elaborated in Williamson (1981). It is briefly discussed in the next section with what is referred to as the 'inhospitality tradition' within antitrust.
2. The quotation is attributed to Turner by Stanley Robinson, 1968, NY State Bar Association, Antitrust Symposium, p. 29.
3. For an interesting commentary and contribution, see Douglass North (1978). The earlier Davis and North book, however, gave relatively little attention to institutional changes that occurred within firms (1971: 143).
4. The term 'local goals' subsumes both the functional goals of a subunit of the enterprise and the individual goals of the functional managers. In a perfectly harmonized system, private goals are consonant with functional goals, the realization of which in turn promotes global goals. Frequently, however, managers become advocates for parochial interests that conflict with global goal attainment. If, for example, R & D claims a disproportionate share of resources – because of effective but distorted partisan representations from the management and staff of this group – profits (global goals) will suffer. Aggressive subgoal (or local goal) pursuit of this kind is a manifestation of opportunism (see below).
5. The phrase is Richard Posner's (1979: 928).
6. For a discussion of this point, see Williamson (1975: 11–13, 109–10).
7. Although the non-strategic tradition inspired by Aaron Director makes insufficient allowance for anti-competitive behavior, it was a useful counterweight to the inhospitality tradition to which it was paired. For a critique of the more extreme versions of this non-strategic – or, as Posner (1979: 932) puts it, the 'diehard Chicago' – tradition, see Williamson (1981).
8. Moral hazard is a technical term with a well defined meaning in the insurance literature. It refers to an *ex post* insurance condition and is clearly distinguished from adverse selection, which is responsible for a troublesome *ex ante* insurance screening problem. Opportunism is a less technical but more general term that applies to a wide set of economic

behavior – of which adverse selection and moral hazard are specific kinds. Unless, therefore, moral hazard is given a broader meaning, the substitution of moral hazard for opportunism focuses attention on a subset of the full range of human and economic conditions of concern.

9. The coexistence of cunning and bounded rationality is troublesome to some. How can economic agents simultaneously be more clever and less competent than the hyperrational man that populates neoclassical models? Is he a maximizer or is he not? This is not a useful dichotomy. Maximizing is an analytical convenience the use of which is often justified by the fact that human agents are '*intendedly* rational' (Simon, 1957b: xxiv). As discussed in the text, however, comprehensive contracting, which is an ambitious form of maximizing, is infeasible. Opportunism has important economic ramifications for this reason.

10. I have reference, of course, to the Arrow–Debreu contracting model.

11. The argument that effective *ex ante* competition for the right to supply service (franchise bidding) vitiates the need to regulate decreasing cost industries sometimes goes through but not always. Incomplete contracting (bounded rationality) coupled with the hazards of *ex post* opportunism place great strain on the franchise bidding mode if assets are durable and specific. For a critique of what I believe was a mistaken assessment of the feasibility of using franchise bidding for CATV, see Williamson (1976).

12. As Knight observes: 'With uncertainty entirely absent, every individual being in possession of perfect knowledge of the situation, there would be no occasion for anything of the nature of responsible management or control of productive activity' (1965: 267).

13. Williamson (1979a and b). Also see Klein et al. (1978) for an illuminating discussion of transaction specific investments in the context of what they refer to as 'appropriable quasi-rents'.

14. Whereas scale economies refer to declining average costs associated with increasing output of a single line of commerce, scope economies are realized 'where it is less costly to combine two or more product lines in one firm rather than to produce them separately' (Panzar and Willig, 1981: 268). Retail outlets that carry many products and brands (drug stores, department stores) presumably enjoy significant economies of scope in the retailing function.

15. Bureaucratic disabilities aside, any given firm could realize all of these production benefits for itself by an appropriate increase in the scale and scope of its activities. Pursuit of this logic however, leads to the following anomaly: all firms, of which there will be few, will be comprehensively integrated and diversified in sufficient degree to obviate the need for market exchange. The fact that we do not observe comprehensive integration – as Coase puts it, 'Why is not all production carried on by one big firm?' (1952: 340) – suggests that the bureaucratic disabilities of internal organization are very serious. But since we do observe that some transactions are organized within firms, this poses the question of which and why. The answer resides in the transaction-cost disabilities of markets that arise when asset specificity and demand externalities appear.

16. Note that the nature of the asset specificity matters. If the assets in question are mobile and the specificity is due to physical but not human asset features, market procurement may still be feasible. This can be accomplished by having the buyer own the specific assets (e.g. dies). He puts the business up for bid and awards it to the low bidder, to whom he ships the dies. Should contractual difficulties arise, however, he is not locked into a bilateral exchange. He reclaims the dies and reopens the bidding. This option is not available if the specific assets are of a human asset kind or if they are non-mobile. See David Teece (1980) for a related discussion.

17. Manufacturers may, of course, decide to integrate into components if work-in-process inspections are much cheaper than final inspections.

18. Franchising will be more prevalent if aggregation economies are present at the distribution stage. It will be inefficient in these circumstances for a single product firm to integrate forward into distribution.

19. The hierarchical decomposition principle is due to Simon (1962, 1973). As he observes,

the anatomy of an organization can be viewed either in terms of the groupings of human beings or the flows and transformations of symbols (1973: 270). He emphasizes the latter, which is in the spirit of transaction-cost analysis.

20. Thus, whereas I argue that the object is to minimize the sum of production and transaction costs, taking output and design as given, the more general problem is to maximize profits, treating output and design as decision variables. A rudimentary statement of the optimizing problem, for a given organization form (f), is to choose output (Q) and design (D) so as to maximize:

$$\pi(Q,D;f) = P(Q,D) \cdot Q - C_f(Q,D;S) - G_f(Q,D),$$

where π denotes profit, P(Q,D) is the demand curve, S denotes combinatorial economies of scope, and C_f and G_f are the production costs and governance (transaction) costs of mode f. Transaction costs become relatively more important to this calculus as the assets needed to support specialized designs become progressively more specific – which they normally will as designs become more idiosyncratic.

Plainly the tradeoffs that run through this optimizing relation are more extensive than my earlier discussion discloses, but a detailed assessment of these is not needed for the types of purposes to which the asset specificity principle is herein applied. Both the externality and hierarchical decomposition principles should likewise be qualified to recognize tradeoffs. Again, however, second order refinements are not needed for the comparative institutional purposes to which these are applied below.

21. The treatment of these matters by Koontz and O'Donnell (1955) is representative.

22. Others who reported that the modern corporation was assuming capital market resource allocation and control functions include Richard Heflebower (1960) and Armen Alchian (1969).

23. Moreover, whereas the line-and-staff structure that the railroads adopted in the 1850s could be said to have been prefigured by the military, there is no such military precedent for the M-form. Rather, the reorganization of the military after World War II has certain M-form attributes.

24. For a discussion of the public policy issues posed by conglomerates, see Williamson (1975: 163–71).

25. The diversification of personal portfolios is not a perfect substitute for conglomerate diversification because bankruptcy has real costs that the firm, but not individuals, can reduce by portfolio diversification. Bankruptcy costs have not sharply increased in the past thirty years, however, hence these differences do not explain the appearance of the conglomerate during this interval.

26. To be sure, the substitution of internal organization for the capital market is subject to tradeoffs and diminishing returns. Breadth – that is, access to the widest range of alternatives – is traded off for depth – that is, more intimate knowledge of a narrower range of possible investment outlets – (Alchian and Demsetz, 1972: 29), where the general office may be presumed to have the advantage in the latter respect. The diminishing returns feature suggests that the net benefits of increased diversity eventually become negative. Were further diversification thereafter to be attempted, effective control would pass back into the hands of the operating divisions with problematic performance consequences.

27. For a discussion of these preconditions – mainly high concentration coupled with high barriers to entry – see Joskow and Klevorick (1979) and Williamson (1981).

28. Had 'normal' managerial preferences prevailed, the U-form, which favored the exercise of those preferences, would presumably have been retained.

29. Recent contributions to the theory of the firm that are held to have a bearing on the study of the modern corporation are Alchian and Demsetz (1972) and Michael Jensen and William Meckling (1976). Both, however, deal with a microcosm much smaller than the modern corporation. Thus Alchian and Demsetz focus on the reasons why technological non-separabilities give rise to team organization. Although small groups may be explained in this way (manual freight loading, whereby two men are required

to lift coordinately, is the standard example), the existence of complex hierarchies cannot be explained in terms of the imperatives of such non-separabilities. (The largest work group which, to my knowledge, qualifies is the symphony orchestra.)

Similarly, while the Jensen and Meckling paper is an important contribution to the principal-agent literature, it does not generalize to the modern corporation – as they expressly acknowledge (1976: 356). Although they conjecture that their analysis can be applied to the large, diffusely owned corporation whose managers own little or no equity (1976: 356), I have serious doubts.

Bibliography

Adelman, M. A. (1961) 'The antimerger act, 1959–1960', *American Economic Review,* May, 51: 236–44.

Alchian, A. A. (1969) 'Corporate management and property rights', in H. G. Manne (ed.), *Economic Policy and Regulation of Corporate Securities*. Washington: American Enterprise Institute for Public Policy. pp. 337–60.

Alchian, A. A. and Demsetz, H. (1972) 'Production information costs, and economic organization', *American Economic Review*, Dec., 62 (5): 777–95.

Arrow, Kenneth J. (1962) 'Economic welfare and the allocation resources of invention', in National Bureau of Economic Research (ed.), *The Rate and Direction of Inventive Activity: Economic and Social Factors*. Princeton, NJ: Princeton University Press. pp. 609–25.

Arrow, K. (1964) 'Control in large organizations', *Management Science*, April 10 (3): 397–408.

Arrow, K. (1969) 'The organization of economic activity: issues pertinent to the choice of market versus nonmarket allocation', in *The Analysis and Evaluation of Public Expenditure: The PPB System*, Vol. 1. US Joint Economic Committee, 91st Congress, 1st Session, US Government Printing Office. pp. 59–73.

Arrow, K. (1971) *Essays in the Theory of Risk-Bearing*. Chicago, IL: Markham Pub. Co.

Arrow, K. (1974) *The Limits of Organization*. 1st edition. New York: W. W. Norton & Co.

Ashby, W. R. (1956) *An Introduction to Cybernetics*. New York: John Wiley and Sons.

Barnard, C. I. (1938) *The Functions of the Executive*. Cambridge, MA: Harvard University Press.

Baumol, W. J. (1959) *Business Behavior, Value and Growth*. New York: Macmillan.

Benston, George J. (1980) *Conglomerate Mergers: Causes, Consequences and Remedies*. Washington, DC: American Enterprise Institute for Public Policy Research.

Berle, A. A. and Means, G. C. (1932) *The Modern Corporation and Private Property*. New York: Macmillan.

Bruchey, Stuart W. (1956) *Robert Oliver, Merchant of Baltimore, 1783–1819*. Baltimore: Johns Hopkins University Press.

Buckley, P. J. and Casson, M. (1976) *The Future of Multinational Enterprise*. New York: Holmes and Meier.

Burton, R. H. and Kuhn, A. J. (1979) 'Strategy follows structure: the missing link of their intertwined relation'. Working Paper No. 260, Fuqua School of Business, Duke University, May.

Cary, W. (1969–70) 'Corporate devices used to insulate management from attack', *Antitrust Law Journal*, 39 (1): 318–24.

Caves, R. E. (1980) 'Corporate strategy and structure', *Journal of Economic Literature*, March, 18 (1): 64–92.

Chandler, A. D., Jr (1966) *Strategy and Structure: Chapters in the History of Industrial Enterprise*. Cambridge, MA: MIT Press.

Chandler, A. D., Jr (1977) *The Visible Hand: The Managerial Revolution in American Business*. Cambridge, MA: Belknap Press.

Coase, R. H. (1937) 'The nature of the firm', *Economica* N.S., 4: 386–405; and in G. J. Stigler and K. E. Boulding (eds) (1952) *Readings in Price Theory*. Chicago, IL: Richard D. Irwin for the American Economic Association.

Coase, R. H. (1972) 'Industrial organization: a proposal for research', in Victor R. Fuchs (ed.), *Policy Issues and Research Opportunities in Industrial Organization: Economic Research: Retrospect and Prospect*. New York: NBER; distributed by Columbia University Press, New York and London. pp. 59–73.

Commons, John R. (1951) *Institutional Economics: Its Place in Political Economy*. New York: Macmillan.

Cyert, Richard M. and Hedrick, Charles L. (1972) 'Theory of the firm: past, present, and future: an interpretation', *Journal of Economic Literature*, June, 10 (2): 398–412.

Davis, Lance E. and North, Douglass C. (1971) *Institutional Change and American Economic Growth*. Cambridge, England: Cambridge University Press.

Doeringer, P. and Piori, M. (1971) *International Labor Markets and Manpower Analysis*. Boston, MA: D. C. Heath and Co.

Drucker, P. (1974) *Management: Tasks, Responsibilities, Practices*. New York: Harper & Row.

Fishlow, Albert (1965) *American Railroads and the Transformation of the Antebellum Economy*. Cambridge, MA: Harvard University Press.

Fogel, William R. (1964) *Railroads and American Economic Growth: Essays in Econometric History*. Baltimore: Johns Hopkins University Press.

Franko, Lawrence G. (1972) 'The growth, organizational efficiency of European multinational firms: some emerging hypotheses', *Colloques International aux CNRS*. pp. 335–66.

Goldberg, V. P. (1976) 'Regulation and administered contracts', *Bell Journal of Economics*, Autumn, 7 (2): 426–52.

Hayek, F. (1945) 'The use of knowledge in society', *American Economic Review*, Sept., 35: 519–30.

Heflebower, R. B. (1960) 'Observation on decentralization in large enterprises', *Journal of Industrial Economics*, Nov., 9: 7–22.

Hymer, S. (1970) 'The efficiency (contradictions) of multinational corporations', *American Economic Review*, May, 60 (2): 441–8.

Jensen, M. C. and Meckling, W. H. (1976) 'Theory of the firm: managerial behavior, agency costs and ownership structure', *Journal of Financial Economics*, Oct., 3 (4): 305–60.

Joskow, Paul L. and Klevorick, Alvin K. (1979) 'A framework for analyzing predatory pricing policy', *Yale Law Journal*, Dec., 89: 213–70.

Klein, B., Crawford, R. A. and Alchian, A. A. (1978) 'Vertical integration, appropriable rents, and the competitive contracting process', *Journal of Law and Economics*, Oct., 21 (2): 297–326.

Knight, Frank H. (1965) *Risk, Uncertainty and Profit*. New York: Harper & Row.

Koontz, H. and O'Donnell, C. (1955) *Principles of Management: An Analysis of Managerial Functions*. New York: McGraw-Hill.

Larson, Henrietta M. (1948) *Guide to Business History: Materials for the Study of American Business History and Suggestions for Their Use*. Cambridge, MA: Harvard University Press.

Livesay, H. C. (1979) *American Made: Men Who Shaped the American Economy*. 1st edition. Boston: Little, Brown.

Mansfield, E., Romeo, A. and Wagner, S. (1979) 'Foreign trade and US research and development', *Review of Economic Statistics*, Feb., 61 (i): 49–57.

Marris, R. (1964) *The Economic Theory of Managerial Capitalism*. New York: Free Press.

Marris, R. and Mueller, D. C. (1980) 'The corporation, competition, and the invisible hand', *Journal of Economic Literature*, March, 18 (1): 32–63.

Marschak, J. and Radner, R. (1972) *Economic Theory of Teams*. New Haven: Yale University Press.

Mason, E. S. (1960) 'Introduction', in E. S. Mason (ed.), *The Corporation in Modern Society*. Cambridge, MA: Harvard University Press. pp. 1–24.

Nelson, R. R. (1981) 'Assessing private enterprise: an exegesis of tangled doctrine', *Bell Journal of Economics*, Spring, 12 (1) 92–111.

Nelson, R. R. and Winter S. G. (1981) *An Evolutionary Theory of Economic Behavior and Capabilities*. Cambridge, MA: Harvard University Press.

North, D. C. (1978)'Structure and performance: the task of economic history', *Journal of Economic Literature*, Sept., 16 (3): 963–78.

Panzar, John C. and Willig, Robert D. (1981) 'Economies of scope', *American Economic Review, Papers and Proceedings*, May, 71 (2): 268–72.

Polanyi, M. (1962) *Personal Knowledge: Towards a Post-Critical Philosophy*. New York: Harper & Row.

Porter, G. and Livesay, H. C. (1971) *Merchants and Manufacturers: Studies in the Changing Structure of Nineteenth Century Marketing*. Baltimore: Johns Hopkins University Press.

Posner, R. A. (1979) 'The Chicago school of antitrust analysis', *University of Pennsylvania Law Review*. April, 127 (4): 925–48.

Radner, Roy (1968) 'Competitive equilibrium under uncertainty', *Econometrica*, Jan., 36 (1): 31–58.

Scherer, F. M. (1980) *Industrial Market Structure and Economic Performance*. 2nd edition. Chicago, IL: Rand McNally College Pub. Co.

Simon, H. A. (1957a) *Models of Man: Social and Rational Mathematical Essays on Rational Human Behavior in a Social Setting*. New York: John Wiley and Sons.

Simon, H. A. (1957b) *Administrative Behavior: A Study of Decision-making Processes in Administrative Organization*. 2nd edition. New York: Macmillan.

Simon, H. A. (1962) 'The architecture of complexity', *Proceedings of the American Philosophical Society*, Dec., 106 (6): 467–82.

Simon, H. A. (1973) 'Applying information technology to organization design', *Public Administration Review*, May–June, 33 (3): 268–78.

Simon, H. A. (1978) 'Rationality as process and as product of thought', *American Economic Review*, May, 68 (2): 1–16.

Sloan, A. P., Jr (1965) *My Years with General Motors*. New York: MacFadden-Bartell.

Sobel, R. (1974) *The Entrepreneurs: Explorations within the American Business Tradition*. New York: Weybright and Talley.

Stopford, John M. and Wells, Louis T., Jr (1972) *Managing the Multinational Enterprise: Organization of the Firm and Ownership of the Subsidiaries*. New York: Basic Books.

Teece, D. J. (1977) 'Technology transfer by multinational firms', *Economics Journal*, June, 87: 242–61.

Teece, D. J. (1980) 'Economies of scope and the scope of the enterprise', *Journal of Economic Behavior Organization*, Sept., 1 (3): 223–45.

Temin, P. (1981) 'The future of the new economic history', *Journal of Interdisciplinary History*, Autumn, 12 (2): 179–97.

Thompson, James D. (1967) *Organizations in Action: Social Science Bases of Administrative Theory*. New York: McGraw-Hill.

Tsurumi, Y. (1977) *Multinational Management: Business Strategy and Government Policy*. Cambridge, MA: Ballinger.

US Federal Trade Commission (1948) *Report of the Federal Trade Commission on the Merger Movement: A Summary Report*. Washington, DC: US Government Printing Office.

Vernon, R. (1971) *Sovereignty at Bay: The Multinational Spread of US Enterprise*. New York: Basic Books.

Wilkins, Mira (1974) *The Maturing of Multinational Enterprise: American Business Abroad from 1914 to 1970*. Cambridge, MA: Harvard University Press.

Williamson, O. E. (1964) *The Economics of Discretionary Behavior: Managerial Objectives in a Theory of the Firm*. Englewood Cliffs, NJ: Prentice-Hall.

Williamson, O. E. (1970) *Corporate Control and Business Behavior*. Englewood Cliffs, NJ: Prentice-Hall.

Williamson, O. E. (1975) *Markets and Hierarchies: Analysis and Antitrust Implications: A Study in the Economics of International Organization.* New York: Free Press.

Williamson, O. E. (1976) 'Franchise bidding for natural monopolies – in general and with respect to CATV', *Bell Journal of Economics*, Spring, 7 (1): 73–104.

Williamson, O. E. (1979a) 'Transaction-cost economics: the governance of contractual relations', *Journal of Law and Economics.*, Oct., 22 (2): 233–61.

Williamson, O. E. (1979b) 'On the governance of the modern corporation', *Hofstra Law Review.* Fall, 8 (1): 63–78.

Williamson, O. E. (1980) 'Organizational innovation: the transaction-cost approach'. Discussion Paper No. 82, Center for the Study of Organizational Innovation, University of Pennsylvania, Sept.

Williamson, O. E. (1981) 'Antitrust enforcement: where it's been; where it's going'. Discussion Paper No. 102, Center for the Study of Organizational Innovation, University of Pennsylvania, May.

Williamson, O. E. and Teece, D. J. (forthcoming) 'European economic and political integration: the markets and hierarchies approach', in P. Salmon (ed.), *New Approaches to European Integration.*

Williamson, O. E., Wachter, Michael L. and Harris, Jeffrey E. (1975) 'Understanding the employment relation: the analysis of idiosyncratic exchange', *Bell Journal of Economics*, Spring, 6 (1): 70–280.

The political environment

Politics is often taught, in the social sciences, on the basis of competing
– philosophical – frameworks or grand theories. Thus liberalism (in the
stricter political sense) or realism (another term used to describe generally
'Right-wing', Conservative values) are contrasted with structuralism
(which has customarily inherited the Left-wing mantles of Marx and
Lenin). Somewhere in the middle, and they would claim, firmly in the real
world, come the pluralists (those who look – in the modern parlance –
to a consensual mix of market and state). The emphasis on competing
frameworks, and the explanation of historical trends from which these
frameworks are derived, has the virtue of allowing judgements to be made
both as to what future political developments, on a society-wide basis, are
likely to be, and what political systems might emerge as best suited to
handle these.

In this book, where relevance to managers is our touchstone, we have
deliberately eschewed these grand debates and have taken the organization
itself, and the possible political impacts upon it, as our prime focus.

Thus, the first chapter, 'Growth in activist groups', by Arion N.
Pattakos, looks at political issues on an almost domestic scale: the impact
of pressure groups upon an organization, and especially of those espous-
ing activism.

Pattakos argues that managers should recognize that activist groups
have become important actors in the development of public policy. An
awareness of, and sensitivity to, the needs and aspirations of such groups
is a basic requirement if managers are to deal effectively with them. In
the chapter Pattakos explores the reasons why such groups may develop
around particular issues and values. He gives examples of the development of activist movements. He describes the characteristics of effective
groups and the highly sophisticated and influential ways in which they
may plan, train, develop and implement strategies and campaigns. He also
then considers how businesses may cope with the challenges posed,
including actively organizing a response.

A point he does not stress but which should be considered, is the need
to be aware of the issue at the root of the activism. Many pressure groups
focus on the injustices they perceive against individuals or the community.
In many, if not most, situations the most effective counter is quite simply
to right the perceived wrong.

The second chapter, 'The transformation of AT & T' by Carol
Kennedy, looks at a specific case at the opposite end of the spectrum:
where a corporation was faced with the whole might of government

ranged against it. It could not hope to prevail against such odds, but had instead to plan to divert rather than directly oppose the challenge. As the result of the rigorous application of 'anti-trust' (anti-monopoly) law, AT & T was broken up into its component parts – the central, 'technology'-based core including the world famous Bell Labs, and the so-called 'Baby Bells' – the regional telephone operators.

The chapter describes the whole process from the legal battle itself through to the results of the divestiture. It might be argued that AT & T did not read early enough the 'weak signals' which gave advance warning of government's intentions, and this itself is a salutary warning about the need for 'tuning in' effectively to developments in the political environment. However, the case also examines how AT & T subsequently managed to survive a shock which might easily have led to its ultimate demise; a lesson about handling the 'fractures' referred to in the first section of this book, just as much as about how to deal with irresistible government pressures. Arguably, IBM, which was at the last minute saved from a similar break-up, has suffered even greater trauma. The sense of relief it felt at not being forced into divestiture in its case led, on the rebound, to a whole series of policies which took that company away from the philosophies which had been at the heart of its success. The story of how AT & T, in contrast, adapted itself to these external changes by transforming its competitive stance holds many lessons for other organizations.

The third chapter, 'The strategic implications of Europe 1992' by Herman Daems, was not included just because of its topicality – though that was a bonus. The prime reason for its inclusion was, rather, to examine the fall-out from one large-scale political initiative. It amply illustrates the many, massive changes which may be forced upon organizations by political decisions which are beyond their control. At the same time it suggests strategies which such organizations might follow in this specific situation, and some of these have more general applicability. Most important of all it clearly shows the paramount need to develop suitable strategies to deal with such 'fractures' in the external – political – environment.

The final chapter in this section explores the relationship between the concepts of reference groups and relative deprivation. The concept of reference groups – the groups with which individuals compare themselves and/or to which they feel they belong, providing them with their frames of reference, of values and standards of comparison – clearly has applicability across a range of contexts, from the political (for example, the political activist groups addressed above) to consumer markets and segments. In this chapter the focus is particularly on the implications of relative deprivation – the sense of deprivation that can occur when individuals compare their own situation with the imagined situation of some other individual or group.

Runciman considers the broader consequences of reference-group formation and relative deprivation within different political and economic contexts, exploring the potential outcomes of individuals' and groups' senses of grievance and inequality. In doing so he raises issues that are highly pertinent to analyses of change in an organization's political – and sociocultural – environment.

Together the four chapters illustrate the range and diversity of political influences which may bear on organizations and which need to be understood and addressed. Management's answer to the challenge of a small activist group may be very different to that when faced with forced divestiture, but even at these extremes the first response should be to try and understand the forces at work before planning how these may be controlled or channelled to the organization's benefit.

7

Growth in activist groups: how can business cope?

Arion N. Pattakos

Ever since the civil rights movement, the Vietnam War and the ecological efforts of the 1960s and 1970s, activist organizations have become major participants in the public policy development process. They are the voices of change. They foreshadow the direction political movements will take. They are voices listened to in legislative bodies. Activist organizations, on a state-by-state basis, made nuclear power in the United States virtually an uneconomic route for society, even in the face of a four-fold increase in oil prices. If business does not engage the activists, they will have the say in what our public policy is and on their own terms. (Jack Mongoven, Issue Strategist)[1]

For more than a decade, close observers of the public policy process have been warning the business community of a significant force to be reckoned with. It has become increasingly clear that agenda setting, decisive input and the shape of outcomes are no longer the almost exclusive province of business, government and elites. A grassroots citizen component has been identified, a component sparked by vocal, articulate and increasingly sophisticated activists. Today, as activists, their groups and their causes, proliferate and gain in power, the need to be attuned to the voice of public interest groups as they influence the public policy debate becomes even more important.

Look to the horizon and beyond, what issues demand the attention of corporations now and in the future? What are the early warning signs that suggest monitoring programs and action plans be designed and implemented? Necessary for answering these questions is evaluated information (intelligence) about the players and where they stand on issues. Business leaders must be aware that activists have become important players in the development of public policy. Saul Alinsky, the activists' activist, in his 1971 work *Rules For Radicals*[2] outlined how to organize grassroots movements for successful campaigns. Since his time, training centers, manuals and other how-to-literature have become readily available to teach activists how to achieve their goals on local, national and international levels.

Reprinted by permission of Pergamon Press PLC from *Long Range Planning*, 22(3) 1989: 98–104.

The issue process

W. Howard Chase in his seminal work *Issues Management: Origins of the Future* (1984) modeled the key processes associated with understanding and managing issues. In describing the interactions between and among citizens, business and government, he advised that although the three are at the heart of the process, '. . . none of the three, by itself, makes public policy. Policy is the end result of their interaction.'[3]

While the government and business components of this interaction are clear to most and seen as paramount by them, citizen input is given short shrift by business as it plans for the future. Long-range corporate planning requires more than the broad, traditional 'will it sell' marketing approach. Such planning requires more than making economic projections and assessing broad political risk and stability. To accomplish effective short- and long-term planning, today's business strategists must consider and assess the impact of their plans on the sociopolitical environment as well. This requires sensitivity to what the activists are doing and what they plan to do.

The citizen component of the issue process is given its highly vocal and articulate voice by activists – a self-appointed dedicated cadre of people who derive their mandate (they believe), strength and motivation from the people. Equally, and perhaps more importantly, many unaffiliated 'citizens' believe activists do speak for them. A wrong or potential wrong is seen and citizen (activist) spokespeople set out to make it right. The impact on business, of course, is rooted in the notion that ultimately corporations and how they operate derive their legitimacy from the people. Standards of what comprises proper, ethical, fair and legal business conduct have changed over the years and will continue to do so. How corporations are perceived is fundamental to these changes.

Though activists may be self-appointed this does not make them wrong (or right) on an issue. Just as business and government are not bad by definition, neither are activists and activism. With many there is room for dialogue and interaction – the trick is knowing with whom one can interact effectively. Some are idealistic or pragmatic while others are intransigent, opportunistic or driven by political agendas; still others see compromise as a cop out. It is important, therefore, to determine motivation in order to understand the basis for activist criticisms and later to establish a foundation for effective dialogue and negotiation. It makes little sense to engage in discussions with those not prepared to talk in good faith.

There are literally thousands of activist groups, here and abroad, focusing on corporations and on one or many issues of concern to them. Collectively, these groups list memberships in the millions.

Over the past several years, events and challenges to corporate governance make clear there is a relationship between the financial bottom line and the concept of the corporate 'good citizen'.[4] Wise business people at the very least hear (not necessarily listen to) what their critics have to say.

Activist movements

An understanding of activist issues and their organizations and knowledge of their plans, capabilities and intentions is a form of insurance and provides corporations with a foundation for timely and effective action.

What follows are generalizations about the development and characteristics of activist movements and their typical strategies and tactics. Of course, two observations can immediately be made about generalizations and any typology: there will be exceptions and there will be variances. Generalizations and typologies, though rarely perfect, are valuable because they provide planners with a benchmark for anticipating the future.

Activist movement development

Robert L. Heath and Richard Alan Nelson[5] model what they view as the developmental stages of an activist movement. They point out that not all movements will go through each of the stages. Activists may achieve goals early or fail to develop a sufficient base to proceed. The stages:

- *Strain*. A movement gets its impetus from a desire to change some condition.
- *Mobilization*. The stage of a movement when it must begin to marshal its power resources.
- *Confrontation*. That moment when the group attempts to force a corporation or government agency to recognize the group and meet its demands.
- *Resolution*. Determining how society can be adjusted to accommodate the results of discussion.

The Heath/Nelson model generally conforms to what the staff of *International Barometer* and I have observed. *International Barometer*, a monthly newsletter published since June 1985, reports on activists, their organizations and issues; it pays particular attention to activist pressures on business.[6] Our assessment of activism follows.

The classic Nestlé case is illustrative of all the stages of activist development. In early 1970, the UN sponsored Protein Advisory Group discussed the problems associated with infant health and nutrition. At one of these meetings an unsubstantiated comment was made that infant formula use in the Third World was responsible for killing millions of babies. In 1973, *The New Internationalist*[7] published 'The baby food controversy' and in 1974, the British charity War on Want published *The Baby Killer*. Following in short order were accusations by Swiss activists that Nestlé was a 'baby killer' – in fact they took the War on Want publication and translated and renamed it *Nestlé Kills Babies*. Nestlé sued sixteen Swiss activists for libel, won the lawsuit (in 1976), obtained a trivial judgment and the activist movement continued to develop. By 1981, Nestlé was the object of a boycott by some 700 organizations in the US and abroad. That year, after two leading US PR firms failed to cope, an issue management team under the direction of Rafael D. Pagán Jr[8] was put together by Nestlé. The crisis team resolved the boycott in 1984. Its resolution was costly in terms of dollars, morale and executive time – it had developed too far before it was recognized that effective action was required.

Strain may occur with a single person perceiving wrong or being wronged followed by the development of a single organization or perhaps several organizations. When several organizations are concerned with the same issue they often go their separate ways at first and probably will not be directly linked, except for some basic exchange of information. Later – during mobilization – as the need for a stronger, coordinated movement is perceived by their staffs or leadership, coalitions or umbrella organizations for those activist groups with the same or related goals are formed. Most groups work in a loose confederation.

Although the exact starting-point (strain) of an issue may be difficult to see, the issue does become evident when activists begin organizing and become vocal. Biotechnology is such an issue. Individual activist groups concerned with various aspects of biotechnology have formed coalitions; conferences have been held and more are planned. International ties have been and continue to be forged; model state laws have been drafted and are being circulated in various states. Activists clearly believe that biotechnology may take a course contrary to the one they perceive should be taken and they are mobilizing their resources.

Mobilization or networking may take many forms. For example, the Pesticide Action Network (PAN) was formed as a world-wide coordinating organization dedicated to monitoring and eliminating the use of toxic chemical pesticides. The US Friends of the Earth (FoE) is an affiliate of PAN and is in the same building with another affiliate, The Pesticide Education Action Program (PEAP), an information clearing house for many environmental groups on this continent. Jay Feldman, the national director of the National Coalition Against the Misuse of Pesticides (NCAMP), is a member of the board of advisers to PAN and its national coordinator in the US. PAN is an affiliate of the much larger International Organization of Consumer Unions (IOCU).

Confrontation usually becomes the burr, stimulating what may be a costly (to business) issue resolution process. Resolution may take many forms: negotiation or compromise; capitulation; laws or regulations (or the reinterpretation of laws and regulations); or, international codes, to name a few.

And, resolution of an issue may be merely temporary. The issue may be regenerated through a variety of factors such as new scientific concerns or the perceived failure of a corporation to follow through with its promises. Two recent examples serve to illustrate: The first one relates to chlorofluorocarbons banned for aerosol use several years ago in the US as a threat to the ozone layer – many thought that would take care of the problem. New international concerns with CFCs arose when evidence showed further ozone depletion. This time, countries focused on CFCs in all their uses (e.g. as a refrigerant, in the manufacture of foam containers, etc.). This led forty-five nations in September to agree to freeze CFC production at current levels by 1990 and reduce CFC use 50 per cent by the year 2000. Further concerns will likely result in more regulation or voluntary curtailment. DuPont, a major CFC manufacturer, announced plans in early April 1988 for a total phase-out. Activists applauded the move and promptly put pressure on other producers. Also in April the fast-food packaging industry said it would stop making cartons, cups and other containers using CFCs by the end of 1988.

The second example shows the Nestlé Corporation – sans Pagán – once again spotlighted in the infant formula controversy. Nestlé was accused on National Public Radio (14 September 1987) of failing to live up to its 1984 agreements that ended the seven-year boycott of Nestlé products. Patricia Young, the activist interviewed on NPR, said, among other things, that she felt 'betrayed'. Ms Young, one-time chair of the International Boycott Nestlé Committee was described by the interviewer as a sweet, grey-haired motherly type.

Resolution of a particular issue does not necessarily mean that an activist group or groups will be disestablished. Some issues have many fronts. The environment as an issue, for example, has many diverse components. In other cases, a group, after resolution of a specific issue, may reinterpret their role. This was the case with the activist organization INFACT, the main boycott-Nestlé protagonist in the US. When the Nestlé boycott was over, rather than go out of business, INFACT polled its membership, giving them a number of choices. Based on the voting, INFACT switched to an antinuclear theme. INFACT, which now describes itself as dedicated to checking the life-threatening abuses of TNCs, presently is promoting a boycott of GE products because GE produces parts critical to major nuclear systems. A 2 September 1987 INFACT news release states that an 'independently commissioned poll' revealed in just one year, two million consumers were already boycotting GE products. INFACT continues to mobilize and it is in the beginning stages of its confrontation with GE. It must be added that the infant formula issue continues to receive attention. INFACT has a spin-off, Action for Corporate Accountability, which devotes its resources to this emotional issue.

Activist group characteristics

Activist groups display many characteristics in common. Activists take the long view and are prepared to stick to their goals for years despite any short-term disappointments. They form coalitions to achieve a mass they alone may not be able to achieve. They have become more sophisticated over the last ten years and make full use of technology (e.g. personal computers and modems are standard, they operate computer bulletin boards and there is even a non-profit high-tech firm set up to help them to do all of this).

They plan and train. This training teaches them how to organize, develop strategies and to negotiate. The Midwest Academy is but one of over thirty centers in the US which exist to train the activist community. It was organized in 1973 to help low and moderate income people 'win concrete results, develop a sense of their own power, and alter the relations of power, all in order to build a more just and humane society', their informational letter states. They claim they have trained more than 20,000 people from more than 900 organizations. They conduct one-week sessions around the country and develop courses for specific needs. Among the subjects presented in their standard seminars are recruiting; leadership; negotiation; power relationships; coalitions; choosing an issue; and strategy.

Activist groups have a ready forum in the media, legislative staffs and state and federal legislatures since activists for the most part are perceived as being altruistic and hence credible. Members of the media see themselves as dedicated to a similar purpose: championing the rights of the people. Many activist groups know how to capture the imagination and interest of a wide audience with media events designed to further their objectives. Few of us have failed to see or hear about Greenpeace members parachuting from smoke-stacks, or fearlessly dashing around in motorized rubber rafts daring whaling ships to run them down. Furthermore, activists are easy to identify with – David against the corporate Goliath, the poor against the rich – set against a backdrop where, 'By the age of 18, the average kid has seen businessmen on TV attempt over 10,000 murders', quoted a Mobil Oil advert appearing in the 26 March 1987 edition of *The New York Times*.

While it is true that activists are 'responsible to no one' in the sense of facing most external consequences of their actions, it is not true in another sense. Activists have their own brand of stakeholders and act the way most academic literature written on the subject of group dynamics suggests groups will act. They have constituencies, internal politics, many have full-time professional staffs and, indeed a bureaucracy. It is important to know who comprises that staff and how they react because, as in most organizations, it is they – much more than the rank and file or nominal leaders – who give detailed direction and shape to the politics and goals of the general membership.

Critics of activist groups maintain that such groups use only anecdotes, which are exceptions to the norm to get their point across, and that they do little research. While anecdotes do provide an immediate trigger to energize and focus supporters and to mobilize the uncommitted, activists also are generating and/or using research to support their positions. There are certainly many varying views available which are supportable by some study, somewhere, that activists can and do take advantage of. Many activist organizations have staff scientists as well as lawyers to help them support their causes.

Activist groups develop campaigns designed to bring the maximum pressure on their targets and they appear to chose their targets well. Campaigns may single out one company (and that company usually is surprised and adopts a 'why me' attitude) or use other methods to create interest and foster support. PAN for example, has identified what it calls the 'dirty dozen' pesticides and has adopted the goal of eliminating them from world-wide use. As mentioned, INFACT has singled out GE as the centrepiece of its campaign. Nancy Cole, INFACT's executive director, told *International Barometer*, 'Our campaigns provide an opportunity for millions of people to be involved. (Targeting) a company which has a lot of public visibility (provides) a way that a lot of people can connect the issue with what is going on.'[9]

In spite of all these apparently positive sounding characteristics, activists are not 10 feet tall. They have their problems too, not the least of which are organizing and executing their campaigns. There are not enough leaders to go around, leaders with ability to motivate and get things done. Volunteer and low-paid labor can only do so much. Lofty principles in the absence of specific achievable goals likely will lead to the disintegration of an organization. Activist groups need action, victories to point to if they are to remain viable.

Activist tactics and strategies

Activists define strategy as a broad plan used to change something. The written plan of a well organized group will specify an ultimate purpose, a grand goal, possibly utopian, and certainly stated in a way to gain adherents and rally support. The plan will outline specific, achievable objectives which are realistic and associated with specific tactics to achieve those objectives. The objectives may be short or long term. Training centers and 'how to' manuals present practical exercises on how to prepare such plans under a variety of scenarios.

If this has a familiar ring to the business leader, it should; this level of sophistication is fundamental to effective planning and execution. And, present-day activists have made that discovery. Some activists may not feel comfortable with such war-like words as 'campaign', 'strategy' and 'tactics', but they use them as clear descriptors of what they need to do to achieve success.

'Tactics means doing what you can with what you have', said Saul Alinsky. The strategy and tactics employed by activists give substance to the principles articulated as his thirteen rules of 'power tactics'.[10] Six are of particular relevance today:

1 'Power is not what you have but what the enemy thinks you have.'
3 'Wherever possible go outside of the experience of your enemy.'
4 'Make the enemy live up to their own book of rules.'
10 'The major premise for tactics is the development of operations that will maintain constant pressure on the opposition.'
11 'If you push a negative hard and deep enough it will breakthrough into its counterside.'
13 'Pick the target, freeze it, personalize it, and polarize it.'

Tactics are the day-to-day actions of any strategy or campaign within that strategy. There are diverse tactics limited in number only by the creativity of the tactician. Activist students are instructed to apply more than one tactic to a target. This insures that multiple pressures are applied from several sources. It is believed that the target, often a corporation, confronted on many fronts, will make a mistake or reveal some vulnerability. An advantage will be posted thereby to the activists.

Part of any strategy is the need to mobilize support. Activists seek such support from many sources: from religious groups, the media, unions, and universities; they lobby at the UN, its agencies and other international bodies; they lobby at all legislative and regulatory levels and may lobby corporations directly; they develop coalitions with other concerned groups, and they certainly seek grassroots – people power – support.

Among their well-used tactics are: economic boycotts (there are some 100 targeting corporations right now in the United States); stockholder resolutions; letter writing and other communications with stakeholders; legal actions; marches; demonstrations; sit-ins; prayer vigils; cooption of employees; media stunts; seminars and lectures; and, the writing and distribution of books, pamphlets and other publications and where possible, exposés. This short list represents a few of the more than 200 specific tactics in use by activist groups.

The extremists

Unfortunately, actions taken by some activist groups or individual sympathizers may go beyond non-violent approaches. Examples of such actions directed at people or property are: the bombing of abortion clinics and harassment of their employees; the bombing of a Bayer A.G. plant in Belgium by an unknown environmental group reportedly supporting Greenpeace's goals; the bombing of and putting sugar in the tanks of Shell gas stations in the Netherlands by anti-apartheid activists; placing dead fish in safety deposit boxes to protest bank policies; environmentalists pounding nails and spikes into trees scheduled to be harvested; stealing animals from research laboratories and promoting rumours in the United Kingdom that Mars candy bars were laced with poison to halt animal experimentation. These are but a few examples. The clear implication is that corporations must be on guard from this type of protest, albeit perpetrated by a minority and usually condemned by the overwhelming majority.

Trends in activism

Activist groups continue to mature and professionalize. *Community Jobs*, published monthly by the Community Careers Resource Center, a non-profit tax-exempt organization, keeps people aware of where 'public interest' jobs are throughout the United States and Canada in its some ten pages of advertisements. Daily, *The Washington Post* runs job adverts from activist organizations. *The National Boycott Newsletter*, published quarterly, advises the activist community of current and new boycotts and identifies sponsors and reasons for the boycott. There are a vast number of activist newsletters and other publications used to keep members of groups mobilized, interested and informed.

All this is to say that activist groups are here to stay for the foreseeable future and discerning their directions is an important and necessary form of 'early warning' for corporations.

Trends we see during the growth of activism:

- More legal and regulatory enforcement (policing).
- Focus on and use of more staff studies (scientific, technical, legal) or outside research to support activist views.
- A continued broadening of issue interests and formation of still larger coalitions and networks.
- Further internationalization of issues and hence groups.
- Continued attempts to influence national legislation and regulation through international agencies and organizations.
- Adoption of issues anywhere in the world and making them felt continents away.
- Continued selection of multinationals as high profile and symbolic targets.
- Multi-level operations – work at national and international levels while moving toward more work at local levels; a top down and bottom up strategy.
- Use of issue management techniques and a wider variety of tactics on a wider selection of stakeholders.
- The formation of alliances with small businesses.
- Extensive use of technology for communication and for information clearing houses.
- Increased appeals directly to electorates, negotiations with political

parties in power and moves to become political insiders; and, the use of canvassing and other 'political' techniques to enhance their power-base.

Look to the future – know your critics

What issues does the future hold for corporations as activist groups promote their agendas? Rhoda H. Karpatkin, Executive Director of the US Consumers Union Inc., and President of The International Organization of Consumer Unions (IOCU),[11] '. . . nominated . . . three issues that should be provoking the attention of consumers and their organizations. . . . The first issue is the consumer's right to be protected from hazardous technologies and the toxic substances associated with them. . . . The second issue relates to . . . corporate behaviour . . ., a pervasive indifference by many corporations to laws, regulations, codes and minimum standards of human decency . . . (the) third issue . . . is that of the poor consumer . . . the specific food, housing and health care problems of poor people.'[12] Of course, the consumer movement is but one of many that are continually developing and implementing plans and campaigns based on their concerns.

How can business cope?

It is easy and dangerous to ignore an issue at its outset. Such ignorance becomes less and less affordable as firms enter an ever more volatile public policy issue environment. The fact that an issue may arise in some obscure corner of the world should not exclude it from consideration and possible impact on corporate operations in other areas of the world. All actors participating in the public policy issue process have access to modern technologies for the rapid communication of ideas. Activist organizations are expanding in number and in membership. Corporations are increasingly under direct or indirect pressure from well-networked activist groups who see themselves as policing the zone where business and society meet.

It is not easy to 'look over the horizon and beyond' but it is necessary for business leaders to do so.

A prudent executive anticipates the inevitable – a problem, a crisis, an issue – even though it may be for some ill-defined future. An understanding – early warning – of activist movements is fundamental to any public policy issue planning process. Implementation of such a plan requires a research, analysis and monitoring system to provide insights on how the plan is working and what changes are required to meet the unanticipated.

Traditional approaches for identifying broad trends which may affect the marketplace are necessary but are increasingly insufficient as corporations position themselves for the future. Activist groups clearly are major participants in developing public policy and bring to bear a further sociopolitical dynamic on how a corporation will be permitted to operate. Thus, activism must be considered in corporate strategic planning and public policy action programs if it is to be effective. The problems posed by this activist dynamic may cause some executives to yearn for the 'good old days' of single dimension government – corporate interaction – but those days are gone.

How can business cope with the growth of activism? A key element is organizing to deal with issues. Are systems established for an appropriate flow of information into and out of the corporation? Has responsibility and authority been assigned for determining policy on an issue, for planning and implementation? Are objective analyses made about issues and pertinent actors? Is action being taken? Are feedback systems in place, so that necessary adjustments can be made as corporate programs unfold?

Solutions to the problems dealing with the citizen–business–government relationship are not easy to arrive at. They take organization, understanding, the application of negotiating skills and the ability to compromise. Basic to any strategic approach to conflict management is an analytical system attuned to the needs of the corporate environment and knowledge of public policy issues and the actors who are involved in those issues. Knowing corporate critics, their characteristics, strategies/tactics and hearing and evaluating what they have to say is a significant input to effective corporate action planning, programing and execution within the public policy milieu.

It is time for corporations to meet activism with activism.

Notes

1. Jack O. Mongoven is President and CEO of MBD Inc., a Washington DC firm specializing in assisting corporations in effective participation in the public policy issue process.
2. Saul Alinsky, *Rules For Radicals: A Pragmatic Primer for Realistic Radicals*, Vintage Books Edition, New York (1972), originally published by Random House (1971). Saul Alinsky died in 1972. Activist literature still quotes extensively from the works of Alinsky.
3. W. Howard Chase, *Issues Management: Origins of the Future*, p. 26, Issue Action Publications Inc., Stamford, CT (1984).
4. Depending on the issue and the effectiveness of the campaign, corporations may have bottom line impacts in varying degrees to their: sales/profits/growth; cost of doing business in the form of adverse laws, regulations, taxes; sanctions imposed on them for violations of laws or regulations; lawsuits; community reaction, e.g. to plant siting; lost executive time; capital availability; relationships with vendors; employee confidence and productivity; and recruitment of quality employees.
5. Robert L. Heath and Richard Alan Nelson, *Issues Management: Corporate Public Policy Making in an Information Society*, pp. 204–21, Sage Publications Inc., Newbury Park, CA (1986).
6. *International Barometer* has been published monthly by Pagan International since June 1985. *The Economic Reporter*, December (1985), said IBs' '. . . methods are to track activists, describe their methods, and profile their leaders to try to give advance early warning of where trouble is likely to come from . . . it seems to be generally encouraging

dialogue', *Mother Jones*, May (1987) said IB is '. . . scrupulously objective' and quoted activist Michael Jacobson as saying that *Barometer* '. . . does provide public-interest groups with an opportunity to send signals to industry'.

7. H. Geach, 'The baby food controversy', *The New Internationalist*, London (1973).
8. Rafael D. Pagán Jr, is president and CEO of Pagan International.
9. *International Barometer*, p. PS-1, April (1986).
10. Saul Alinsky (1972/1979), pp. 126–48. See note 2.
11. IOCU is headquartered in the Hague and has two regional headquarters, one in Maylasia (for Asia), and the other newly opened in Uruguay (for Latin America) and has plans to open an office in Africa. It has some 160 affiliates in over fifty countries and has official NGO status with various UN agencies – WHO, ECOSOC, UNIDO, UNICEF, and FAO. NGO status enables the IOCU to submit position papers, to review and comment on the position papers of others and to sit on panels of experts.
12. Rhoda H. Karpatkin, 'Changing issues, changing agendas: winning for the consumer in the next 50 years', address before the 32nd annual conference of the American Council of Consumer Interests, St Louis, MO, 9 April (1986). Ms Karpatkin was elected to another three-year term as President of IOCU at their September 1987 congress held in Madrid. She also is President of the US Consumers Union. *International Barometer*, October–November (1987) issue provides on-the-scene coverage of the IOCU Congress.

8

The transformation of AT & T

Carol Kennedy

The oldest and largest US multinationals, and those who work in their upper corporate echelons, exude a kind of pride and purpose rarely found in their European counterparts. Perhaps it has something to do with having their roots in the heroic age of American business, when enterprise and engineering were together literally pushing out the frontiers and forging the ethos immortalized in 1925 by President Calvin Coolidge: 'The business of America is business.'

No US corporation was prouder than mighty American Telephone and Telegraph, or had a greater sense of its own destiny, which may have been partly to blame for the fate that overtook it in 1981–4. A federal anti-trust action had been looming for years, but it was totally unexpected that AT & T would lose – and agree to lose – so much; nothing less than the breakup of the entire Bell system of regional telephone companies, known affectionately to generations of Americans as 'Ma Bell'.

Although the company kept its research and manufacturing core, and was freed for the first time to compete in information age markets, it is arguable – and no doubt will be argued in business school case studies for years to come – whether a less hubristic strategy on AT & T's part in the 1970s could have delivered more from the US Justice Department. After all, in 1956 the company had been promised 'no real injury' in future anti-trust cases in return for its exclusion from the then fledgling data-processing industry.

AT & T is still a mighty force in US industry, ranking fourth by market value in the *Forbes 500* of 1988. It retained the rights to provide a long distance telephone service, the so-called 'Long Lines'; its equipment manufacturing subsidiary, Western Electric, now renamed AT & T International, and the renowned Bell Laboratories, the world's most fertile source of electronics inventions. Bell Labs have some 20,000 patents to their credit, including such fundamentally world-changing technologies as radio telephony, cable TV, lasers, the transistor and the silicon chip.

Since the release from its thirty-year undertaking not to enter the computer market, a rich global potential lies open to it, though some of its international ventures, notably that with Olivetti, have proved troublesome.

Reprinted by permission of Pergamon Press PLC from *Long Range Planning*, 2(3) 1989: 10–17.

The company is still, as Vice President John L. Segall admits, feeling the after-effects of a gigantic culture shock as the deeply imbued public service philosophy of founding president Theodore Vail has been forced to give way to aggressive competition in the marketplace. To cap a singularly difficult period in the company's history, just as its new strategy was in place and beginning to run, chairman and chief executive James Olson died unexpectedly of cancer in May 1988. In December 1988, it reported the first annual loss since its foundation in 1885, following a much larger than anticipated write-off of obsolete long-distance equipment.

AT & T still, in the words of a senior international executive, has 'a high concept of its own destiny', but that destiny is not quite so clear-cut and immutable as it seemed in 1980, when AT & T was the largest corporation in the world, unquestionably pursuing the mission laid down by Theodore Vail in 1909 – 'One System, One Policy, Universal Service.' That mission, known to AT & T veterans as 'POTS' – Plain Old Telephone Service – was to provide a 'universal service' at the lowest price for the average customer. Heroic myths abounded in the company of AT & T employees who kept the service running, linking America coast to coast, through blizzards, floods and all manner of natural disasters. And undeniably the mission had succeeded: the Bell System was widely acknowledged as the most technologically advanced and efficient in the world.

At divestiture, after nearly a century of existence, the company boasted assets of $150bn, revenues in excess of $40bn, profits in excess of $7bn and more than one million employees. (Today's much leaner corporation has assets of $38.4bn, sales of £33.6m, and employs 370,000.) AT & T was one of the soundest of Wall Street's blue-chip stocks, renowned as a haven for widows' savings.

When George Saunders, the chief defence lawyer at the anti-trust trial, stood up to begin his plea, he was able to declare without hyperbole that he represented 'the greatest business enterprise this world has ever produced'. And he added: 'Let there be no mistake: the government is here to destroy that enterprise.'

There was, undoubtedly, an element of hostility in Washington to a corporation widely perceived as arrogant and overconfident of its power. John DeButts, the company's patrician southern chairman in the early 1970s, spent millions of dollars fruitlessly lobbying for the so-called 'Bell Bill', which would have preserved the old single system had it got through Congress.

Deregulation

But the company could have detected the shape of its future as early as 1968, when the Federal Communications Commission (FCC) took the first steps towards deregulating the telecommunications business by opening up the terminal equipment market to competing companies. (Before 1968, AT & T owned almost every private telephone and business switchboard in the US, and leased them profitably to its captive customers.)

The FCC decision was known as 'Carterfone' after Thomas Carter of Carter Electronics, who pushed through a successful anti-trust suit against AT & T enabling him to 'patch' his mobile and car phones into the AT & T network. Its significance was immense for independent telephone companies, who were now free to interconnect with AT & T's switched phone network. Users could buy equipment from any supplier and simply plug it into the AT & T network.

Microwave Communications International

In 1969, another threatening market was set down when the FCC allowed Bill McGowan's fledgling Microwave Communications International (MCI) to enter the lucrative 'private lines' business between two major industrial cities, Chicago and St Louis. Companies with offices in both centres could save enormously by using MCI's direct line service, which was bounced by microwave technology off terminals set at intervals between the two cities, instead of dialling into AT & T's switched long-distance network. With supreme irony, microwave technology had been first developed in Bell Labs.

MCI prospered and began aggressively to expand. In 1972 it announced plans to extend its service to 165 cities from coast to coast across America. AT & T could no longer ignore this pushy upstart. Many of its regional company presidents, led by Charles L. Brown of Illinois Bell (later to succeed DeButts as AT & T chairman), urged a strategy of direct confrontation by lowering prices wherever the giant corporation was in competition with MCI.

AT & T finally adopted that strategy, but at the cost of a delay that gave the rival time to develop its strength. At bottom, there was a cultural resistance: to John DeButts, AT & T's founding principles of universal service to all had been so bred in the bone of a forty-year career with the Bell system that he found it difficult to respond in entrepreneurial fashion to MCI's flagrant 'cream-skimming' tactics in high-profit business areas.

Until DeButts became chairman in 1972, indeed, AT & T had never even had a marketing department. For more than ninety years it had operated like a utility; far from having to market it products, it *was* the marketplace. The company's profit margin or 'rate of return' was fixed by the FCC and state regulators as a percentage of its costs – usually between 10 and 15 per cent. As its costs rose, so did its profits: it was hardly a system that fostered economy or the trimming of overheads.

The R & D programme was managed by a committee and was not as responsive to market pressures as it should have been. There was no mechanism for integrating marketing and research. The company was run by engineers and the overwhelming factors in determining the characteristics of new products were technical and technological. AT & T's attitude to the marketplace was epitomized by the president of one of its operating companies, New York Telephone, who remarked of his marketing director: 'We don't have anything to sell, so I don't know what he does.'

What the whole Bell System did have, however, was a service motivation second to none. DeButts believed implicitly that this was the result of the company's historic regulated monopoly status: should the corporation be cut loose upon the rough seas of competition, DeButts felt, 'we would be a different business, and I for one would feel the poorer for it'. Yet he understood the need for some internal change and hired one of IBM's top marketing experts, Archibald McGill, to set up new marketing systems.

McGill saw his task as steering the strategic direction of the company from being technologically driven to being financially and customer-driven in the IBM mould, using financial evaluations in place of technological ones and replacing the concept of a uniform telephone service by a drive to identify and appeal to discrete groups of consumers. To those long nurtured on POTS – they were said in AT & T to have 'Bell-shaped heads' – such talk was heresy. Outside the corporation, McGill's appointment prompted suspicion that AT & T was trying to get the best of both worlds; preparing to compete while attempting to hold deregulation at bay until it was ready to handle it.

The anti-trust suit

When, belatedly, AT & T did hit back at MCI's challenge, cutting its prices in MCI areas and negotiating toughly on interconnection fees, McGowan riposted by filing a huge anti-trust suit in the spring of 1974. In a bitter sequence of events for AT & T, judgement was finally handed down in MCI's favour just as the federal anti-trust trial got under way in 1981. AT & T's bill was $1.8bn – the biggest anti-trust loss in US history.

Well before that, however, it was clear to many at AT & T that an era was passing irrevocably into history. MCI was heading to become a billion dollar corporation by 1980 and it was estimated that between 1977 and 1980, the free-for-all in the equipment market would bite away half of Western Electric's market share, much of it going to Japanese manufacturers. Charles Brown of Illinois Bell, who succeeded DeButts on the chairman's early retirement in February 1979, was one who did clearly see the need for a more competitive stance.

In 1978, McKinsey's advised the company to change its public utility structure to that of a competitive firm. Similar proposals had been fiercely resisted in 1973, but Brown was determined to implement them.

Early in 1978 he appointed a task-force to recommend restructuring based on market segment rather than departmental objectives. The whole financial basis of AT & T was to be changed, from plans made largely on technical grounds to decentralized budgets from each segmented business, each competing for resources from a central management body.

The fall of the Bell System

As Peter Temin of MIT and Louis Galambos of Johns Hopkins University explain it in their lucid and scholarly study *The Fall of the Bell System* (1987), commissioned by AT & T to record the divestiture while personal experiences remained fresh, the switch from domination by engineers to domination by marketeers was matched by a shift in basic power structures.

Ever since Vail's time, the regional company presidents had set policy and interacted with AT & T while the operating vice presidents ran the businesses – reflecting the corporate relationship of AT & T chairman and chief executive officer. Under reorganization, operating VPs would be replaced by the heads of the business segments, reporting directly to the company presidents. A whole proving ground of management succession had been wiped out.

Although management stresses were considerable (and may have influenced DeButts' decision to retire two years early), Brown pushed ahead, spelling out clearly what the new era would mean. In a Chicago speech entitled 'Meeting change with change', delivered in November 1978, Brown described how high technology businesses – the direction in which AT & T would have to expand – required advanced marketing strategies. Ma Bell, he said, was a symbol of the past. 'Today, ours is a business that knows it is not we, AT & T, but the customer who knows best. Mother Bell simply doesn't live here any more.'

Internal changes and stirring speeches were not, however, going to halt the looming federal anti-trust case. Brown faced several alternatives, all of them unpalatable. Loss to AT & T was inevitable; either vertical (from the equipment subsidiary and Bell Labs) or horizontally (from the regional telephone companies). The former would be far more damaging to AT & T as it faced the rapidly enlarging IT markets for integrated telecommunication systems.

Hopes of a limited divestiture were dashed, ironically enough, by the incoming, business-friendly Reagan administration in 1981. The new assistant attorney-general, William Baxter, was 'a man on an ideological mission', in the words of Temin and Galambos (1987). He resisted even the arguments of defence secretary Casper Weinberger that the anti-trust case should be dropped because the AT & T network was a national strategic asset, and declared he would 'litigate to the eyeballs'.

Brown was left with one effective option – to divest the operating companies. This would have the advantage of leaving a vertically integrated central AT & T core, well placed through Western Electric and Bell Labs to compete in information age markets. It would remove the company from the uncomfortable spotlight of public policy. But it would also mean surrendering all responsibility for a national telephone network, thus destroying forever the Bell System.

It was, as Temin and Galambos (1987) write, 'the biggest single decision that an American businessman has had to make in the last century. . . . He accepted the fact that his best option was to break up the Bell System.'

The AT & T board was naturally unhappy but accepted Brown's decision without a major revolt, realizing, in Temin and Galambos' (1987) words, that 'the unthinkable had become . . . unavoidable'. Abandoning the Bell System was the only way for AT & T to extricate itself from the massive judicial, regulatory and legislative firepower aimed at it.

The Baby Bells

Agreement was reached, the trial was stopped and on 1 January 1984, a much slimmed-down and altered AT & T opened for business. In all, it has lost three-quarters of its previous assets. Out of its twenty-two former operating companies were carved seven regional holding companies – the so-called Baby Bells – each with between $15bn and $20bn in assets. This had been chosen as the most financially viable size, on the model of two successful predivestiture companies, Pacific Telephone and Southwestern Bell. (Brown wanted AT & T to retain ownership of the Bell name and logo, but the judge awarded it to the 'Baby Bells' after Tandy Corporation objected that it would give AT & T an unfair advantage in selling phone equipment to its former subsidiaries.)

The Baby Bells have since gone from strength to strength. Between them they provide local phone service to around 80 per cent of the US population and their revenues ranged in 1987 from $8bn (Southwestern Bell) to $12.3bn (BellSouth). 'They are just like cash registers', observes one Wall Street analyst. In years to come they are expected to break out of 'plain old telephone service' into all sorts of transmission facilities over the phone lines, including cable television; perhaps even competing against the remaining fiefdom of Ma Bell, long distance services. At present they are prohibited by the divestiture terms from doing this, though they have been able to squeeze some other concessions such as data-base transmission, seen as a huge market.

While the Baby Bells flex their muscles in pleasurable and profitable freedom, albeit in some frustration at their remaining restraints, the cultural trauma for the management of the old 1m-strong AT & T has been enormous. Vice President Segall, who was placed in charge of divestiture planning by Charles Brown, compares it to the 'Big Bang' theory of the universe, whose experimental verification won two Bell Labs physicists the Nobel Prize in the mid-1960s. Yet job losses were minimal – nine out of ten Bell System employees stayed in the same job after divestiture, even working for the same supervisor, and shareholders did better out of the breakup than before. (All three million shareholders retained their stock in AT & T and in addition were given proportionate values in the local companies, which have expanded so aggressively since divestiture.) As for the telephone service itself, Theodore Vail would have been proud of the seamless way it carried on over the transition, though some residential users have since found some deterioration in the repair service.

Managing the crisis

For the skilful short-term management of crisis, indeed, much credit must go to the durability of Vail's old Bell System culture, though it acted as a drag-anchor in other respects. As Segall (1986) told a conference in Hong Kong two years after divestiture: 'Employees performed as if they were involved in the restoration of telephone service following a devastating hurricane, fire, flood or snowstorm . . . a company composed of 1m employees and $150bn in assets, having 3m shareholders, needed to be reorganized in 24 months! Few companies in the world could have carried out such a task with the efficiency of the Bell System.'

Yet the deeply embedded values of the system meant also that, as one manager observed: 'Employees reacted to the news much in the way they would have done if a close family member had been suddenly killed in a accident.'

It was a massive exercise in the management of change. AT & T executives, says Segall (1986), followed the maxim of Robert Louis Stevenson: 'Keep your fears to yourself, but share your courage with others.' In briefings across the length and breadth of the land, they stressed the bright future that telecommunications could offer in the information age. 'The task that management faced', said Segall in Hong Kong, 'was nothing less than mapping out a new course for the future, and redesigning an institution to pursue that course, bringing with it an understanding and dedicated workforce.' This would involve deep changes in 'the theory or vision of the firm – and in the processes by which it would be managed'.

The transformation

Three main transformations were required, as Segall (1986) outlined them:

- What had been a telephone company for nearly a century had to become a company whose business was the movement and management of information.

- What had been a domestic American company had to become international.
- What had been a government-regulated monopoly had to become a competitive company dictated by the marketplace.

To accomplish these, changes were required in six sectors:

1 The corporate structure was reshaped into a decentralized organization of strategic business units, known in AT & T as 'Lines of Business' (LOB). Each LOB was to be a profit centre focused on a particular market or business segment, with autonomous decision-making within operational and financial boundaries set by AT & T headquarters, which would also spot and facilitate synergies between, say, silicon chip manufacture and computer system sales.

2 The planning process was completely redesigned. 'As recently as 1970,' recalled Segall, 'when AT & T officials were asked "Who is the Bell System's chief planner?", it was not uncommon for them to answer, in dead seriousness, "Theodore Vail".'

   The Bell System was operationally oriented and run largely on management by objectives. Continuing evaluations and long-range strategic planning were, for the most part, regarded as unnecessary. No planning group as such existed in the old Bell System, apart from a 'cabinet' of AT & T top officers and the presidents of Western Electric and Bell Labs. They met on alternate Mondays and in between came meetings of the so-called 'Odd Monday' group, consisting of the AT & T chairman and those reporting directly to him. This eventually became the Executive Policy Committee, responsible for long-range planning, but no strategic planning system as such was set up until 1982/3.

   Post-divestiture, each LOB would be responsible for its own five-year plan, subject to corporate review and approval to ensure compatibility with corporate strategies and priorities in the allocation of resources. There would be strong emphasis on flexible strategies focused on markets and market segments, both corporate and LOB.

3 People were brought in from outside the corporation at all levels to impart new perspectives and expertise, especially in marketing. An important aspect of this strategy was to 'attract individuals with a bias towards risk-taking and to make all parts of the company more sensitive to the competitive marketplace', as Segall explained. (Management development in AT & T had, until McGill's appointment, traditionally been from 'within the ranks'.)

4 A major revision of corporate training programmes was required at all levels, stressing the importance of understanding customers' needs and competitors' strengths and weaknesses in the fast-changing global information marketplace. 'A key objective of this refocused training is to build into the new corporate culture an acceptance of ever-changing market conditions and, more important, the ability to adapt quickly to those changes', said Segall.

5 Incentives were encouraged by new compensation and reward schemes. Individual and organizational awards for reaching and exceeding sales and financial targets are now part of AT & T's compensation packages.
6 International corporate alliances were actively pursued in order to gain entry and expertise in markets around the world. In just over a year, AT & T arranged with six of the top European computer companies to adopt Unix, AT & T's standard for a software operating system; went into a joint venture with Philips for the marketing of switching and transmission equipment in Europe; arranged with Wang to produce compatible computers and document standards; took a 25 per cent interest in Olivetti, manufacturer of the PC6300 computer sold by AT & T in the US; went into a new computer communication company in a joint venture with several of Japan's leading electronics companies including Hitachi, Fujitsu, Mitsubishi Electric and Sony; set up a plant to manufacture telephones in Singapore and entered joint ventures with companies in Taiwan (digital switches), Korea (switches and fibre optic equipment); with Rockwell, Honeywell and Data General (swapping data between computers and switches), and with Telefonica of Spain (to design and manufacture integrated circuits).

Commenting on this in 1986, Segall said: 'We have moved significantly into the international marketplace in a shorter time, we believe, than any other company in modern times.'

The new mission

Divestiture cost AT & T dearly in its demands on management and strategic planning time. It cost in other ways, too. In *The Fall of the Bell System* (1987), Temin and Galambos compared the state of corporate shock to 'Vienna after World War I . . . (AT & T) has had to reduce the size of its internal bureaucracy, to develop new leadership paths and – most importantly – to define a corporate mission appropriate to its new business.'

This was done formally in 1980 in AT & T's report to stockholders:

No longer do we perceive that our business will be limited to telephony, or, for that matter, telecommunications. Ours is the business of information handling, the knowledge business. And the market that we seek is global.

Not as boldly inspirational, perhaps, as Vail's 'One System, One Policy, Universal Service', but appropriate to a far more complex and sophisticated business environment.

Implementing the new mission has not been easy. Some of the expected new directions did not materialize – for example, the great jousting between AT & T and IBM which was predicted after deregulation. IBM remains a full-time computer manufacturer with an interest in telecommunications, while AT & T manages a national telecommunications network and sells computers principally to facilitate switching functions in that network. As Temin and Galambos (1987) explain: 'The two firms overlap to some extent – in electronic transmission of data, for example – but are almost completely in different markets.'

How far and in which directions it would go into information technology, and how much the company would continue to rely on telephony were broad strategic questions following divestiture, but there were also difficult technical matters of finance to be resolved in the change from a regulatory to a cost accounting system. One of the most complex aspects was the breakup of billing systems which had been, as Segall said in a 1988 interview, 'a bit of a black art . . . whereby we shared the benefits of a decreasing cost per unit in technology in long distance with the exchange companies. In the Bell System they were principally our companies but also independent telephone companies. . . . These were huge amounts of money, at the time of divestiture about $7bn–$8bn. The entropy level of the organization was very high.'

How then does AT & T see its strategic direction now, and the change to a new corporate culture? Visiting Vice President Segall (who has responsibility for corporate planning under Vice Chairman Morris Tanenbaum) in AT & T's headquarters building in midtown Manhattan, one gets a clear impression that this is still a company with a special sense of mission and destiny.

Until divestiture, the New York headquarters was a remarkable 1957 building at 195 Broadway, once described by the *New York Times*'s architectural critic as 'a temple to the god of the telephone'. The roofline above its rising tiers of Ionic colonnades was crowned with a gilded sculpture known as 'The Spirit of Communication' – a naked youth bound round with coils of wire. When the company sold 195 Broadway, the statue was removed to the white marble lobby of the new AT & T Building on Madison Avenue, popularly known as the 'Chippendale Building' because of its broken-pediment skyline.

Most of AT & T's management business is now carried on at Basking Ridge, New Jersey, and the company has leased out most of the Madison Avenue building, retaining the two top floors, mainly for board meetings surveyed by the portraits of Vail and Alexander Graham Bell.

Whatever diverse activities the information age holds for AT & T, telephony is expected to continue producing growth, a matter of some satisfaction for Segall, whose long career with New York Telephone gives him a proprietorial pride in the Manhattan panorama spread beneath his office windows. Telecommunications services produced approximately half AT & T's revenue stream in 1987, with strong volume growth. 'Telephony is not a dead end, it's a major area of evolution', says Segall.

In its bid to internationalize fast through alliances, the company acknowledges lessons learned through hard experience. 'Nothing fails like success', says Segall, quoting Britain's Dean Inge, to point up the dangers of relying too complacently on technological quality at the expense of marketing.

> We were wonderfully successful. We had some of the best technology the world has ever seen, and we still do. It was natural for us to assume that the world would come running with great enthusiasm to embrace us. But the world doesn't work that way.
>
> We didn't have any contact with the end-users of what we wanted to sell, whether telephone instruments, computers or whatever. We had no marketing or sales infrastructure. Large telephone systems we could sell to the PTTs, but in every country there is big political persuasion to use its own and not to welcome foreign suppliers. There were lessons of marketing, lessons in understanding political realities, cultural sensitivities and the approach to each country. So we are re-assessing those approaches now.

One problem with its foreign relationships may be, as the journal *International Management* suggested, that AT & T is perceived as having too American an image in the world at large. Segall concedes the criticism has a point: 'We *are* too American. I don't know how we can hurry that.'

Lessons will be drawn from the setbacks with Olivetti ('we just did not have an international product line poised to go through Olivetti') and there will be 'much closer alliances in terms of product manifestation'. In early 1989, those lessons appeared to be bearing fruit when AT & T was chosen as the foreign partner for Italy's state telecommunications equipment company. The agreement with Italtel could be a significant bridgehead into the European telecoms market as Italy gears up for a five-year modernization plan.

If by 1992 there is a common tariff on data in Europe, Segall sees great opportunities in that area. 'I'm also a strong believer that there will be communications and commerce on a much broader scale with Eastern Europe. One of Gorbachev's main planks is to double civilian telecommunications capacity and introduce computers at every level in the USSR. We would have to plan for that.'

Part of Segall's responsibilities is to look at potential new markets, and he emphasizes the difficulties here of having part of the business still under the regulatory eye of the FCC. 'Any entry into new markets with respect to some of these complex networks must be approved by the FCC: that's terrible both in terms of what can be done for the customer and in terms of our planning. I do not want to under-estimate the penalties and burdens. I'm not the resident Pollyana. My role is to cast doubt on the aspirations of other groups.'

In some respects, ironically, the power of the FCC is felt more after divestiture than in the days when Washington was seeking ways to cut the old monolithic AT & T down to size. This will continue through the early 1990s as the FCC decides the crucial issue of long-distance equal-access payments.

In many ways, as the study by Peter Temin and Louis Galambos (1987) concludes, divestiture as an experiment in competition remains 'an enormous gamble'.

Bibliography

Coll, Steve (1988) *The Deal of the Century: The Breakup of AT & T*. New York: Simon and Schuster.

Segall, John L. (1986) 'Dealing with Change: Cosmic, Corporate and Personal'. Paper given at the Human Resources Conference in Hong Kong, 8 January.

Temin, Peter and Galambos, Louis (1987) *The Fall of the Bell System*. Cambridge: Cambridge University Press.

9

The strategic implications of Europe 1992

Herman Daems

How 1992 will shape competition

The immediate effect of the 1992 project will be a decline in the costs of doing business in a European market. The decline comes from a lowering of the costs of crossing borders. Several factors will be responsible for lower border-crossing costs. First, the costs of shipment will go down as there will be fewer administrative hurdles at border-crossings, less time will be lost in waiting for custom clearance and shipment rates will go down as deregulation forces road haulage companies and airlines to compete more aggressively on price. Second, as goods and services cross borders fewer product adjustments will be necessary in order to satisfy local legislation and standards. As a consequence of the lowering of the costs of crossing borders, companies will be able to expand their geographical markets in Europe. A company located in Belgium which before could only serve the Belgian market will after 1992 be able to compete in such neighbouring markets as Germany, Holland and France. But this applies also to its competitors located in those countries. As companies will increasingly be able to penetrate each other's markets, traditional market boundaries will disappear and competitive arenas will be redrawn.

Rivalry

The disappearance of traditional market boundaries increases rivalry and leads to competitive battles. In some markets the battle will be fought on the basis of costs, as companies that have opportunities for lower costs because of a more cost-efficient location of their production facilities or because of unexploited economies of scale and unused productive capacity will try to use their cost advantage to improve their competitive position. But in other markets the battle will be over product specifications, as products that currently are not available in some markets can be supplied to such markets after Europe has become a border- and barrier-free economy.

Reprinted by permission of Pergamon Press PLC from *Long Range Planning*, 23(3) 1990: 43–8.

Rivalry will particularly intensify in the short run. Indeed, companies will be eager to take advantage of the enlarging markets. Production facilities where opportunities for economies of scale exist will be expanded. When competitors simultaneously move to grab the cost advantages associated with expansion, a fierce battle can be expected because in many industries demand growth will not be sufficient to absorb the expansion of capacity. Another reason why rivalry will become more intense is that collusive market sharing arrangements will break down as traditional market positions come under pressures. In many industries companies are aware that the race to use capacity to fully exploit economies of scale and the breakdown in collusive market practices may be detrimental for industry profits. Therefore, companies in such industries as electronics and power generators have actively been pursuing mergers and strategic alliances. Through such mergers companies can rationalize capacity building and capacity utilization. Intra-industry mergers are already reducing the fragmentation of market structures and are increasing market concentration. Over the long haul this process of concentration will make rivalry less intense. The Commission is very concerned about this development and as a consequence has stepped up its efforts to monitor and police mergers and acquisitions that strengthen the market dominance of the key players in an industry.

Buyer power

Competition in European markets will intensify as a consequence of increased rivalry but increases in buyer power will also play a role. After the directives of the 1992 project have been implemented, buyers will have more options than ever before of obtaining goods and services from suppliers all over the European community. Buyers or arbitrageurs will compare prices in different European markets and will purchase products where prices are lowest. It will consequently be much more difficult to sustain the currently high levels of price discrimination in European markets. For multinational companies with nationally organized sales organizations in various European countries that have decentralized pricing, the increased buyer power can create many problems. German customers who have always bought from the German sales organization will now have the option of buying directly from the Italian sales organization of the company. As a consequence of 1992 it will be necessary to restructure national sales organizations in order better to coordinate their pricing and their promotional activities.

Companies may also find that their local customers disappear. This is specifically the case for companies that serve markets of intermediate products. The 1992 project forces industrial buyers to rationalize their production facilities. This will lead to the closure of production facilities. A company that has served a specific production facility of an industrial buyer may find that by 1992 the facility is being closed down.

Power of suppliers

Suppliers will also gain power because with the expected decline in the cost of border-crossing costs they not only have the option to supply local users but they can also deliver goods and services to users in other European markets. In this way suppliers will no longer be at the mercy of their traditional local users. It is also possible that some of the traditional suppliers will re-locate to a production site in another European country. This will effect the organization of purchasing and the logistics of supply.

Entry of new competitors

The Europe 1992 project will also have an impact on the entry of new competitors. As suggested above, for companies already located within the European Community the lowering of the border-crossing costs will make it easier to penetrate new geographical markets. For companies like the Japanese car manufacturers, who so far have tended to serve Community markets with imports, it is not entirely clear what will happen after 1992. Some fear that they will be locked out and therefore they are trying to invest in new production or assembly facilities in the Community or to buy up existing companies. The direct investments bring new and efficient capacity to the European market and therefore they are likely to heat up competition in European markets. Some attempts are being made in Europe to impose restrictions on the plants that are being built by non-Community firms. The restrictions typically are local content requirements.

Substitutes

The threat to a local industry's profitability from the development of substitute products and services is probably in the short run not very great. But over the long haul the larger internal market will make it possible to increase the efficiency of the product development process and will speed up product innovation.

Above, it was shown that the creation of a single European market impacts on the five critical forces of competition: rivalry, buyers, suppliers, new entrants and substitutes. The impact is such that competition will become more intense over the short run in the Community markets. It is obvious that the effect of 1992 on the intensity of competition will differ from industry to industry. But whatever industry a company is in it should evaluate the implications of the increased competition for the company's competitive strategy.

The strategic implications of Europe 1992

Here are some fundamental questions that a company should consider as it reviews its European business strategies.

- Will the company's competitive position be sustainable as competition heats up?
- What can the company do to shore up its position?
- In what European markets should the company compete and how should the company serve those markets?
- How should the company use its existing production facilities?
- Where should the company locate its various value activities?

Competitive position

Companies that have built their competitive position on a low-cost strategy must evaluate to what extent their costs position will be eroded by the 1992 project. Two factors can be responsible for the erosion of the cost position.

Economies of scale
As markets enlarge because borders disappear and barriers diminish, opportunities arise for exploiting unrealized economies of scale. Some companies are in a better position than others to take advantage of these opportunities. The larger competitors in the industry will find it easier than the smaller ones in the industry to build a cost position on the basis of economies of scale, because they can most credibly make the investments to expand their production facilities. Very often the larger competitors are located in the larger countries. Competitors in large European countries will also benefit as national product standards become more homogeneous. Such competitors already have large volumes in their home country to achieve economies of scale and will be able to ship products to other European countries without having to incur costs for adjusting products to other standards. The cost position of the large competitors will also improve relative to the cost position of the smaller ones because the large competitors will be able to drastically cut the number of different product varieties they need to produce to serve all European markets. If the shift from national to Community standards imposes a one time adjustment cost on the companies to achieve compliance the larger companies again are in a better position than the smaller ones because the larger competitors will be able to spread the adjustment costs over a larger volume. For all these reasons it can be expected that competitors from the larger countries will have an advantage in defending cost-based competitive positions.

Cost-efficient locations
Companies with cost-efficient locations for their production facilities are in a better position to defend a cost-based competitive position as Europe 1992 becomes a reality than the companies that have not yet been able to invest in cost-efficient locations. The cost-efficiency of a location can come from lower labour costs, fiscal advantages offered by the country where the facility is located or from the transport savings that can be gained from the central position of the

production sites. These factors usually work in opposite directions. Countries, like Greece, Spain and Portugal with the lowest labour costs are less centrally located than countries like Belgium and the Netherlands. Consequently, labour intensive plants will be moved to South European countries while plants that manufacture products that are subject to high transportation costs will be concentrated in the centre of Europe.

For companies that rely on a strategy of product differentiation the threat to the sustainability of their competitive position comes from the following three factors.

New products   As a consequence of freer markets, products that thus far have not been offered in a specific European market may by 1992 be introduced in that market. If such products offer different characteristics to consumers they may well start eroding the position of the established products.

Price/value ratio   A substantial threat to differentiation strategies comes from sudden declines in price/value ratios. Market integration will enable some producers of differentiated products to realize economies of scale which in turn will give them the opportunity to price competing differentiated products out of the market.

Economies of scale in marketing   Differentiation strategies are often highly dependent on marketing efforts. As 1992 approaches increased competition among media will make it cheaper to develop brand images for differentiated products on a European scale. The logistics of distribution can also be improved because of the 1992 project. It will no longer be necessary to build distribution organizations along national boundaries and consequently cost savings will be available.

Defending a competitive position

What can companies do to avoid losing their competitive advantage in the new Europe? Basically the company can try to reverse the various threats that I described above. Instead of waiting for its competitors the company should try to move first. This suggests that one of the critical elements in shoring up the company's competitive advantage in a business will be timing. Companies that wait until all the directives are implemented will find that their most dangerous competitors have already moved upon them. But moving early may not be enough. As I argued above, small players are bound to have a substantial handicap in exploiting the opportunities for economies of scale. Such players should evaluate if they can move from a cost-based advantage to a differentiation-based advantage. Despite the homogenizing of product standards, differentiation-based strategies are going to be easier in the post-1992 markets because companies will be able to reach small market niches in a variety of

European countries, and in this way the company will be able to build sufficient volume for an efficient production of the differentiated products. Smaller companies that have decided to defend a differentiation-based advantage may want to look for partners based in other Community states but with skills complementary to their own in order to facilitate the introduction of their products in markets that they have not entered so far. The complementarity of the skills is necessary because such complementarity makes it easier to create a more stable alliance between the partners. If differentiation is not feasible the smaller players may want to consider selling out to a larger player in the industry.

Mergers are also an alternative when the major players want to impose some order as the industry prepares itself for the transition to a post-1992 era.

Market coverage strategies

In what markets should a company compete and how should it be present in such markets? In order to make the discussion of the question specific I look at the question from the point of view of a Dutch company as it considers the Italian market. The question raises many complex issues but within the context of the 1992 project there are two elements that are of particular relevance. I have put them together in Figure 1. The first element (the vertical axis in Figure 1) that the Dutch company needs to consider is the competitive strength of the local competitors in the Italian market. The second element (the horizontal axis) is the cost of crossing the Italian border with goods for delivery to the Italian market. These costs not only include the custom clearance costs and the costs of transportation but they also cover the costs of adjusting products to Italian specifications. I will distinguish between the pre-1992 period and the post-1992 period. In the past when the border-crossing costs were high the Dutch company opted to create its own production facility in Italy to serve the market there because the Italians were weak competitors in their own market. The Dutch company preferred to invest in an Italian subsidiary because local production was cheaper than importing the goods from Holland. The fact that the Italians were weak was crucial for the decision of the Dutch company because if the Italians had been strong the Dutch company would probably have stayed out of the Italian market. In the post-1992 era the situation will change because the border-crossing costs decline. The Dutch company is now evaluating whether it should reverse its earlier investment decision and close down its Italian subsidiary. As long as its Italian competitors remain weak it makes sense for the Dutch company to close its Italian subsidiary as the Dutch company has spare capacity in its other European subsidiaries and as it can exploit economies of scale in those subsidiaries. The story would of course be different if in the past the Dutch company had decided to stay out of Italy. As a consequence of the 1992 project the Dutch company

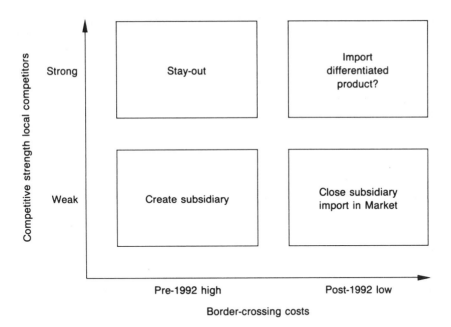

Figure 1 *Analysis of the 1992 effect on market coverage strategy*

would probably want to reconsider the import opportunities in the Italian market, the more so because the position of its Italian competitors may have weakened for reasons that I described before. In fact the Dutch company may well have good chances for market success if it were able to differentiate its products *vis-à-vis* the products supplied by the locals.

Optimizing the existing production facilities

With the help of Figure 2 a company can analyse what it needs to do with its existing production facilities. The two critical elements are: the opportunities for economies of scale (vertical axis) and the size of the market it can reach and serve from its plants. Again a distinction can be made between the pre-and the post-1992 period. If the company operates its plants at full capacity and no cost savings can be obtained from drastic expansions in the scale of its plants, the plants will typically serve local markets in an efficient way. For such a company not much will change in the post-1992 era. The plants will continue to serve local markets. However, if the company operates plants with inefficient sizes at less than full capacity the company will be forced to drastically restructure its plants in order to become competitive in the post-1992 era.

Configuration of value activities

Where should the company locate its value activities in the new Europe? Again this is a complex question but a good analysis of it can be made

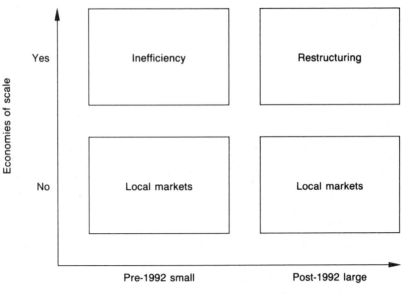

Figure 2 *Analysis of the 1992 effect on abilization of production plants*

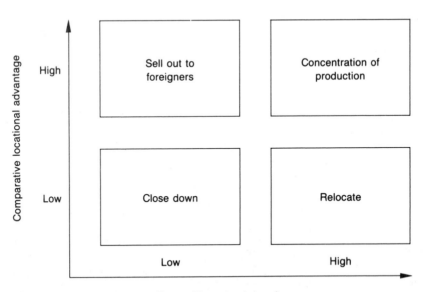

Figure 3 *Analysis of the 1992 effect on location of production centres*

with the help of Figure 3. The relevant dimensions to consider are: the Community-wide competitive strength of the company in such value activities as production, R & D and distribution and the locational advantages of a specific European country for these value activities. I will consider the case of a German company that wants to evaluate the configuration of its value activities. If the German company expects that it can hold on to its competitive position in the post-1992 era and if Germany offers the best European location for doing product development and manufacturing then there are no reasons for the company to relocate its activities. However, if because of high labour costs and transportation costs Germany no longer is the best European location for that value activity then the company should move its operations to other European locations that have lower labour costs or are more centrally situated in Europe. The story changes when the German company expects to irreversibly lose its competitive strength post-1992. In that case, its strategic options depend on the locational advantages of Germany for the value activities of the company. If Germany has no locational advantages then the threatened company should prepare for closure. However, if Germany is an ideal location then the company may want to sell out to a stronger foreign competitor or look for a foreign partner to shore up its competitive position.

Organizational consequences

There will also be organizational implications of the 1992 project. Companies that thus far have relied on national organizations to manage their European operations will need to take a hard look at that organization. Many companies, Philips is a prominent example, are doing this already but many have found that there is a lot of resistance to the re-organization from the previous national powerhouses that feel threatened by the restructuring. The re-organization should help middle-sized companies that thus far have developed competitive strategies at national levels to integrate those strategies into a Community-wide competitive strategy, if not into a global strategy.

Several functions and activities will need to be re-organized to take full advantage of the single European market. The product development activity can now be organized at a Community-wide level because adjustments to the new homogeneous product standards should be coordinated. In this way it will also be possible to speed up product development and to make the process more efficient. Purchasing should be organized in such a way that the company can take advantage from increased competition among suppliers. The logistical organization of supply must also be reviewed. Major changes could occur in the coordination of production operations. Some plants will be expanded while others will close down or take on new assignments. The physical distribution will no longer be organized along national lines and a rationalization of distribution centres will become possible. Sales organizations should continue to have a national prospective because they will have to respond to the typical national characteristics of the markets that will still be there after 1992. But the sales organizations will need to be coordinated at a Community level, because otherwise customers will take advantage of price and promotional differences between countries. The free movement of capital – if it is realized as planned – will make it possible to further centralize the finance function. Finally, the human resource function will have to prepare managers and workers for more cross-cultural cooperation.

10

Relative deprivation and the concept of reference groups

W.G. Runciman

The related notions of 'relative deprivation' and 'reference group' both derive from a familiar truism: that people's attitudes, aspirations and grievances largely depend on the frame of reference within which they are conceived.

The term 'relative deprivation' was originally coined by the authors of *The American Soldier*, the large-scale social-psychological study of the American army which was carried out during the Second World War. The authors of *The American Soldier* do not give any rigorous definition of relative deprivation,[1] but its general sense is immediately apparent. If A, who does not have something but wants it, compares himself to B, who does have it, then A is 'relatively deprived' with reference to B. Similarly, if A's expectations are higher than B's, or if he was better off than B in the past, he may when similarly placed to B feel relatively deprived by comparison with him. A strict definition is difficult. But we can roughly say that A is relatively deprived of X when (i) he does not have X, (ii) he sees some other person or persons, which may include himself at some previous or expected time, as having X (whether or not this is or will be in fact the case), (iii) he wants X, and (iv) he sees it as feasible that he should have X. Possession of X may, of course, mean avoidance of or exemption from Y.

Relative deprivation may vary in magnitude, frequency or degree. The magnitude of a relative deprivation is the extent of the difference between the desired situation and that of the person desiring it (as he sees it). The frequency of a relative deprivation is the proportion of a group who feel it. The degree of a relative deprivation is the intensity to which it is felt. It is obvious that the three need not coincide. The proportion of a group feeling relatively deprived may be quite independent of either the magnitude or the intensity of the relative deprivation, and relative deprivation may be just as keenly felt when its magnitude is small as when it is large. Relative deprivation should always be understood to mean a *sense* of deprivation; a person who is 'relatively deprived' need not be

Extracted from Chapter 2 in W.G. Runciman, *Relative Deprivation and Social Justice*. (London: Routledge & Kegan Paul, 1966).

'objectively' deprived in the more usual sense that he is demonstrably lacking something. In addition, relative deprivation means that the sense of deprivation is such as to involve a comparison with the imagined situation of some other person or group. This other person or group is the 'reference group', or more accurately the 'comparative reference group'. The addition of 'comparative' is made necessary because 'reference group' can be used in two other senses which will not necessarily overlap with the comparative sense. It can not only mean the group with which a person compares himself; it can also be used to mean either the group from which he derives his standards of comparison or the group from which the comparison is extended and to which he feels that he belongs.

Any one person will have a multiplicity of reference groups, membership, comparative and normative. These may vary not only from topic to topic, but even on a single topic they could in theory change from one moment to the next. But on broad issues of social equality, the relative deprivations common to a group or class will be fairly consistent. Hyman, in his original paper, makes the point that despite the enormous multiplicity of possible reference groups, the number habitually used by any one person is small, and particular reference groups are likely to be specified in the context of particular problems.[2] It is true that the same people will give different answers when the questions 'What sort of people are you thinking of as "people like yourself"?' or 'Who do you compare yourself with?' are asked in different contexts. But on topics where social inequalities are at issue – as opposed to topics where purely individual differences are involved, such as intelligence or physical strength – the answers given are likely to follow a fairly stable pattern.

The most difficult question of all, however, is how far a person's reference group should be seen as the cause or the effect of his other aspirations and attitudes. This is particularly difficult with comparative as opposed to normative groups. In the language of survey research, should they be treated as a dependent or an independent variable? There are two ways of looking at the problem. On the one hand, we could say that a person who sees his opportunities as limited will choose a comparative reference group not too far from his present situation, so that his magnitude of relative deprivation is accordingly kept low. On the other hand, we could say that because he only compares himself with groups close to his own position his goals are limited, and his magnitude of relative deprivation is by this means kept low. Which description is correct in any given case?

It will almost always be safe to say that the influence is reciprocal; but there may be no certain means of distinguishing between cause and effect, or of detecting which of several possible reference groups is the influence acting on a particular attitude.[3]

The question must, therefore, always be asked in two separate parts: first, what determines a person's choice of reference group? second, what results from the choice? There may be a spiral effect in the direction of either a higher or a lower magnitude of relative deprivation. A comparison with someone much better off may produce consequences which will encourage a further comparison with someone better off still, or a comparison with someone worse off may be conducive to a relative contentment in which no comparisons leading to a sense of grievance will be likely to obtrude. But the particular comparison chosen is the crux of the relation between inequality and grievance.

The most famous finding, in the literature on reference groups comes from the evidence of a survey rather than an experiment. It is one of the findings reported in *The American Soldier*. In the Military Police, where opportunities for promotion were very poor, satisfaction with opportunities for promotion was found to be higher than in the Air Corps, where opportunities for promotion were conspicuously good.[4] This result is certainly not what common sense would initially lead one to expect. If the finding had been that the better the chances of promotion, the more likely people were to be satisfied about it, this would have appeared an unnecessary demonstration of the obvious. But it is only when the notion of reference groups is introduced that the actual finding can be readily explained.

This is, in effect, the explanation given by the investigators. They do not use the term reference group, but they comment that what is needed is 'the theory that such opinions by soldiers represent a relationship between their expectations and their achievements relative to others *in the same boat with them*'.[5] The implications of this idiomatic but imprecise phrase are more fully brought out by Merton and Rossi. Those who were not promoted in the Military Police tended to compare themselves with the large number of their fellows who were also not promoted, while those few who had been promoted were likely to appear to themselves to have done relatively better. In the Air Corps, by contrast, the man who was not promoted would be likely to compare himself with the large number of his fellows who *had* been promoted, while these, though successful, would appear to themselves to have done relatively less well. This explanation, once put forward, is intuitively as well as statistically convincing. It does not have the certainty of an experimental result since we cannot be sure that, for example, entrants to the Air Corps did not share traits of character which might incline them to different attitudes from those of the Military Police. But the finding is quite striking enough to lead us to look at the general relation between inequality and grievance in terms of reference group choices.

If we turn from the effects of the choice of reference group to its possible cause, the choice seems in this instance to be numerically determined. The more people a man sees promoted when he is not promoted himself, the more people he may compare himself with in a situation where the comparison will make him feel relatively deprived. This arthimetical determinant of satisfaction is emphasized in *The American Soldier* and, given the appropriate assumptions, can be extended and formalized. On a pure model of this kind, assuming random comparisons, there will be definable points where the frequency of relative deprivation and thereby the likelihood of dissatisfaction with promotion will reach their maximum and minimum.[6] But the actual extension of opportunities for promotion need not be the only determinant of this sort of effect. In the first place, it may be some other influence which causes those who have been promoted to be taken as a comparative referent. In the second, some other group may be taken as a referent because of a belief that its opportunities are better (whether in fact they are or not).

On the 'pure' numerical model, the frequency of relative deprivation will be at a minimum when either everybody or nobody is promoted; in between, it will rise and fall as actual mobility rates rise. But the assumption that relative deprivation will be least frequent where promotion opportunities are worst is not intuitively very convincing. Unless people literally cannot conceive of a society in which social mobility is possible, it is plausible to suppose that some, at least, of the members of a subordinate class will feel relatively deprived in relation to their superiors. They will not, of course, be taking as a reference group members of their own class who have risen from it, as in the example of the Military Police; their sense of grievance will rather stem from their comparing the classes as such. But the effect is the same – they will be tempted to compare themselves with people placed above them. Under what circumstances, therefore, will the correlation hold between a higher rate of mobility and a lower rate of satisfaction with the system of social inequality? In the words of Merton and Rossi,

> . . . it is scarcely probable that this relationship between actual mobility rates and individual satisfaction with mobility chances holds throughout the entire range of variation. If promotion rates were reduced to practically zero in some of these groups, would one then find an even more 'favourable opinion' of promotion chances? Presumably, the relationship is curvilinear, and this requires the sociologist to work out toward the conditions under which the observed linear relationship fails to obtain.[7]

Suppose we assume a society in which the rate of upward mobility increases progressively and evenly over time. Assume also that the unpleasantness of subordination and therefore the intensity of grievance among those who feel it, is constant throughout. If it is true that a little mobility produces less frequent dissatisfaction than does more mobility, and also that zero mobility produces more frequent dissatisfaction than does a little mobility, then the relation between the mobility rate and the frequency of relative deprivation in any given population might look something like Figure 1.

I must emphasize as strongly as I can that this use of a graph is purely illustrative. It might seem tempting to label the four points on the curve slavery, feudalism, industrialization and democracy; but this could never be properly quantified and tested, even if these terms could be satisfactorily

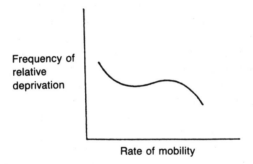

Figure 1

defined. The use of the graph is rather that it directs our attention to particular points along the progress of a society towards greater equality for the members of its subordinate strata. If the assumption represented in the graph is correct, and if it can be applied outside of occupational mobility rates to other topics relevant to social equality in general, then there are some points between which satisfaction rises as equality spreads, but others between which an improving situation leads to a higher, not lower, incidence of relative deprivation.

The readiest illustration of an advance towards equality leading to an increase in relative deprivation is the common observation that revolutions are apt to occur at times of rising prosperity. Although no one would suggest that this is more than a part of the explanation of any particular revolution, historians of various times and places, including eighteenth-century France and twentieth-century Russia, have noticed the tendency for overt discontent to be relatively rare in stable hardship and to rise alike in frequency, magnitude and intensity as opportunity is seen to increase. The argument is stated at its most succinct by Tocqueville in discussing the French Revolution: 'Thus it was precisely in those parts of France where there had been most improvement that popular discontent ran highest. . . . Patiently endured so long as it seemed beyond redress, a grievance comes to appear intolerable once the possibility of removing it crosses men's minds. . . . At the height of its power feudalism did not inspire so much hatred as it did on the eve of its eclipse.'[8] To take an example closer to the present study, it has been emphasized by Henry Pelling in his account of the origins of the Labour Party that in late nineteenth-century Britain 'the immediate onset of what economic historians now call the "Great Depression", so far from encouraging Socialism and the break-up of the Liberal Party, actually discouraged working class militancy and destroyed the "advanced" elements then in existence'.[9] Furthermore, 'The period of [the workers'] greatest political and industrial advance (1888 to 1891) was a period of comparative prosperity.'[10] Such a tendency can perhaps be explained by the cautious pessimism which hardship inevitably breeds. But this, in effect, is to say that in hard times comparative reference groups will be more restricted than in good, which is a part of the generalization being put forward.

This does not mean, however, that if times get sharply worse the frequency and intensity of relative deprivation may not be heightened. It is only poverty which seems irremediable that is likely to keep relative deprivation low. Marx and Engels were not foolish to hope for economic crises as the catalysts of revolution, for when a stable expectation is suddenly disappointed this is at least as likely to promote relative deprivation as when an expectation is suddenly heightened. What is common to both situations is that people are made aware of not having what they have been brought to think it feasible or proper or necessary that they should have. The upsetting of expectations provokes the sense of relative deprivation which may in turn provide the impetus for drastic change. Where apparently stable expectations are disappointed, the comparative reference group is likely to be the previous situation of the membership reference group. But when expectations are rising faster than the likelihood of their fulfilment, it is both more interesting and also more difficult to ascertain what has determined the choice of reference group by which the feeling of relative deprivation has been engendered.

The likelihood of a rise in dissatisfaction accompanying an advance towards equality will of course vary greatly from one topic to another. But the important conclusion which follows from the discussion so far is that there is no stronger initial reason to expect the resentment of inequality to correlate with relative hardship than with relative good fortune. Apart from historical examples which suggest themselves, a particularly striking example of a curvilinear relationship between inequality and grievance is furnished by a piece of recent research carried out in the United States. In a study of the effects of a tornado on a community wholly unprepared for it, it was found that

> the feeling of being relatively better off than others *increases* with objective loss up to the highest loss category . . . The highest proportion feeling less deprived than others is among those with medium personal loss – some injury to a household member, or death to a non-household member or a close friend. Among those with serious personal losses, those with only medium property damage were subjectively worse off and less active than those with high property damage.[11]

As is shown in the discussion from which this quotation is taken, these apparently paradoxical results can at once be explained by bringing in the notion of reference groups. Those hardest hit correspond to those at the left of the graph in Figure 1. But those only a little way from where the disaster struck most severely are likely to contrast themselves with those hardest hit, and by this standard they are likely to feel fortunate to have escaped as lightly as they did. Those at the edge of the disaster area, by contrast, are less likely to be aware of the situation of the severest sufferers and more likely therefore to feel relatively deprived by comparison with those who suffered little or no loss of any kind. Finally, those outside the scope of the study altogether will, we may safely assume, have no occasion to feel relatively deprived at all. This is a remarkably apt illustration of just the sort of curvilinear relationship which the promotion example suggested.

Consider the first low point on the curve. In the Military Police, or among the Arkansas households where only medium loss has been suffered, the low frequency of relative deprivation is plausibly explained by saying that for these people things are visibly not as bad as they could be; at the same time, the situation of a number of comparable people who are very much better off is not readily brought home to them. Relative deprivation, therefore, is likely to be low in magnitude and intensity as well as in frequency. The same seems often to be true of a subordinate class in a larger social system. In the absence of an external stimulus, the limited reference groups by which relative deprivation is kept low (in any or all of the three senses) tend to be self-perpetuating. This feedback effect generated by modest comparisons underlies many familiar generalizations about the hold of habit, the correlation between poverty and conservatism, or the unambitiousness of the underprivileged. Once the vicious circle has been broken, this may set off a rising spiral of expectations and comparisons which will continue until a new equilibrium is reached. But some external influence is needed. The interesting question, therefore, will always be what first broke the equilibrium at the lower level and so gave rise to the change of reference groups.

One of the most obvious of such external influences is war. It is often said that war is the most effective impetus behind social change, and although it is not always clear what is meant by this, a part of the process supposed to occur is the dislocation of familiar standards of reference. Expectations are first of all heightened by the feeling that some tangible rewards will result from victory. But as well as this, new comparisons are generated in two different ways. First, the underprivileged strata who are seen to have shared the exertions and suffering of war in equal measure with their social superiors are encouraged to feel a common aspiration with their superiors for a joint share in a better world. Second, the purely physical disturbances of war bring the members of different classes into more immediate contact with each other than is ever likely to occur in peacetime. The result is that the magnitude, frequency and intensity of relative deprivation are all markedly heightened among people whose previous reference groups had been much closer to their own immediate situation.

War, however, is not the only disturbance by which reference groups may be upset. It is one of the biggest; but disturbances can often be brought about simply by the receipt of news. Orwell, in *The Road to Wigan Pier*, describes a man saying to him that there was no housing problem until people were told about it; or in other words, a sense of relative deprivation was aroused as soon as a different standard was introduced from outside. For people to be told that their economic or social situation is bad may be enough to convince them that it is, even if they had not been thinking so before. The proverbial stirring-up of discontent performed by revolutionaries and agitators depends precisely on their persuading people to judge their situation in terms of comparisons which it had not previously occurred to them to make. In the same way, education can upset traditional reference groups and heighten the general level of aspiration; better close the schools, as Ernest Bevin said in 1920, than create aspirations and then deny them. Conversely, religion can sometimes restrict aspirations; if it teaches that the existing order is just, it can inhibit those comparisons between one stratum and the next which might lead to the system's overthrow. The subversive potentialities of knowledge derive from its capacity to act as an independent influence on reference groups and thereby create relative deprivations where they did not exist before.

A third disrupter of reference groups is economic change. Prosperity can break the vicious circle between poverty and conservatism by making people aware of the possibility of a higher standard than it would previously have occurred to them to hope for. Conversely, a decline in prosperity, if not too violent, can restrict the sense of relative deprivation by inhibiting comparisons with more fortunate groups. There may at the same time be an influence the other way round – prosperity may, for example, result in turn from the urge to realize higher aspirations, as in Schumpeter's theory of the entrepreneur. But for the mass of the population, war, or education, or economic change are external influences by which their attitudes and expectations are altered. If it is true that the sense of inequality in society depends on the choice of reference groups, then the influences behind reference group choices will be the determinants of the relation between grievance and inequality. In particular, they will explain this relation when it is most discrepant – that is, when those at the bottom seem least discontented with the system which places them there.

Political theorists of many different persuasions have wondered at the acquiescence of the underprivileged in the inequalities to which they are subjected, and have explained this acquiescence in terms of ignorance, or habit, or traditionally restricted expectations.

It is dangerous to generalize too freely from this into talking about the 'unambitiousness' of the underprivileged, since the distance between a person's situation and his reference group may be equally large whether he is a labourer's son who wants to be a craftsman or a solicitor's son who wants to be a high court judge.[12] It may well be that the magnitude of the relative deprivations which are felt by the underprivileged is no greater than the magnitude of those felt by the very prosperous. The point is rather that whatever the relative magnitudes of relative deprivation, those near the bottom are likely, even in a society with an egalitarian ideology, to choose reference groups nearer the bottom than self-conscious egalitarianism would imply. Or to phrase it more carefully, they are likely to modify their reference groups in such a way that their aspirations are diverted from those goals which the rags-to-riches myth misleadingly holds out for them.

This more circumspect phrasing is made necessary by the alternative implication suggested by Merton. In a paper entitled 'Social structure and anomie',[13] Merton has argued that those who find themselves denied the positions which the egalitarian myth has led them to believe are open to them may be driven to adopt high but 'deviant' ambitions. In the American culture, success is mandatory; those to whom conventional success is denied because of their inferior position will therefore tend to seek success of a less conventional or even legitimate kind. Merton advances this argument without recourse to the notion of reference groups – which is surprising, in view of their relevance to it and Merton's own discussion of reference group theory. But if we translate his argument into these terms, it can be summarized by saying that the American ideology encourages the underprivileged to make extravagant reference group comparisons; but since the relative deprivations to which these give rise are demonstrably unlikely to be satisfied, the original reference groups may be modified by the adoption as goals of more feasible but less respectable positions of wealth and influence. The result is that 'deviant' ambitions are chosen by members of the underprivileged strata more frequently than would occur in the absence of the cultural norm of success for all. The ideology of egalitarianism influences reference group choices which in turn help to promote 'deviant' behaviour.

This argument might seem to be incompatible with Hyman's. Merton suggests that an egalitarian ideology promotes large ambitions among the underprivileged, while Hyman emphasizes rather their adjustment to the depressing realities of inequality. If, however, we keep in mind the caveat about 'unambitiousness', it is clear that the two amount to the same. Even in a society where the ideology of egalitarianism is most powerful, those at the bottom modify their ambitions in accordance with the facts of their situation. They may, it is true, continue to feel relatively deprived of wealth and success to a greater extent than they would in a society where equality was held neither desirable nor possible. But their reference groups will not be those implied by a literal adoption of the belief that there is a place at the top for everyone. Even where equality is an article of faith, the facts of inequality tend to restrict those feelings of relative deprivation which they might be thought to stimulate. The 'normal' situation, where inequality is not seen to be markedly diminishing, is for reference groups to be close to home.

There is, however, one difficulty involved in generalizing about reference group choices which is largely concealed by the sort of examples which I have cited. In talking about soldiers in the Military Police, or auto workers in Michigan, we are talking about men in a situation where only limited kinds of comparison are relevant. When Chinoy talks to auto workers about their occupational aspirations, it is safe to assume that they are answering as self-conscious auto workers; if they cite a reference group outside of their occupation, it is by contrast with their occupation that it should be interpreted. Similarly, when an interviewer talks to soldiers about promotion opportunities, the framework of the discussion is necessarily delimited, since a small and clearly definable population includes all the relevant candidates for reference group comparisons. But if we move from this to talking about resentments of inequality in the context of a total society, then the scope of reference group choices, both comparative and membership, becomes enormously enlarged. What happens when people make comparisons in more than one of their various capacities, and these capacities have different rankings in the hierarchy of the society to which they belong?

The problem has received some attention among American social psychologists under the headings of 'status-consistency' and 'status-crystallization'.[14] Given people who belong at the same time to social categories which are differently ranked, the problem is to discover how far their attitudes or behaviour are influenced by their awareness of the discrepancies in the status of their differently ranked roles. It has been suggested, for example, that such people are likelier than others to adopt liberal political attitudes. But attempts to generalize along these lines have been subjected to some effective criticism, and no very illuminating conclusions have emerged from the studies so far carried out. It seems agreed that it is a mistake to look at status as though it were unidimensional, and that 'all forms of status inconsistency are psychologically disturbing';[15] but this hardly needs saying. The significance of status inconsistency for the relation between inequality and grievance is intuitively obvious. A person who occupies two different roles or categories may well be driven by his awareness of the discrepancy between them into a resentment of the status accorded to him in his lower-ranked role. When, for example, manual workers achieve a greater equality of reward, but not of status, with workers who used to be above them in both, then it is probable that their frequency of relative deprivation of status will rise in proportion as their relative deprivation of income is appeased.

There is, however, yet another possible difference in the nature of the relative deprivation which they will feel. This is the difference which I briefly mentioned earlier. The manual worker whose prosperity has heightened his relative deprivation of status may have come to feel that his occupation as a whole is insufficiently esteemed.[16] But suppose that his prosperity rather leads him to identify with those in other occupations whose level of reward is the same. If his disparate statuses (in the sense of high reward but low esteem) influence his attitudes in this rather different way, then he will not so much wish to rise in social prestige within his membership reference group as out of it.

This is the one final distinction in types of relative deprivation which

Table 1

| | | Relatively deprived because of own position as member of group | |
		Satisfied	Dissatisfied
Relatively deprived because of group's position in society	Satisfied	A	B
	Dissatisfied	C	D

is relevant to the relation between inequality and grievance. A person's sense of relative deprivation will be affected not only by which of several membership reference groups is the basis for his chosen comparison; it will also be affected by what he feels about its relation to his comparative group. The two will, of course, share at least the common attribute without which a sense of relative deprivation could not be engendered at all. But suppose a person succeeds in reaching a position of equality with his comparative group. Did he want to rise out of his membership group, or with it? If the first, then he was dissatisfied with his position as a member of what he saw as his group; if the second, then he was dissatisfied with the position of what he saw as his group relative to other groups in the larger system. The difference between the two is obvious, but important. It is also closely bound up with the person's choice of normative reference group.

The distinction can be conveniently represented in the form of a four-fold table, see Table 1.

It would, of course, be unwarrantable to assume that any single person, who may occupy a variety of roles and hold a variety of attitudes to them, can arbitrarily be assigned to one or another of these four categories. But as long as it is clear that the four categories are no more than ideal types, then it may be useful to describe them in a little more detail.

Type A could perhaps be labelled 'orthodox', since it covers anyone who is neither ambitious within his group nor resentful on its behalf. It is, however, perfectly possible for a person to be anxious to change the structure of his society without himself feeling relatively deprived. Type A, therefore, will not only include the studious conformist or the successful social climber; it will also include the prosperous altruist who is not himself relatively deprived, but is at the same time driven by guilt or conviction into radical attitudes. In addition, Type A will include those who are low in the social hierarchy but who, for whatever reasons, are not in fact resentful of their position. It is the members of Type A who show how Durkheim's problem comes to be solved – how, that is, people who do not have very much become comfortably convinced that they have no right to more – and who exemplify all the most glaring disparities between inequality and grievance.

Type B, by contrast, covers the sort of 'striver' who is dissatisfied with his present situation, but not in a way that gives him common cause with others like him. A hypothetical example of Type B is the junior executive balked of promotion. He can be presented in such a way that he appears a rather greedy and unpleasant sort of person, but this may be unfair. He might, for example, be a poor but talented artist who feels that his merits are unrecognized, or an intelligent adolescent denied a university scholarship, or an unemployed man refused the scale of benefit to which he is entitled under the regulations in force.

Type C includes all the exemplars of the strong lateral solidarity traditionally found within the working class. But members of Type C need not belong only to a group which resents the inequalities to which it is subjected in the hierarchy of economic class. The member of a religious movement or a minority race may equally feel only a collective relative deprivation, and have no wish to improve his personal position in relation to any of the social categories to which he feels that he belongs. In general, the relative deprivations of Type C are those which play the largest part in the transformation of an existing structure of social inequalities.

Type D, finally, consists of those most relatively deprived of all, who are dissatisfied both with the position of their group and also with their membership of it. Their ideal type will be the tribune of the plebs – the man who not only feels the deprivations and injustices imposed on his class but who explicitly aspires to lead or even ultimately to rule his class in the course of securing redress on their behalf. Individual examples of Type D have had striking effects on the course of history. But for the purposes of the present study the two most interesting types are B and C. In order to refer to them, and to the two types of relative deprivation which they exemplify, I shall use the terms 'egoist' (for Type B) and 'fraternalist' (for Type C).

Neither term is entirely satisfactory, but it is better to use existing words in a specialized sense than to have recourse to neologisms. Although 'fraternalistic' relative deprivations are more naturally suggestive of a working-class person and 'egoist' of a middle-class person, this need not be so by definition. There is nothing to prevent a working-class person feeling relatively deprived within but not on behalf of his class, and, as we shall see, middle-class people are very capable of fraternalistic relative deprivation. There is, however, a significance in the fact that 'fraternalism' is traditionally characteristic of the working, and 'egoism' of the middle-class; and a part of the answer to the relation between inequality and grievance might lie in the circumstances by which the working class has been influenced in the direction of egoistic rather than fraternalistic relative deprivations. The difference between the two, indeed, can be redefined in terms of normative reference groups. Consider once again the example of a working-class person whose comparative reference group is the middle class, or a section of it. If his normative reference group is the working class, then his relative deprivations will in principle be fraternalistic; if it is the middle class, they will be egoistic.

The distinction cannot in practice be applied quite so easily as this suggests. Not only can the notion of a normative reference group not be rigorously defined, but it need never imply any one particular comparison out of the range of relevant inequalities. A manual worker may well think of himself as belonging to the 'middle-class' (whatever this means to him) and whether or not he feels relatively deprived will depend on the comparisons which he makes as a self-styled middle-class person. Furthermore, his assessment of others in what he sees as his class will in turn affect whether his relative deprivation, if he feels one, is of a fraternalistic or an egoistic kind. But once the answers to these more detailed questions can be ascertained, or at least inferred, then the relative deprivation which he feels – with whatever intensity – can in principle be fully described.

It will be clear from the account I have given that none of these terms lend themselves to completely strict definition; but they do provide a framework within which the relation of inequality to grievance can be discussed with reasonable precision. Whatever term is used for it, relative deprivation lies at the heart of this relation. The way in which comparative reference groups are chosen, the membership reference group which gives the comparison its basis and the normative reference group which either exacerbates or mitigates the perception of inequality contain between them the answer to why inequalities are or are not regarded with a resentment proportionate to their magnitude. The only term which has been left altogether undefined is inequality itself.

Notes

1. Samuel A. Stouffer et al., *The American Soldier, I: Adjustment During Army Life* (Princeton, 1949), p. 125.
2. Hyman, 'The psychology of status', p. 47.
3. On the way that this problem can prove insuperable in the absence of experimental evidence, see the abstract of Norman Kaplan, *Reference Group Theory and Voting Behavior* (PhD thesis, Columbia University, 1955), in *Dissertation Abstracts* XV (1955), p. 1458. Whether the influence is that of a comparative or a normative reference group, it may be impossible to establish which of several possible choices is a determinant of attitudes.
4. Stouffer, op. cit., pp. 250–3.
5. Ibid. p. 251.
6. See James A. Davis, 'A formal interpretation of the theory of relative deprivation', *Sociometry* XXII (1959), pp. 280–96.
7. Op. cit., p. 236, n. 7.
8. A. de Tocqueville, *The Old Regime and the French Revolution* (Garden City, NY, 1955), pp. 176–7.
9. H. Pelling, *The Origins of the Labour Party 1880–1900* (London, 1953), p. 6.

10. Ibid., p. 8.
11. Allen H. Barton, *Social Organization Under Stress: A Sociological Review of Disaster Studies* (National Academy of Sciences – National Research Council; Washington, DC, 1963), p. 63. The particular study was carried out in Arkansas by the National Opinion Research Center.
12. See L. T. Empey, 'Social class and occupational aspiration: a comparison of absolute and relative measurement', *American Sociological Review* XXI (1956), p. 704; and cf. S. Keller and M. Zavalloni, 'Classe sociale, ambition et réussite', *Sociologie du Travail* IV (1962), p. 2.
13. Reprinted in *Social Theory and Social Structure*, Chapter IV.
14. See initially Gerhard E. Lenski, 'Status crystallisation: a non-vertical dimension of social status', *American Sociological Review* XIX (1954), pp. 405–13.
15. Elton F. Jackson, 'Status inconsistency and symptoms of stress', *American Sociological Review* XXVII (1962), p. 469.
16. For example, the effect of higher wages on miners as described by N. Dennis et al., *Coal is Our Life* (London, 1956), p. 76 could be rephrased in these terms.

The social environment

Organizations operate in complex national and international sociocultural environments, within which individuals' and communities' values and lifestyles shift over time. Slow, sometimes imperceptible as these shifts may be, they can clearly have profound implications for organizations. We see these implications most obviously in the marketing sphere, where changing consumer values and lifestyles lead to new opportunities for new products (and significant threats to existing products which fail to adapt to such changes).

The need to be aware of developments in the sociocultural environment is well known to many managers. In this section, however, we examine this arena from somewhat different perspectives to those found in most of the management literature. Again we draw on other social sciences, particularly sociology and cultural studies.

In the first chapter, taken from *The Expressive Revolution*, Bernice Martin examines the longer-term impact of the 'counter-cultural revolution' of the 1960s. She shows how the values of the so-called 'counter-culture' of that period were not, as might have been expected, abandoned in the more austere 1970s, but instead were absorbed within mainstream culture. Many of the motifs of 1960s' counter-cultural protest about, for example, self-expression, 'authenticity' and so on, have become part of the accepted vocabulary and symbolism of everyday social life.

Martin also argues that the counter-culture of the 1960s was both a product and an agent of structural changes occurring 'in the very fabric' of advanced industrial societies. She explores the nature of those changes in a range of spheres including the political and the commercial, where ideas about 'authenticity' and expressiveness have become integral to many products' imagery and presentation.

Debate about the demise of 'modernism' and the emergence of a new 'postmodern' era has been central within the social sciences for some time. In the second chapter, 'After the masses', Dick Hebdige explores a number of issues raised by the thesis of a postmodern era, in particular the central role of 'signs and symbols' in modern life. He discusses the impact of market research, which has produced pervasive classifications of social categories – 'yuppies' being the most obvious example. These cut across traditional demographic categories to map a 'social world of desire'. Hebdige also argues that a sociology of aspiration could well combine the critical and diagnostic resources within sociology and cultural studies with the descriptive and predictive knowledge available from market research. The reverse is, of course, also true.

In the third chapter, 'Some remarks on informal work, social polarization and the social structure', Pahl explores the nature of the 'informal' economy and its consequences. He argues that a key consequence of current patterns of informal work is to reinforce rather than redress contemporary patterns of inequality. Certain households, particularly those with 'core' rather than peripheral workers, become increasingly advantaged while others become increasingly disadvantaged.

In addressing the informal economy and its impacts, Pahl brings to our attention an aspect of society's economic life that is ignored by most economists and management theorists but is nevertheless of considerable potential significance to them.

The final chapter by Mike Featherstone, 'Lifestyle and consumer culture', again addresses the 'consumer culture' and the centrality within this of matters of style, self-expression and 'a stylistic self consciousness'. In the consumer culture, material goods operate as symbols and communicators in relation to self and identity rather than simply as functional utilities.

Featherstone also reminds us that assumptions about a pluralistic, self-expressive 'autonomous' consumer culture need to be balanced with the awareness that particular tastes and lifestyles are not free-functioning. They are importantly mediated by processes of legitimation occurring within embedded social structures such as class, gender, race, etc.

In these various ways, all these chapters address sociocultural worlds within which organizations are enmeshed. Going beyond 'market-mapping' they offer managers important 'food for thought' about the nature and impact of changes in those worlds.

11

The expressive revolution

Bernice Martin

If one looks only at the superficial, theatrical extravaganza of the 1960s, the happenings, demonstrations, psychedelia and the rest, it is easy to assume that the counter-culture was merely trivial, ephemeral, a minor footnote in the margin of cultural history. From the viewpoint of the counter-culture's pioneers, it looks like a failed revolution. The argument of this book is that it was more significant than the first and less than the second. The counter-culture was an index to a whole new cultural style, a set of values, assumptions and ways of living which Talcott Parsons, with uncharacteristic exaggeration, has called the 'Expressive Revolution'.[1] The 1960s were the transformation point. They exemplified for society at large, in striking ways, processes which would expand the frames within which expressive possibilities were currently contained. By the mid-1970s many things which had seemed traumatic, shocking, revolutionary in the previous decade had been incorporated into mainstream culture. The pioneers of the 1960s had genuinely sought to remove the frames altogether, but in the event the consequences were less drastic. The frames stretched, sometimes a long way from their former contours, but they ultimately reasserted their nature as limits and margins.

Yet within the expanded frames culture had institutionalized much of what the counter-culture had stood for. If it ever was truly a *counter-*culture (this point will be discussed later), it had certainly ceased to be so by the mid-1970s because its most characteristic methods and messages had been appropriated by mainstream culture.

In this chapter I want to concentrate on the nature of the social system in and on which the changes of the 1960s operated. The argument is that the counter-culture was a particularly colourful symptom, herald and agent of structural changes which were occurring in the fabric of advanced industrial societies. The 1960s' aspiration to let the jinnee out of the bottle was itself the product of social change.

Advanced industrial societies are materially prosperous and minutely differentiated in terms of the division of labour, the structure of social institutions and the distribution of social roles. This development contains a central problem and contradiction: it gives with one hand and takes

---

Extracted from Chapter 2 in Bernice Martin, *A Sociology of Contemporary Cultural Change.* (Oxford: Basil Blackwell, 1981).

away with the other. What it gives is affluence and a new possibility of freedom and individuality; what it takes away is natural social rootedness and automatic structures of belonging. Material plenty releases both people and resources from the immediate disciplines of survival so that whole populations are enabled to discover layers of 'expressive' needs – self-discovery and self-fulfilment, richness of personality, variety and depth of relationships – as legitimate and at least half-feasible aims. So 'experience' can become a positive, sought-after value; and mere 'coping' with the exigencies of one's material and social situation is no longer enough.

At the same time structural differentiation specializes and fragments experience so that more and more people find their lives split into separate enclaves of partial and specialized role-playing inside large and often impersonal institutional structures. Little is left beyond the privatized sphere of family as a place where it is unequivocally legitimate to be an integrated person with full affective and expressive rights. The consequence of this contradiction is twofold. First, it focuses the perception and social vocabulary of expressive fulfilment on the private and the personal: the very idea of fulfilment comes to imply individualized and personalized experience; the expressive sphere itself thus holds up a mirror to the egoistic and anomic normality of modern society. Second, it implies a socially structured deafness and blindness to fulfilment based not on individual choice and free affect but on custom, security, tradition, limits and ascription. This deafness and blindness is not total but involves yet another contradiction. Modern society's most natural social resource is the association. Expressive needs are thus pervasively 'organized' in voluntary and state-provided associations – from yoga clubs to the doctor's surgery. But this is precisely a manifestation of the very specialization and fragmentation which makes expressive fulfilment both so urgent and so elusive. Thus the vocabulary of institutionalization *per se* becomes as suspect as it is pervasive: bureaucracy, organization, structure can thus be anathematized, while at the same time a vision of a lost golden age or millennium around the corner can idealize purified community as the only acceptable form of the collective pole of experience to balance the privatized role of personal expressiveness. Thus the pure collective and the pure individual form the dynamic duality inside the myth which drives the Expressive Revolution.

Of course, these tendencies are very unevenly developed across the range of milieux which form modern society. Traditional and semi- or quasi-communal enclaves protected from the ravages (and benefits) of differentiation, mobility and fragmentation continue to exist in all social classes, and particularly among the 'respectable' working class. Moreover, by a further twist in its logic, differentiation enables a growing enclave in each society to specialize in expressive activities as a form of work while other enclaves specialize in the instrumental sphere. The arts, the mass media, the universities, the Churches, and the caring professions are *par excellence* in the expressive category, while the commercial, industrial and technological spheres constitute the major arena of instrumental activities. Thus the Protestant ethic confronts its antithesis on the disputed boundary between expressive and instrumental worlds. Daniel Bell[2] has made much of this point. He argues that the techno-structure of advanced industrial societies generates an ideology which places a high value on rationality, calculation and efficiency, while the cultural sphere – what (following Parsons) I have called the 'expressive enclave' – isolates an ideology of self-fulfilment, spontaneity and experiential richness. Thus the ideological trajectories of the differentiated subcultural spheres of industrial society pull in contradictory directions and institutionalize an unresolved tension at the centre of society (what Bell calls the 'cultural contradictions of capitalism').

I have deliberately left out so far all mention of the political sphere, which Bell treats as the third semi-autonomous, subcultural sphere and which, in my view, is the most difficult to make sense of. With echoes of an older and now much battered convergence hypothesis, Bell argues that the imperatives of the political sphere are equality and participation. My own immediate response is sceptical. It may be that Bell's formulation is suggestive but unsatisfactory precisely because politics is a sphere in which the instrumental and expressive imperatives confront each other, vying for supremacy. One consequence of the contest could be the adoption of some expressive *rhetoric* in capitalist (if not in state Communist) societies, whatever the nature of the political conflict.

In a discussion of the nature of modernism, Eisenstadt argues that from the time of its invention by Western European society modernism has always had two by now near-inextricable facets, one symbolic or ideological and the other technical/industrial.[3] Modernism in its first guise has always involved something analogous to a religious mission, in this case a Romantic ideology of individual rights, wider participation and self-determination (national and individual) and the acceptance of perpetual change as a way of life. It has exported these values to the populations of the Third World, along with tractors, penicillin and napalm. Thus for Eisenstadt the ideological/political components of modernism are precisely the precursors of the values of the Expressive Revolution: both are offshoots of the Enlightenment and of Romanticism, and both have a structural, but not a one-way-determinist, relation to the nature of industrialism and structural differentiation.

All this is by way of prelude to the vexed question of whether the Expressive Revolution is and was inevitably politically radical or even revolutionary. Certainly, in the 1960s the counter-culture was popularly seen as intrinsically Leftist. But if we accept the argument so far about the nature and derivation of the Expressive Revolution we would need to demur on two grounds. First, the progeny of the Enlightenment and Romanticism are already provided with a full range of political positions consonant with expressive values ranging from bourgeois liberalism through Romantic revolution to ultra-individualist anarchism. Indeed, it takes only a slight effort of the imagination to see how a style of politics like Burkean conservatism could be presented as caring for whole, integrated persons and allowing them to get on with the important expressive things of life by taking politics out of the sphere of controversy. In a very serious sense the expressive value system is *a*political, concentrating as it does on the individual, experiential dimensions and mistrusting the wider institutional nexus as impersonal, distorting and coercive.

At another level, however, the forces which release expressive needs also widen the possibilities of political dissent. A greatly expanded cultural class specializing in expressive work roles becomes the repository of anti-materialist and anti- or non-instrumental values which thus, for that class, form the locus of the sacred. The cultural class is distanced and protected from the Puritan disciplines of the economic sphere and can afford Utopian perspectives which reject the compromises and opportunism of practical politics and economics. It is perfectly poised to espouse what Weber called *Wertrationalität* or an antinomian and charismatic pursuit of absolute ends, and to despise and attack *Zwekrationalität*, the functional rationality of means which dominates the economic sphere. Thus a vocal and eminently visible wing of the Expressive Revolution was and remains anti-capitalist and anti-bourgeois and embraces every radical position between Maoism and anarchism. Other factors have colluded with this tendency.

In brief then, my argument is that the values of the Expressive Revolution, the *placet experiri* of the 1960s, is not inextricable from the political Left. The relationship is contingent, not essential. The Left-wing intelligentsia, partly because of its impasse *vis-à-vis* the affluent proletariat and partly through a professional *hubris* that took the tools of its trade for the key to the universe, adopted the values and techniques of expressiveness and thus gave them a contingent but highly visible radical colouration. The counter-culture of the 1960s looked revolutionary in its first flowering (hence the 'counter') and indeed was experienced as such by many of its early innovators. The wider society too was initially convinced of the 'revolutionary' nature of the new phenomenon, both because of its evident outrage and because so many of the counter-culture's practitioners declared themselves revolutionary. Yet underneath the red clothing was a beast of a different colour, or perhaps a chameleon able to take on *any* political colouring. The general argument, then, is that the so-called counter-culture was advance warning of the much wider and less spectacular thrust of the Expressive Revolution into the whole hemisphere of personal/cultural activities in advanced industrial society. It was a specialist and exaggerated form of a phenomenon which is affecting all spheres of society, though to different extents and at different rates. What it 'countered' was not so much traditional cultural values as the contrasting hemisphere of instrumentality and power, work and politics. The counter-culture was historically continuous with the humanistic/expressive values of the traditional cultural elite, and merely pushed Romantic individualism to ever more extreme lengths in contradistinction to the bureaucratic and bourgeois individualism[4] of the instrumental enclave. That bifurcation is increasingly an institutionalized feature of advanced industrial society.

Two particular social facts have contributed to the swift incorporation of the values of the expressive counter-culture into the mainstream of social life. The first is the fact that the social group which acted as the main carrier of the expressive values, even in its most revolutionary guise, was a cultural elite located close to the status, if not to the power centre of industrial society. The main home of the anti- or non-instrumental values of the counter-culture was and remains the upper middle class in the expressive professions – the arts, education (particularly higher education), the mass media and the caring professions and semi-professions. There is a high degree of self-recruitment in all these areas, particularly at the upper status level of each field, and while this cultural class is functionally distinct from the traditional political and industrial elite, it is linked to the power centre by strong ties of family and by common educational experience. It is, for example, a commonplace of post-1960s research that the academic and professional classes contributed a disproportionate share of their progeny to the counter-cultural student movement of the 1960s. Any movement located quite so close to the centre is unlikely to suffer total repression: the power centre will accommodate where it can so as to stave off a split in the societal hub.

The second fact is associated with the normal processes of legitimation in complex societies. Shils offers a persuasive analysis of the tension between the 'sacred centre' and any geographical, status or cultural 'periphery' which challenges that centre or makes a bid for independence from its control.[5] A complementary thesis is offered by Kolakowski.[6] Shils argues that the media of communication in modern society make it easier for the centre to control or interfere with the idiosyncrasies of peripheries because these deviations or challenges are both more visible and more accessible to penetration. Peripheries attempt to infiltrate the centre, while the centre offers certain concessions in return for the periphery's relinquishing of its ambition of total autonomy. The result is an interpenetration which systematically reduces the difference between the culture of centre and periphery respectively. Kolakowski suggests that one favourite means which the centre has always employed in the face of a revolutionary movement within the society is to deploy the style and techniques of that revolutionary movement against it. He calls this the Counter-Reformation offensive, on the model of the Roman Church's response to the German Reformation. Elements of both Shils' and Kolakowski's processes clearly occurred between the late 1960s and the mid-1970s, aided by the fact that the counter-cultural 'periphery' in question was no agglomeration of the dispossessed but rather a budding cultural elite. One of Shils' cardinal points is that the values and lifestyle of the group at the societal centre naturally partake of the quality of sacredness. The counter-cultural 'periphery' was in fact not so much a periphery as the rising generation of 'culture specialists' at the societal centre. Thus the privileged social locus of the new wave of expressive values was inherently likely to assist the diffusion of those values because of the radiation effect of the cultural 'sacred'.

Certainly, by the early 1970s the political and commercial centre, as well as the older generation of the cultural class itself found that hints of 'authenticity' and expressiveness helped sales and strengthened images. By these means many of the motifs of counter-cultural protest in the 1960s were transformed into the normal vocabulary of symbolic expression and now serve to reinforce assumptions that modern man has the right to subjective experience of a range and quality which most societies in the history of the world would have regarded as Utopian or absurd. (Many, of course, would also have regarded it as very distasteful.)

It might be argued that the 1960s were able to 'afford' an expressive extravaganza because it seemed to most Western people in that decade that a never-ending economic expansion and rise in standards of living was one of the givens of life in industrialized societies. In the 1970s and 1980s, the prospects of galloping inflation, unemployment and zero or negative rates of economic growth might be expected to call into doubt the assumption that expressive values were the luxury product of an already past prosperity and of a misplaced sense of economic security. Certainly, it would be plausible to argue that the end of effortless affluence might help to account for the partial rehabilitation of the values of the Protestant ethic in the 1970s – signalled, for example, by the conversion of many hippies into disciplined Jesus freaks, or by the rediscovery of the value of sequence and structure in education. But these are perhaps only natural corrective mechanisms that operate when the pendulum has swung too far for viable social organization: and there are counter-indications too.

First, the transformation of what in the 1960s were esoteric motifs of the counter-culture into widely accepted themes is too pervasive to be ignored or denied: political tactics of disruption, pioneered by yippies, hippies and the like, are now used as routine modes of pressure-group activity; photographic and narrative techniques of brokenness and ambiguity developed in the Underground currently feature in women's magazines and popular television programmes: Monty Python and the Goodies brought surrealism into even the lower-middle-class parlour; the cultural representation of sexuality in all its forms is far more explicit; authority is seldom able to legitimate itself with the old vocabulary of authority *per se* but only by means of a populist and anti-hierarchical rhetoric; and so on. So much of what was counter-cultural in the 1960s is now an unnoticed and accepted part of the givens of the 1980s, like the nude pin-up girl in the daily newspaper (or the nude boy in *Cosmopolitan*), or the assumption that it is pure anachronism to expect children to defer to adults or to use respectful modes of formal address to their elders. The process has gone furthest in the middle-class expressive professions, but it has also affected general cultural assumptions and many aspects of leisure-time style, even among those whose working lives are dominated by the instrumental milieu. In particular, it has infiltrated deeply the cultural vocabulary of the media of mass communication. One may, of course, wonder how deep the transformation has been and whether isolated and specialist items of expressiveness have been inserted in peripheral, private and interstitial niches or used in mass culture for the same old purposes of profit and easy titillation. Yet a shift in cultural norms has undoubtedly occurred, and one needs to explain why things which the market would not take in the 1950s now form the staple fare of the mass-communication industry.

The second indication of the increased salience of expressive values is to be found in the instrumental sphere itself. Ideas which are now regarded as politically and economically realistic responses to, say, ecological pollution or inflation often began as the freaky notions of angry, way-out hippies, yippies or cranks in the 1960s – the campaign to conserve the world's energy and fuel resources, the extirpation of waste, the drive for individual families and localities to become self-sufficient in food and basic necessities, 'survival strategies', the 'simple life' as the solution to everything from early redundancy to the besetting diseases of twentieth-century urban life (obesity, cardiac arrest, stress, and so on). Politicians have to take account of the popularity of anti-bureaucratic and 'small is beautiful' values which have spread outwards from the counterculture and now reinforce political claims for, say, devolution or the abandonment of high-rise flats as the natural policy in urban housing programmes. So while it may be true that the Expressive Revolution and its counter-cultural storm-troopers were in part at least products of industrialized affluence, expressive values do not automatically lose their cultural hold when relatively modest checks on the growth of that affluence make themselves felt. A traumatic world recession might be a different matter, but short of that, increments of expressive possibility do not in any simple way seem to depend on stockpiles of material goods in themselves; indeed, the emptiness of consumer materialism is one of the strong messages of the Expressive Revolution. Ironically, of course, it is a message which can be processed and packaged by the very consumer materialism it began by rejecting and can be used to sell anything from breakfast foods and cosmetics[7] to gardening tools, seeds and do-it-yourself equipment. Above all, of course, it is used to advertise get-away-from-twentieth-century-technology holidays – by jet plane.

In sum then, the gist of my thesis is that the extravagant counterculture of the 1960s was largely a medium of cultural transmission and transformation. It drew attention to, and familiarized the wider society with a range of expressive values, symbols and activities by showering them forth in their most extreme and dramatic form. The process of the 1970s has been to shift the various cultures and subcultures to accommodate an expansion of expressive possibility inside their various styles. This results in very different constellations from context to context and has set off a number of defensive movements which resist the wider value shift by focusing on particularly evocative symbols – from opposition to fluoridization and pornography (that is, symbolic pollution) to the rising conversion rate of neo-Puritan sects like Jehovah's Witnesses or the Moon Family. But though the movement to expressiveness is selective and uneven, it nevertheless has every appearance of being inexorable.

The most salient feature of the counter-culture of the 1960s was the symbolism of anti-structure. It was essentially a pitting of freedom and fluidity against form and structure. Expressiveness in the 1960s was a long and concerted attack on boundaries, limits, certainties, conventions, taboos, roles, system, style, category, predictability, form, structure and ritual. It was the pursuit of ambiguity and the incarnation of uncertainty. Yet it was also its own opposite, and in this lay a fundamental dilemma. I argued earlier that the Expressive Revolution idealized not only the pure, self-defined and self-determining individual but also the purified collectivity, the perfect community. So the anti-structure and anti-rituals of its symbolic system were contradicted by a search for new, purified rituals and symbols of belonging to a collectivity which could transcend the specificities and limits of time, place and cultural milieu.

The picture is further complicated if one considers the scenario against which the counter-culture of the 1960s played out its symbolic tableaux. Structural differentiation was certainly making its inexorable way through the British social structure, bringing increments of specialization, mobility and privatization to new segments of society. Yet it was spreading unevenly and still left relatively untouched some 'traditional' enclaves, particularly among the upper working classes. Even more than these social changes, full employment and unprecedented general affluence were making the aspiration to new levels of expressive fulfilment more than a pipe dream for the normal citizen. Yet the frames within which these possibilities were experienced – family systems, class and regional cultures, institutional arrangements for recreation and collective activity, role sets and the like – mostly dated from a past in which expressive priorities were *not* the central imperatives. And it is as well to remember that a frame needs only the passing of one generation before it is inherited as 'traditional'. Some loosening of the older boundaries and structures was already occurring in post-war Britain, but an expansion of expressive possibilities was filtering down the status hierarchy only slowly and up to the 1960s had affected mainly the most obviously 'private' spheres, such as marriage, sexual relationships, parenthood, concepts of 'mental health' and the 'integrated personality' and patterns of personal leisure activity. But normal social life was still littered with the symbolism of belonging and of structure, demarcations (between kin and non-kin, friend and stranger, Us and Them, public and private, male and female, adult and child, authority and obedience, everyday and festive, work and leisure) which formed the grammar and syntax of living. Rhythms, rituals and ceremonials were woven into the fabric of social behaviour. It was these frontiers which came under concerted attack from the counter-culture, and it is hardly surprising that the initial response of most of the conventional world was an outraged sense that its very being, its contours of self, were being assaulted.

Notes

1. T. Parsons, 'The educational and expressive revolutions'. Two special University of London lectures given at the London School of Economics, Spring 1975.
2. D. Bell, *The Cultural Contradictions of Capitalism*. Heinemann, London, 1976.
3. S. N. Eisenstadt, 'The tradition of modernity'. Mimeo. Paper given at the Centennial Symposium of the Hebrew Union College, Jewish Institute of Religion, Jerusalem, April 1976.
4. The bourgeois individualism sometimes snapped back at its counter-cultural detractors. See e.g. A. Rand, *The New Left: The Anti-Industrial Revolution*, Signet Books, New York, 1971.
5. E. Shils, 'Centre and periphery: selected papers 2', *Essays in Macrosociology*, Chicago University Press, Chicago, 1975.
6. L. Kolakowski, 'The concept of a counter-reformation'. The 1976 Hobhouse Memorial Lecture given at Bedford College, University of London, May 1976.
7. Mary Quant cosmetics *par excellence*. They were both expensive and packaged with pictures and names redolent of wholesome, 'natural', rural life ('Country Clay'), or additionally echoing the Flower Power era ('Middle Earth'). The Smirnoff Vodka advertisements are probably the cleverest and most blatant examples of the use of a jet-set version of counter-culture motifs to sell a luxury product to middle-and lower-income customers.

12

After the masses

Dick Hebdige

Few people – whatever their political persuasion – looking at Britain in the 1980s would deny that we are living in new times. The crucial question is how far are the long-term global shifts in cultural, political and economic life mapped out under the heading of new times intrinsically connected to the rise of the Right? One way of opening up this question – if only to present a 'worst case' scenario – is to see how these same shifts have been interpreted in recent debates on postmodernism.

Before looking at postmodernity, we have to consider the era it supposedly replaces. Marshall Berman sets out in his book *All That Is Solid Melts Into Air* (1983) to provide a sketch of modern times by tracing out the connections between three terms. First, *modernization* refers to the economic, social and technological innovations associated with the rise of capitalism. Second, *modernity* describes the radically transformed character of life under capitalism most clearly visible in the great European and American cities of the nineteenth and twentieth centuries. Lastly, there is *modernism* – the answering wave of experimental movements in the arts linked again to the capitalist metropolitan centres. Together these radical modernist innovations, from symbolism and cubism to surrealism and stream-of-consciousness writing, set out to articulate the experience of modernity. The terms of this engagement with modern life were always critical, whether modernists were rejecting 'mass culture', negating bourgeois norms and values or seeking to align themselves with progressive social forces. In the case of the International Style of modern architecture and the Bauhaus ideals of industrial design (the so-called 'machine aesthetic') the ambition was to merge with the modernization process itself in order literally to build a better world founded on rational principles (e.g. 'form follows function').

But it is precisely this equation between modernity, progress and rationality that has itself been brought into question in the 'postmodern' era. At the core of this question lies the 'legitimation crisis'. If modernity is a condition in which 'all that's solid melts into air' then all the old institutions and centres of authority – from religion to royalty – which guaranteed stability and continuity in earlier epochs and more traditional

---

Extracted from Stuart Hall and Martin Jaques (eds) *New Times: The Changing Face of Politics in the 1990s.* (London: Lawrence and Wishart, 1989). pp. 76–93.

societies are prone to crisis and contestation. If ideals like truth and justice are not underwritten by divine authority then how is authority to be guaranteed? If all values are flattened out beneath exchange then how are true and lasting values to be established? One of the quests within modernity has been to find ways of resisting this tendency towards the relativization of all values and claims to power by grounding knowledge and legitimating authority so that they are placed beyond question.

According to the French philosopher, Jean-Francois Lyotard, this 'legitimation crisis' has been solved through the invention of what he calls 'the great meta-narratives' of the modern period. By this he means all those overarching belief systems originating in the Enlightenment – from the belief in rationality, science and causality to the faith in human emancipation, progress and the class struggle. These great stories have been used over what he calls the past 'two sanguinary centuries' to legitimate everything from war, revolution, nuclear arsenals and concentration camps to social engineering, Taylorism, Fordist production models and the gulag. The collapse of faith in these meta-narratives heralds what Lyotard calls the 'postmodern condition'. None of the 'centres of authority' legitimated by these collapsed meta-narratives – including that essential 'holding operation', the modern nation state – survives the transition into new times, at least as the latter are defined in postmodern theory.

What replaces them for the American Marxist critic, Fredric Jameson, is the universal 'logic' of the market. For Jameson, the global spread of capital has meant that all such centres are either destroyed or have been made over and absorbed by the interlocking cultural and economic systems that make up 'late capitalism'. In the process the political and cultural maps of the modern period have been redrawn so that the old oppositions – science versus art, fact versus fiction, Left versus Right, high culture versus low culture, mass culture versus 'progressive' modern art and so on – no longer hold. In the postmodern world no values prove 'timeless', 'authentic' or 'oppositional' forever when absolutely everything from the price of pickled mushrooms on a Polish street corner to definitions of desirable art in the West moves with the market.

At the same time, the 'radical' nature of modernism has been called into question in two ways. First, modern art is no longer marginal or oppositional: the 'masterpieces' of the modern 'tradition' now fetch astronomical prices at auctions and sit comfortably within the gallery system, and university and polytechnic arts curricula; TV ads routinely use all the shock effects of modern art. Second, as part of a process of critical review, the canon of High Modernism has been brought to book for its 'Eurocentrism', its 'masculinist' stress on transgression and transformation, its downgrading of everything that does not fall within its definition of what is important, women's art, domestic culture and reproduction, black and Third World art, 'bourgeois' and 'socialist' realism, peasant and working-class white, 'mass' culture, middle-brow and high culture, non-metropolitan culture, etc. Far from being 'progressive', it is condemned for its partriarchal values, its aggressive change-the-world heroism, its colonialist plundering of 'primitive' Third World art. But you do not even need the benefit of hindsight to see that any link between modernization, modernism and utopia is no longer tenable. That link has been dramatically broken – and not just in capitalist societies.

The contention within a lot of postmodernism that today there is no centre is not just a gesture of solidarity with these excluded, repressed or exterminated 'others'. It demands a review of priorities and a rethinking of terms like 'representation' and 'power' at so fundamental a level that any description of the crisis of the Left that does not take it seriously just will not be productive. But the contention also has specific ramifications at both the macro and the micro levels within theories of postmodernism and postmodernity. For Jameson it indicates the end of locality altogether as the multinational character of the late late show of capitalism reduces everything to its own image. The implication here is that we will soon be able to watch *Dallas* or eat a Big Mac in any part of the inhabited world.

At the same time, the point where we 'experience' all this and make sense of it as individuals has allegedly been made over too. The 'sovereign subject' – central to Enlightenment models of rationality, science and the individual – is itself 'de-centred' from the throne of authority. It is de-centred in theory by the *new* 'sciences' – psychoanalysis and Marxism. But in the twentieth century it is also de-centred *practically* in the West by the rise of mass consumption and advertising. As the 'consumption economy' has developed, so the value of commodities is seen to derive less from the laws of economic exchange governing the market or from the ability of products to satisfy primary needs as from the way they function *culturally* as *signs* within coded systems of exchange.

This provides the key for the critique of the Marxist theory of value put forward by the French champion of postmodernity, Jean Baudrillard. For Baudrillard, the distinction between 'real' and 'false' needs upon which Marxist economics is based collapses as consumption becomes *primarily* about individuals and groups using commodities like a language to make out taste and status *differences* between themselves. In his later work, commodities and signs are seen to merge completely as the opposition between what things look like and what is really going on begins to dissolve in the 'hyper-reality' of the media age. This process – what he calls 'implosion of the real' – supposedly displaces all models of rational critique. It is no longer possible for us to see through the appearances of, for instance, a 'free market' to the structuring 'real relations' underneath (e.g. class conflict and the expropriation by capital of surplus value). Instead, signs begin increasingly to take on a life of their own, referring not to a real world outside themselves but to their own 'reality' – the system that produces the signs.

It is at this point that Baudrillard grafts a global theory of postmodernity onto a global theory of cultural postmodern*ism* to produce a scenario which is well and truly apocalyptic – 'fatal', to use Baudrillard's words. In this world of surfaces TV takes over from the real as the place where real things happen only if they are screened (real things here include profits made on the screens of computer terminals by dealers juggling prices on the international money and commodity futures markets). In such a thoroughly *imaged* universe – the world of Reagan–Gorbachev photocalls, Thatcher visits to Gdansk and HRH's *Vision of Britain* – 'politics' becomes largely an adjunct of PR and showbiz even when the etiquette is breached (e.g. the attack on a newscaster on air by lesbian activists to publicize opposition to Clause 28). Rational critique and the will to change the world are replaced by what he calls the 'ecstasy of communication' – a state characterized by 'banal seduction' and 'mindless fascination' where any kind of judgement – not just artistic but moral and political – becomes impossible.

Clearly a great deal more is at stake in the apocalypse laid out by Baudrillard than a shift in the mode of production. But it is also clear that he offers a kind of picture of *some* of the changes that make up new times.

However much we want to resist the chilly extremism of this kind of analysis, it is clear that the 'information revolution' has implications far beyond the extension of financial services and the further diminution of our civil rights. The sheer volume and variety of information may conceal the fact that the shifts are qualitative as well as quantitative. One result of the print boom for instance, associated with desk-top publishing, Wapping and the end of hot-metal trade unionism, is that more and more publications compete for advertising revenue tied to increasingly fragmented and specialized markets. Manic competition at the bottom end of the tabloid market has led editors to abandon the distinction between entertainment and information, as TV soap gossip crowds out 'hard news' on the front pages. Although the tendency is not new, in recent years it has been intensified to the point where hype creates its own 'reality' so that some of the dailies now carry the 'Aliens From Outer Space' stories pioneered in the notorious *Sunday Sport*.

What sense would an orthodox Left analysis make of this decline of standards? It would probably begin by mentioning the circulation war, perhaps citing American precedents. It might go on to condemn the 'Aliens Turned Our Son Into An Olive' style of story as degraded entertainment, even as part of the ideology of authoritarian populism in which all 'aliens' (gay men, the loony Left, black youths, the IRA, acid house fans, etc.) are defined as a threat to the 'family of the nation', as part of the unassimilable enemy within.

But such analyses would be inadequate in so far as they remain tied to an outmoded 'economy of truth'. They fail to acknowledge how far the ground has shifted. For what is also at stake in such mutations of the codes of journalism is the whole 'information order' upon which meaningful debates over issues of this kind rely. The survival of the public realm – a forum of debate where the conflicting interests and ideologies struggle to define reality – in turn depends upon the public's ability to discriminate *in the last analysis* between what is true and what is not. If the generalized scepticism towards mainstream media reportage moves beyond issues of 'fact' and interpretation – (what happened when, where and why and what does it mean?) – to question the line between truth and lies itself then the whole 'economy of truth' collapses.

The idea of a verifiable information order, however precarious and shifting, however subject to negotiation and contestation by competing ideologies, does not survive the transition to this version of new times. After all, it is not as if anybody is really being asked to believe in aliens. Instead they are being invited to relinquish the right to believe in the verifiability of public truths *per se*. Such a stretching of the codes of journalistic licence beyond the limits established in the early days of the mass-circulation press may free the readers from any obligation to believe in the bourgeois myth of disinterested truth by offering itself as a kind of joke in which the reader is invited to participate (the 'joke' is how low can we go?), but its potential dangers are also pretty clear: today aliens from Mars kidnap joggers, yesterday Auschwitz did not happen, tomorrow who cares what happens? Here the so-called 'depthlessness' of the postmodern era extends beyond the integration of signs and commodities into saleable 'lifestyle packages', beyond the tendency of the media to feed more and more greedily off each other, to affect the very function and status of information itself.

The struggle over the meaning of modernity, national identity and the past offered a significant point of tension in Britain throughout the late 1980s – a point of tension which is there to be cracked open in the current controversy around the role of design and architecture in British life. Thatcherite definitions of 'Britishness', national heritage and national pride have sought to align the 'shape of the future' with a selective image of the past so that even the disruptions and upheavals of today's 'communications revolution' are drawn into the charmed circle of national tradition through the analogy with the Industrial Revolution and the Victorian railway boom (the connection is especially pointed in London were the great nineteenth-century railway termini are being redeveloped as luxury hotel, leisure centre, office and shopping mall complexes).

At the same time, within architecture where the term was first popularized, 'postmodernism' has been used to describe developments as different in conception and appearance as the nostalgic, neo-Georgian repro-kitsch of Quinlan Terry, a planned nineteen-storey grey, pink and red office block in the City of London and the 'discreet' horizontal 'groundscrapers', huge, lateral, deep-plan dealing rooms located nearby, sometimes concealed behind the original facades of a block of 'historic buildings'. 'Postmodernism' here has functioned largely as a cover for unrestrained development for profit. Some of the attacks on modernism are literally reactionary – *anti-* rather than *post*modern. Some grow out of an allegedly populist challenge to the arrogance and authoritarianism of Modern Movement architecture while others use style and fashion rather than function as a metaphor for the shift out of Fordism into new times. It is significant that whereas the most celebrated examples of Modern Movement buildings tended to be office blocks rather than housing schemes, the examples of *post*modernism most frequently cited in the architectural journals are supermarkets, shopping malls and leisure developments. In fact, the 'postmodern city' may well be the product of what David Harvey calls 'voodoo economics' where finance capital moves in to occupy the hollowed-out centres left by a declining manufacturing sector with the leisure, heritage and retail industries providing architectural light relief. To counter the argument that the culture of postmodernism heralds an entirely new epoch it is worth considering the sober fact that some of the most feted examples of 'modern' *and* 'postmodern' architecture have been banks; from Mies van der Rohe's designs which helped to transform the skyline of Chicago's financial sector in the late 1930s to Richard Rogers' Lloyds building or Terence Farrell's designs for the revamped City of London.

What is clear is that in Britain the tower block has become a powerful symbol of a superseded socialist era. In the current debates, the tower block's collapse is used to point up the weaknesses of that other larger edifice – the postwar corporate state, with its mixed economy, its embattled health services, its strained, unlikely social and political consensus forged in the white heat of Harold Wilson's modernizing techno-jargon. The acquisition a few years ago by Thatcher of a neo-Georgian Barratt home in an 'executive estate' in Dulwich marks the ideological cut-off point from failed utopia to new realism, from council-house Britain to 'enterprise culture', from stately-home and country-house conservatism to the tougher, 'fairer' contours of the 'property-owning democracy'.

Yet beyond all the ideologizing, nobody – not even architects – would claim that the original 1960s' tower blocks were ever widely popular. There is a vast literature within sociology devoted to the librium addiction and loss of community associated with Britain's 'vertical streets'. The enthusiastic responses to Prince Charles' vision of Britain as first and foremost a landscape to be conserved rather than designed, testified to the strength of popular feeling on the issue. The affirmation within certain types of postmodernism of the particular against the general; the decorative, the 'fantastic' and the 'aspirational' against the 'rational', the 'formal' and the 'academic'; the desirability of maintaining continuity with the past, the reverence for the 'human scale', are all themes that can be articulated to a more imaginative and democratic, more innovative and pluralist version of socialism. In the words of Alexei Sayle: 'No more living 200 feet in the air in a thing that looks like an off-set lathe or a baked bean canner.'

Some theorists go further and claim the *end* of history and political agency altogether. According to Baudrillard, for example, the masses were the invention of the modern period: one of the myths used to legitimate Fordist projects as diverse as 'the dictatorship of the proletariat', parliamentary democracy and selling soap powder. The decline of Fordism exposes the myth of the masses as an active force so completely that we live today – to quote the title of one of Baudrillard's books – literally 'in the *shadow* of the silent majorities' so that all meanings 'implode' into the 'black hole' left by the masses' disappearance.

Postmodern pessimism of this kind is symptomatic of the crisis of a particular intellectual formation (male, white, European) shaped in the crucible of student politics in 1968. The 'end of history' argument can be safely written off as the product of a bunker mentality spawned among a generation of liberally educated 'critical' theorists by the disappointment that set in after the Road to Damascus radicalizations of 1968. Institutionally located intellectuals are marginalized at the best of times and are likely to feel even more redundant in the face of 1980s' 'new realism', new vocationalism, and 'enterprise culture'. But the legacy of 1968 is, of course, itself contradictory. The student uprisings highlighted the decline of workerism, productivism and hierarchical, centralized party politics. But they also heralded the growing importance of cultural and identity politics, the politics of gender, race and sexuality, the ecology and autonomy movements. In the light of these new cultural and political forms and the emergent communities of interest attached to them, the pertinent question becomes not *has* history but rather exactly *whose* history is finished?

What is of course so often forgotten in the hype surrounding postmodernism today is that there is a tradition of cultural socialism closer to home that is rooted in a similar scepticism towards the notion of the 'masses'. The late Raymond Williams always insisted that the 'mass' was a category intellectuals tended to reserve contemptuously for other people, never for themselves. And if, after all is said and done, we still have need of meta-narratives then *The Long Revolution* (Williams, 1963) may ultimately prove more *useful*, more progressive and empowering than the one that frames the theory of postmodernity because it acknowledges the fact that faith and idealism are themselves part of the historical process, vital constituents of the political *will*. It is also possible that something like a sociology of aspiration might grow out of the less totalizing approach to 'ordinary people' that Williams recommends.

One of the features of post-Fordist production is the leading role given to market research, packaging and presentation. While it does not literally *produce* the social, it is none the less the case that marketing provided the dominant and most pervasive classifications of 'social types' in the 1980s (the yuppie is the most obvious example). We use these categories as a kind of social shorthand even if we are reluctant to find ourselves reflected in them. We live in a world and in bodies which are deeply scored by the power relations of race and class, sexuality and gender but we also live – whether or not we know it consciously – in a world of style-setters, innovators, sloanes, preppies, empty nesters (working couples with grown up families), dinkies (dual-income-no-kids), casuals, sensibles, the constrained majority, and today's prime targets, the pre-teens and woofies (well-off-older-folk).

These are the types outlined in commercial lifestyling and 'psycho-graphics' – forms of research which do not present descriptions of living, breathing individuals so much as hypothetical 'analogues' of 'aspirational clusters'. In other words the new intensive but speculative forms of market research are designed to offer a social map of desire which can be used to determine where exactly which products should be 'pitched' and 'niched'. All these types could no doubt be translated back into the old language (it would perhaps be relatively easy to return them to the axis of social class) but everything specific would be lost in the translation.

It is clear that such research methods and the marketing initiatives associated with them have been developed precisely to cut across the old social–sexual polarities. The parameters are designed to be transcultural and transnational (the spread of 'psychographics' in the UK is linked to the drive to go pan-European in preparation for 1992). We may find such forms of knowledge immoral, objectionable or sinister – a waste of time and resources which is unforgiveable in a world where people are starving and in a country where people are still sleeping in the streets – but the fact is that they do actively create and sustain one *version* of the social. They depend for their success on the accurate outlining and anticipation (through observation and interviews with 'target' subjects) not just of what (some) people think they want but of *what they would like to be*. A sociology of aspiration might begin by combining the considerable *critical* and *diagnostic* resources available within existing versions of sociology and cultural studies with the *descriptive* and *predictive* knowledge available within the new intensive market research to get a more adequate picture of what *everybody* says they want and what they want to be in all its radical plurality. The challenge would then be to produce and distribute the required goods and services more efficiently, and equitably than the opposition. Such a mix of traditional academic/ social work and commercial/marketing knowledge functions would take the Left beyond the ghetto of 'miserabilism' to which it is regularly consigned by the loony Right. Such a shift would require what certain forms of postmodernism recommend: a scepticism towards imposed general, 'rational' solutions; a relaxation of the old critical and judgemen-tal postures although it emphatically does not necessitate a retreat from first principles and primary objectives: a commitment to social justice, equality of opportunity, and social welfare. The identity and faith on which Left politics have traditionally been founded remain in place. But beyond that a new kind of politics – as flexible and responsive to new demands and initiatives as the software that powers post-Fordist production – will have to be envisioned. It may well be true that the two great collective identities through which the masses came together to 'make history' in the last 200 years – the first associated with nation, the second with class – are breaking down today in the overdeveloped world. But new 'emancipation narratives' are being written round collectives other than the imaginary community of nation or the international brotherhood of socialist *man*.

Bibliography

Appignanesi, L. and Benninton, G. (eds) (1986) *Postmodernism*. ICA Documents 4, Institute of Contemporary Arts, London.

Baudrillard, J. (1979) *The Mirror of Production*. Telos Press.

Baudrillard, J. (1981) *For a Critique of the Political Economy of the Sign*. Telos Press.

Baudrillard, J. (1983) *Simulations*. Semiotext(e).

Baudrillard, J. (1984) *In the Shadow of the Silent Majorities*. Semiotext(e).

Baudrillard, J. (1988) *America*. Verso.

Berman, M. (1983) *All That Is Solid Melts Into Air*. Simon and Schuster.

Foster, H. (ed.) (1985) *Postmodern Culture*. Pluto.

Harvey, D. (1989) *The Condition of Postmodernity*. Oxford: Blackwell.

Lyotard, J. F. (1984) *The Postmodern Condition: A Report on Knowledge*. Manchester: Manchester University Press.

Morris, M. (1988) *The Pirate's Fianceé: Feminism Reading Postmodernism*. Verso.

Poster, M. (ed.) (1988) *Jean Baudrillard: Selected Writings*. Oxford: Polity.

Williams, R. (1963) *The Long Revolution*. Harmondsworth: Penguin.

13

Some remarks on informal work, social polarization and the social structure

R.E. Pahl

Some years ago I raised a number of questions about the role and function of various forms of work outside employment. In particular I urged that strategies of 'getting by' needed to be explored in order to see whether those forced or expelled from the constraints of wage labour had alternative work strategies or ways of getting by that might compensate them, either by providing opportunities to exercise skills that were less in demand in the labour market or by getting money and other rewards informally (Pahl, 1980). Responding to my own challenge, I undertook a major research project – the results of which have been published over the past four years (Pahl, 1984, 1985a, 1987a, 1987b; Pahl and Wallace, 1985, 1988; Wallace and Pahl, 1986). Others have documented for Europe more generally the growth of 'concealed employment' (OECD, 1986c) and the 'shadow economy' (Gaertner and Wenig, 1985; Smith 1986). The debate in Europe has been substantially advanced as a result of the work of these and other researchers (Inchiesta, 1986). American scholars by contrast, have suffered from a certain degree of parochialism and a lack of theoretical sophistication: even as recently as 1987 authors of an article in the *American Journal of Sociology* bizarrely used employment in small firms as a surrogate measure of the informal sector (Portes and Sassen-Koob, 1987).

However, it is generally well understood that the term 'informal economy' is an all-embracing and imprecise term that can include domestic work in and around the house, carried out without cash payments by household and non-household members, as well as criminal or quasicriminal activities at the place of employment and elsewhere. Self-employed people very often have the most scope to work 'off the books' themselves or to employ others on a 'cash in hand' basis. Much of this activity is designed to avoid paying value added tax, national insurance and income tax. It also saves substantial time and paperwork.[1]

Reprinted by permission of Hodder and Stoughton Ltd from *International Journal of Urban and Regional Research*, (June 1988), 12(2): 247–66.

Many have commented on the growth of the self-provisioning work that is based on expanding home and car ownership and the availability of new tools and 'do-it-yourself' products that democratize skills (Gershuny, 1983; Pahl, 1984). Until the last twenty-five years or so, most people would have used specialist craftsmen to carry out tasks such as painting, decorating and minor building works, yet now a variety of new products enables many more people to do such work for themselves. They may or may not save money; their calculations are not necessarily strictly economic, since the very act of doing the work for oneself may provide satisfaction, so that even if the job takes longer, it is done 'better'. Insofar as this satisfaction in self-provisioning is non-pecuniary, then it is unlikely that it can be readily subcontracted to others. Part of the pleasure is to enjoy one's own craftsmanship or home-baked/grown produce.

There is also much informal work arising out of the tasks involving time, effort and, sometimes, money that are done for members of a family, friends and neighbours for which no payment is expected or required in direct response, but which may imply some specific or generalized form of reciprocity in the future (Sik, 1988). Such activity provides the threads that make up the rich tapestry of life and can extend from exchanging drinks or baby-sitting to the use of more complex skills, such as coaching a child for an examination or repairing the engine of a car.[2]

This is not the appropriate context to present a comprehensive typology of informal work, although that would certainly serve a useful purpose in avoiding over-enthusiastic generalizations based on limited studies in specific social and geographical contexts. However, listing different forms of work simply for the sake of it is unlikely to further substantially any scholarly purpose. It is more important to record significant empirical variation and then move on to more substantive and theoretical issues (Pahl, 1988).

The cumulation of all forms of work

My purpose in this chapter is to focus on the distributional consequences of informal or unrecorded work, in so far as they may affect the system of stratification in the society as a whole. I intend to argue that the distributional consequences of the pattern of informal work in industrial societies is to reinforce, rather than to reduce or to reflect, contemporary patterns of inequality.

However, it must be acknowledged that many commentators continue to argue otherwise. First, there is an assumption that unemployed people are able to mitigate their circumstances by resources gained in the 'black economy'. For example, it has been claimed that 'with high unemployment more and more people are getting caught up in the web of the underground economy' (Parker, 1982: 33). This is in danger of becoming a social scientists' folk myth. It reappears in the Portes and Sassen-Koob article cited above where the authors confidently assert, with absolutely no supporting evidence, 'Efforts of displaced workers to escape chronic unemployment and to supplement paltry official relief expand the supply of labour available for informal activities' (Portes and Sassen-Koob, 1987: 55). Another view focuses less on the black economy but more on the domestic economy or what I have elsewhere termed self-provisioning (Pahl, 1984; Pahl and Wallace, 1985). It has been asserted that as the demand for labour is reduced in the formal economy, more time will be available for people 'to produce more goods and services in the domestic economy' (Rose, 1985: 33). Third and finally, there is the claim that, for poor working-class households in particular, there is a kind of social capital in more established neighbourhoods and communities, which enables those in misfortune to be supported by others who have resources of time, money, goods and services to bestow on their more deserving comrades. Such assumptions are based on putative collectivist and solidaristic tendencies among both kin and non-kin, brought about by long-standing social relationships that have been cemented through propinquity. While there may be some discussion about how far such community supports have been eroded by urban renewal and consumerism, many commentators still emphasize this response to adversity. Thus, Lowenthal, writing in the context of cities in the United States, asserts that:

> although needs may go unmet and thus give rise to problems such as poor health and substandard housing . . . many needs are provided for not through money income, but by the social networks and mutual aid systems that people participate in. (Lowenthal, 1981: 11)

These three putative responses of the unemployed or disadvantaged, namely in engaging in remunerated activity in the 'black economy', becoming more active in the domestic economy and becoming more vigorous in their use of local support networks, can be adduced severally or collectively to justify more punitive attitudes towards unemployed people in Britain and other countries committed to monetarist or Reagonomic economic policies. Thus, when the British government issued a discussion document on employment, *The Times* commented as follows in its leader column:

> Everyone of us knows from our own experience that there is a huge unofficial economy at work, much of it concentrated in the labour market where it makes a mockery of the raw unemployment figures. Many of those people who are on the dole are in part-time work and we all know it. That explains why, though 'everyone cares' as the white paper states, nobody seems to care very much. There may as yet be insufficient public understanding of the origin and nature of Britain's structural unemployment, but there is a universal knowledge and understanding that the black economy, and the high level of benefit, between them seem to make it all tolerable. (*The Times*, 29 March 1985)

Such assertions by leader writers, politicians, economists and others are rarely supported by empirical evidence (Pahl, 1985b). In addition to my own work on the Isle of Sheppey between 1977 and 1986, other studies in Brighton, Kidderminster, South Wales and elsewhere provide strong contrary evidence (cited in Pahl, 1987a, 1987b). Not only are unemployed people *less* likely to own their own dwelling and cars, coming as they do disproportionately from the less-skilled occupations, but they are also much more likely to be reported on by their neighbours. In order to do much of the self-provisioning and minor building work that is done, people need, in addition to free time, tools, transport and social contacts. Informal work, unsurprisingly, requires informal contacts and these are more likely to be found at work or after a good evening's drinking. The unemployed cannot, be definition, get access to the first and, being poor, cannot risk getting involved in the second. The local working-class community may be less of a source of support and more a context for informal spying and reporting as resentful neighbours are more concerned to hold everyone down to a common level (Seabrook, 1982).

Detailed evidence to support this position has now been published quite extensively, and I feel that it is possible to quote from a previous work without further substantiation – we conclude:

> That rather than one form of work being a substitute for another (e.g. work on the side substituting for formal employment), there appeared to be a process of polarization which resulted in those in formal employment being *more* likely to do more self-provisioning and informal 'black work' as well. This cumulation of certain forms of work resulted in some very busy productive households at one pole and, at the other pole, households unable to engage in little more than communal reciprocity and scavenging – indeed some households could not even engage in these forms of work. (Wallace and Pahl, 1986: 120)

My argument, therefore, is that certain households are becoming increasingly more fortunate, whereas others are becoming increasingly more deprived. Thus, to put it positively, some – but certainly not all – households with 'core' workers and other members of the household also in employment (either full- or part-time) are able to achieve and to maintain high household incomes and substantial affluence, despite the individually weak labour market position of some of their members. In very broad terms, the decline of male full-time employment in manufacturing has been offset by growth of female part-time employment not only in services but in manufacturing industry also. These low wages may be legally low because the hours worked are so few or illegally low because the individual is being paid in cash and has no firm base on which to claim more. Such part-time workers are less likely to be in households headed by an unemployed worker and much more likely to be in households in which there is an established full-time worker. This coming together of the core and peripheral workers in bed, if not in the union movement, must do much to defuse social conflict. Those already in employment are in the best position to help other members of their family find employment and, with their multi-earner affluence are more likely to own their own homes, own cars, boats, holiday homes and so forth. The more goods and property they own, the more extra work can and needs to be done. Men in certain occupations are particularly privileged. Those on shift work or whose job allows them more free time during the day or at certain times of the year are particularly well placed. Firemen and university teachers are two occupations well set to provide opportunities for moonlighting. Similarly, some of those in part-time employment, who contribute to a relatively comfortable collective household income, can enhance their standard of living by doing small jobs for cash – cleaning, having a stall in an antique market, caring for the elderly or for handicapped people for which they get paid, possibly in cash, and so on.

Once it is established that a proportion of middle-class households increase their incomes and enhance their lifestyles by pulling all forms of work into their households, the question then arises as to the wider social implications of these tendencies.

If increased household real incomes are a function of multiple earners at a particular stage in the life-cycle, then whilst certainly not all may benefit from this period of affluence, it could be argued that there need be no long-term shift in the stratification order. If, however, this period of affluence, even if relatively short-lived, enables households to buy a house they would otherwise not be able to afford, or to buy a bigger house, or a holiday home, or to accumulate capital through astute operations in the housing market or in any other way accumulate substantial inheritable resources, then the households not able to enjoy this period of advantage may suffer a longer term setback. I return to this point below.

The indications are now that households based on 'core' workers are permanently advantaged throughout the life-cycle and the cumulation of further component wages (that is wages inadequate to support a household, even a single person on his or her own, but which provide sufficient incentive for those in households that already have other earners for such wages to be acceptable as components of those households' income) and involvement in all forms of work leads to increasing household privilege and advantage. Those in employment are most likely to find employment for other members of their households and, likewise, in households without earners in employment it is less likely that members will hear of job opportunities (Cooke, 1987; Payne, 1987).

There are indications that these work-rich households are not necessarily segregated in islands of privilege where job opportunities are more favourable. Between September 1981 and September 1984, the number of males in full-time employment in the United Kingdom declined absolutely by 580,000. However, in the case of female *part-time* jobs there was a net growth of 77,000 new jobs and this increase took place remarkably evenly throughout the country (Department of Employment, 1987: Table 1). Every region showed a substantial increase in female part-time work and, as A. R. Townsend has shown, even the regions that overall showed little or no employment growth had pockets where there was quite substantial growth. By carrying out his analysis at the level of 380 travel to work areas (TTWAS), he shows that whilst employment rose in only 115 of these TTWAS, female employment rose in 166, part-time employment in 227, service sector employment in 220 and jobs in insurance, banking and services in 303 (MSC, 1986: 12). Thus, assuming that female part-time workers are almost entirely contributors of component wages to households, then those that become the more privileged multi-earner households (i.e. relative to those with only one modest 'family' wage) are spread reasonably evenly throughout the country. The polarization between households engaging in all forms of work and the households that are work-deprived is as likely to be within the same street as between regions or areas of the country. These new patterns of social and economic advantage and disadvantage appear more fragmented than has been the case in the past. There are geographical variations to be sure but these are possibly of declining significance, although research in this area is controversial (Hall, 1987).

These work-rich households can be easily observed on local authority housing estates (although they are not, of course, confined there) since, typically, they have bought their dwellings and have changed the visual style of the frontage. There may be a different style of rendering, a new front door or porch and perhaps new windows and roof tiles. Clearly these are an asset that are likely to produce considerable capital gains. Such houses are bought at a substantial discount – long-established tenants may have paid in 1986 no more than £10,000 for a house worth between £20,000 and £30,000 or more. After a period of five years the house may be sold on the open market, or passed on to children. This is a substantial advantage and, as the Sheppey survey showed, the work-rich households combine formal and informal work to create a new affluent lifestyle which is likely to draw them apart from friends and neighbours (Pahl, 1984: Chapters 11 and 12). However, it must also be recognized that in areas of economic decline homeownership can constitute a burden where some houses may be, in effect, unsaleable and the mortgage repayments could become a serious financial burden.

This new division between relatively rich and poor households of wage labourers is not based on the specialized craft skills that created a labour aristocracy in the nineteenth century. I am not describing a new labour aristocracy defined solely in terms of individual or collective position in the sphere of production. The new privileged households are a product of a number of distinct elements which may include all or a selection of the following:

1 a core worker with flexible skills in modern, non-smoke-stack industries, or a worker with security of tenure and with substantial free time to engage in a second job or informal work – on Sheppey, stevedores and firemen fit this category well;

Table 1

a) Social class of head of household by proportion of multiple earners England and Wales (10% Sample) 1981 (economically active and retired heads).

		Percent of multiple earners		
		1	2	columns 1 and 2
			Earners	
Social class		Two only	Three +	
I	Professional occupations	40	8	48
II	Intermediate occupations	38	11	49
IIIN	Skilled workers – non-manual	34	10	44
IIIM	Skilled workers – manual	37	15	52
IV	Partly skilled occupations	32	14	46
V	Unskilled occupations	28	14	42
All economically active and retired heads		34	12	46

b) As above, but taking as *n* the total number of households with at least one earner.

	Earners		
	Two only	Three +	
I	44	9	53
II	44	13	57
IIIN	41	12	53
IIIM	42	18	60
IV	39	17	56
V	35	17	52
All households with at least one earner	42	15	57

Source: OPCS Census, 1981: *Household and Family Composition England and Wales* (10 per cent sample), Table 8.

2 a partner also in employment, whether full- or part-time;
3 other household members in employment, whether full- or part-time, contributing component wages to the household income;
4 the household lives in an owner-occupied dwelling;
5 members of the household have individually or collectively substantial skills, enabling them to engage in self-provisioning for themselves and for neighbouring households. This improves the quality of their lives, saves money and helps in building up stocks of reciprocity with friends and relatives.

These advantages may provide greater benefit in the declining or depressed regions of the north of Britain. The cost of living is likely to be less, so that other things being equal, a given household income provides more opportunities.

This emphasis on the *household* as the salient social and economic unit, rather than the individual, has important implications for contemporary social structure. Whilst the occupational structure based on individual jobs typically produces a hierarchically structured pyramid of advantage, these new tendencies allow a sizeable proportion of households incorporating low or modest incomes to have a higher position in the hierarchy as a result of their collective household work practices. Overall, 34 per cent of all households have two earners and a further 12 per cent have three or more earners. Indeed, if one takes those households with no economically active members out of the calculation, then 57 per cent of all households are multiple-earner households (see Table 1). Amongst those households with multiple earners, social class III (skilled-manual) is the category most likely to have multiple earners with as many as 60 per cent in 1981. Working-class households are no less likely than middle-class households to have three or more earners. The high proportions in the professional and intermediate occupations is curious; it is to be expected that unmarried, economically active working-class children will remain in their parental home, whereas one might have expected their middle-class counterparts to be in higher education or (if they are in employment) to be sharing accommodation with their peers. It is crucially important to remember that the processes that create modest affluence in the middle of the social structure are a necessary means of getting by at the bottom of the social structure. Where the 'chief earner' has a low income, the extra earnings provided by component wages may still do no more than raise the income of such households to the level of the single incomes of more privileged 'core' workers.

The effect of this cumulation of advantage in some households through a benign spiral of mutually reinforcing elements contrasts with the malign spiral to be found in neighbouring households. The combination of time, tools and technology leads to the more high-paid multiple-earner households gaining even more. Paradoxically, the growth of sophisticated tools for 'do-it-yourself' enthusiasts has reduced the money-earning capacity of those who have manual skills but have little income. Those without specialized craft skills but with relatively high household incomes can buy the technology and do a better job. Informal work outside employment is thus *more* dependent on work in employment to provide the necessary income. This helps to underline the Matthew effect: to them that hath, more is given, whereas to them that have little, even that which they have is taken away. This process is severely accentuated by the fact that those whose income is made up of state benefits, whether they be unemployed or state pensioners, get their increases based on a rise in *prices* through a formula related to the cost-of-living index – which, in recent years has provided increases of some 3 or 4 per cent per annum. Those in employment may with the support of the unions, have received increases of some 7 or 8 per cent per annum. There is thus an *annual* 3 or 4 per cent points discrepancy compounding the inequalities between those in secure employment and those on state benefits. This compounding polarization is in direct conflict with the British government's stated objective in the 1985 Green Paper on the *Reform of Social Security*, which categorically stated that *all* groups in society should have 'a share in the long-run increase in national prosperity' (Volume 3: 16). The government effectively made this impossible when, in 1979, they removed this guarantee for the poorest elements in society by abolishing the uprating formula which had hitherto been tied to earnings. By substituting a formula related only to changes in prices, the government has legislated for a scissors effect to remain permanently in British society.[3]

New divisions within the working class?

The process of polarization, based on distinctive work practices, may be reinforced by other divisions and lines of cleavage in British society. A substantial literature has emerged which has reviewed the future of the British Welfare State (Taylor-Gooby, 1987) and distinctively documents inequalities in access to housing and forms of housing tenure (Hamnett, 1984, 1987), in access to health and service facilities (Macintyre, 1986; Whitehead, 1987) and, most significantly, access to employment. After six years of Mrs Thatcher's government, an official departmental report concluded 'Unemployment . . . has now displaced old age as the main reason for low income' (DHSS, 1985: I: 13). Academic commentators, less coy in their terminology, have noted the increase in poverty. Thus Piachaud, in an authoritative review, concluded that increased unemployment has:

> far outstripped old age as the major characteristic of poverty: between 1979 and 1983 the number of people in unemployed families receiving Supplementary Benefits tripled to 2.6 million, whereas the number over pension age fell slightly to 1.9 million. . . . Extrapolating to 1987 suggests that about one million more men, one million more women, and one million more children are now living at Supplementary Benefit level than was the case in 1978. (Piachaud, 1987: 23)

Poverty is increasingly understood to be a women's issue. Taking a poverty level of 140 per cent of Supplementary Benefit, the two types of household most likely to be in poverty are elderly women living alone and lone mothers – 61 per cent in each case (Glendinning and Miller, 1987: 13–14).

Furthermore, the poor are becoming relatively poorer:

> Compared with incomes in general, SB levels have fallen considerably – for a couple on the ordinary rate from 61 per cent of personal disposable income *per capita* in 1978 to 53 per cent in 1987. . . . The overall picture since the Conservatives took office is of those dependent on SB falling further behind the rest of the population. (Piachaud, 1987: 22 and see also Townsend et al., 1987)

Core, established workers may be strengthening their position but they are proportionately declining in numbers, whereas the 'flexible' workers – that is all other workers who are not full-time permanent employees – are increasing. One estimate, based on Department of Employment Labour Force survey data, indicated that the numbers of 'flexible' workers rose by 16 per cent to 8.1 million between 1981 and 1985, whereas the permanent total fell by 6 per cent to 15.6 million. These definitions are not without their problems but, if accepted, the workforce may be neatly divided into two-thirds 'permanent' and one-third 'flexible' (Hakim, 1987a: 43).

Those in the 'flexible' sector are unlikely to get sufficient wages to support themselves and will certainly not have enough to support dependents adequately. Much of the sharp increase in married women's activity rates over the past twenty years, particularly in part-time employment, is related to the fact that their husbands are in full-time employment. Indeed, if male full-time workers become unemployed then there is a greater likelihood that their wives will also become unemployed. This is because of the way the British Supplementary Benefit system works: any earnings over £4 are deducted from the male entitlement. Thus, if before the man's unemployment the couple were earning £185 a week (£140 + £45), the extra £45 would make a substantial difference to the domestic budget. With the male chief earner unemployed there would be no incentive for his partner to continue her part-time job for a net gain of only £4 a week. This may go some way to explaining why, in 1983, only 30 per cent of unemployed male heads of households had their wives in employment against 58 per cent of males in employment (*Social Trends*, 1984: Table 4.27). Thus, peripheral workers are most likely to contribute component wages to an existing household budget rather than attempt to support a separate household on the low incomes of part-time or 'flexible' work. Flexible workers appear to have increased at much the same rate in the other nations of the European Community where the overall picture is very similar to that of Britain (Hakim, 1987b: 553).

So far we have considered the processes whereby certain 'work-rich' households can accumulate more income from a combination of different forms of employment, from more self-provisioning and from other forms of informal work as well. Money makes more money and access to employment provides more access to employment and other forms of work as well.

Notes

The first part of this chapter was originally presented at the symposium 'Wohlfahrts Produktion Zwischen Markt, Staat and Haushalt', ZiF Bielefeld, 18–20 September, 1986. The second half of the chapter, which begins with the section 'New divisions within the working class', was written in August 1987 and presented to the Sixth Urban Change and Conflict Conference, University of Kent at Canterbury. This is part of a programme of work supported by the Joseph Rowntree Memorial Trust. I am grateful to my colleague Chris Pickvance and other members of the Editorial Board for comments on an earlier draft of this paper.

1. In my own fieldwork, on the Isle of Sheppey in Kent, I came across one small factory that assembled furniture in which the owner employed no one officially. He relied

entirely on part-time labour which he paid in cash 'off the roll' of bank notes in his back pocket. It does not, of course, follow that this system is necessarily illegal. Obviously, much depends on the honesty of those involved: they may all report their payments where this is appropriate.

2. Some have put forward the suggestion that this might provide an informalization of welfare state services and hence resolve some of the current problems in maintaining adequate levels of provision in that sphere (Heinze and Olk, 1982). More recent feminist critiques have led to greater caution in making such suggestions (Ungerson, 1987).

3. This point was dramatically illustrated by Mary Goldring, an economist with very wide journalistic experience, who produced a well-researched documentary on *Two Nations on the Same Street* for the BBC in March 1987. Taking part in the programme was Bill Jordan, president of the Amalgamated Engineering Union. He was asked to account for the wage increases when a general assumption is that unions have lost much of their former power. Mr Jordan's answer, as published in *The Listener* (2 April 1987) was as follows: 'Because the workforce put pressure on them. While we hear about the reduction in official strikes, the records will show that the number of unofficial stoppages are still running very high. If you don't believe it, just look at the fact that earnings are growing now at about 7.75 per cent. Now at an inflation rate of something like half that figure, that tells you what sort of pressures are being exerted.'

Bibliography

Auletta, K. (1982) *The Underclass*. New York: Random House.

Cooke, K. (1987) 'The withdrawal from paid work of the wives of unemployed men: a review of research', *Journal of Social Policy* 16: 371–82.

Courtney, G. *Isle of Sheppey Study*. Technical Report. London: SCPR.

Dahrendorf, R. (1987) 'The erosion of citizenship and its consequences for us all', *New Statesman*, 12 June.

Department of Employment (1987) 'The 1984 census of employment and revised employment estimates', *Employment Gazette*, January: 31–53.

DHSS (1985) *The Reform of Social Security*, Vol. 1–4. Cmnd 9517-20. London: HMSO.

Gaertner, W. and Wenig, A. (eds) (1985) *The Economics of the Shadow Economy*. Heidelberg: Springer Verlag.

Gershuny, J. I. (1983) *Social Innovation and the Division of Labour*. Oxford: Oxford University Press.

Glendinning, C. and Miller, J. (eds) (1987) *Women and Poverty in Britain*. Brighton: Wheatsheaf Books.

Hakim, C. (1987a) 'Homeworking in Britain', *Employment Gazette*, 95: 92–104. Reprinted in R. E. Pahl (ed.) 1988.

Hakim, C. (1987b) 'Trends in the flexible workforce', *Employment Gazette*, 95: 549–60.

Hall, P. (1987) 'The anatomy of job creation: nations, regions and cities in the 1960s and 1970s', *Regional Studies*, 21: 95–106.

Halsey, A. H. (1987) 'Social trends since World War II', *Social Trends*, 17: 11–19. London: HMSO.

Hamnett, C. (1984) 'Housing the two nations: socio-tenurial polarization in England and Wales 1961–1981', *Urban Studies*, 43: 389–405.

Hamnett, C. (1987) 'A tale of two cities: socio-tenurial polarisation in London and the South East 1966–1981', *Environment and Planning A*, 19: 537–56.

Heinze, R. and Olk, T. (1982) 'Development of the informal economy', *Futures*, June: 189–204.

Inchiesta, (1986) *Economia Informale, Strategie Familiari e Mezzogiorno*. No. 74. October–December.

Lidbetter, E. J. (1933) *Heredity and the Social Problem Group*, Vol. 1. London: Edward Arnold.

Lockwood, D. (1981) 'The weakest link in the chain: some comments on the marxist theory of action', *Research in the Sociology of Work*, 1: 435–81.

Lowenthal, M. (1981) 'Non-market transactions in an urban community', in S. Henry (ed.), *Can I Have It in Cash?* London: Astragal Books.

Macintyre, S. (1986) 'The patterning of health by social position in contemporary Britain: directions for sociological research', *Social Science in Medicine*, 23: 393–415.

Macnicol, J. (1987) 'In pursuit of the underclass', *Journal of Social Policy*, 16: 293–318.

McMahon, P. J. and Tschetter, J. H. (1986) 'The declining middle class: a further analysis', *Monthly Labour Review*, 109: 22–7.

Missiakoulis, S., Pahl, R. E. and Taylor-Gooby, P. (1986) 'Households, work and politics: some implications of the division of labour in formal and informal production', *International Journal of Sociology and Social Policy*, 6: 28–40.

Morris, L. P. (1985a) 'Local social networks and domestic organisation', *Sociological Review*, 33: 2.

Morris, L. P. (1985b) 'Renegotiation of the domestic division of labour', in B. Roberts et al., (eds) 1985.

MSC (1986) *Labour Market Quarterly Report*, June.

OECD (1986a) *Labour Market Flexibility*. Report of the Group of Experts, Paris: OECD.

OECD (1986b) *Flexibility in the Labour Market: Technical Report*. Paris: OECD.

OECD (1986c) *Employment Outlook*. Paris: OECD.

Pahl, R. E. (1980) 'Employment, work and the domestic division of labour', *International Journal of Urban and Regional Research*, 4: 1–20.

Pahl, R. E. (1984) *Divisions of Labour*. Oxford: Basil Blackwell.

Pahl, R. E. (1985a) 'The restructuring of capital, the local political economy and household work strategies', in D. Gregory and J. Urry (eds), *Social Relations and Spatial Structures*. London: Macmillan.

Pahl, R. E. (1985b) 'The politics of work', *The Political Quarterly*, 50: 331–45.

Pahl, R. E. (1987a) 'A comparative approach to the study of the informal economy'. Paper presented to the ASA Annual Convention, Chicago.

Pahl, R. E. (1987b) 'Does jobless mean workless? Unemployment and informal work', *Annals of The American Academy of Political and Social Science*, 493: 36–46.

Pahl, R. E. (1988) *On Work: Historical, Comparative and Theoretical Approaches*. Oxford: Basil Blackwell.

Pahl, R. E. and Wallace, C. D. (1985) 'Household work strategies in an economic recession', in N. Redclift and E. Mingione (eds), *Beyond Employment*. Oxford: Basil Blackwell.

Pahl, R. E. and Wallace, C. D. (1988) 'Neither angels in marble nor rebels in red: privatisation and working-class consciousness', in D. Rose (ed.), *Social Stratification and Economic Change*. London: Hutchinson.

Parker, H. (1982) 'Social security foments the black economy', *Journal of Economic Affairs*, 3.

Payne, J. (1987) 'Does unemployment run in families?', *Sociology*, 21: 199–214.

Piachaud, D. (1987) 'The growth of poverty', in A. Walker and C. Walker (eds), *The Growing Divide: A Social Audit 1979–1987*. London: Child Poverty Action Group.

Portes, A. and Sassen-Koob, S. (1987) 'Making it underground: comparative material on the informal sector in western market economies', *American Journal of Sociology*, 93: 30–61.

Roberts, B., Gaillie, D. and Finnegan, R. (eds) (1985) *New Approaches to Economic Life*. Manchester: Manchester University Press.

Rose, R. (1985) 'Getting by in three economies: the resources of the official, unofficial and domestic economies', in J. E. Lane (ed.), *State and Market*. London: Sage. Also available as a pamphlet from Department of Politics, University of Strathclyde.

Runciman, W. G. (1974) 'How divided is Britain', *New Society*, 23 May.

Saunders, P. (1986) *Social Theory and the Urban Question*. 2nd edition. London: Hutchinson.

Sik, E. (1988) 'The reciprocal exchange of labour in Hungary', in Pahl, 1988.

Smith, S. (1986) *Britain's Shadow Economy*. Oxford: Clarendon Press.

Taylor-Gooby, P. (1987) 'The future of the British welfare state: public attitudes, citizenship and social policy under the Conservative governments of the 1980s'. Paper presented at the conference on The Welfare State: Functions, Critiques and Alternatives, University of Salamanca, July. Mimeo, University of Kent at Canterbury.

Townsend, P. et al. (1987) *Poverty and Labour in London*. London: Low Pay Unit.

Ungerson, C. (1987) *Policy is Personal: Sex, Gender and Informal Care*. London: Tavistock.

Wallace, C. D. (1984) *Informal Work in Two Sheppey Neighbourhoods*. Final Report to the ESRC. Appendix II. Grant No. G/00/23/0036.

Wallace, C. D. and Pahl, R. (1986) 'Polarisation, unemployment and all forms of work', in S. Allen et al. (eds), *The Experience of Unemployment*. London: Macmillan.

Whitehead, M. (1987) *The Health Divide*. London: Health Education Council.

14

Lifestyle and consumer culture

Mike Featherstone

The term 'lifestyle' is currently in vogue. While the term has a more restricted sociological meaning in reference to the distinctive style of life of specific groups (Weber, 1968; Sobel, 1982; Rojek, 1985), within contemporary consumer culture it connotes individuality, self-expression, and a stylistic self-consciousness. One's body, clothes, speech, leisure pastimes, eating and drinking preferences, home, car, choice of holidays, etc. are to be regarded as indicators of the individuality of taste and sense of style of the owner/consumer. In contrast to the designation of the 1950s as an era of grey conformism, a time of *mass* consumption, changes in production techniques, market segmentation and consumer demand for a wide range of products, are often regarded as making possible greater choice (the management of which itself becomes an art form) not only for youth of the post-1960s generation, but increasingly for the middle aged and the elderly. Three phrases from Stuart and Elizabeth Ewen's *Channels of Desire* (1982: 249–51), which they see as symptomatic of the recent tendencies within consumer culture, come to mind here: 'Today there is no fashion: there are only *fashions*'; 'No rules, only choices'; 'Everyone can be anyone.' What does it mean to suggest that long-held fashion codes have been violated, that there is a war against conformity, a surfeit of difference which results in a loss of meaning? The implication is that we are moving towards a society without fixed status groups in which the adoption of styles of life (manifest in choice of clothes, leisure activities, consumer goods, bodily dispositions) which are fixed to specific groups have been surpassed. This apparent movement towards a postmodern consumer culture based upon a profusion of information and proliferation of images which cannot be ultimately stabilized, or hierarchized into a system which correlates to fixed social divisions, would further suggest the irrelevance of social divisions and ultimately the end of the social as a significant referent point. In effect the end of the deterministic relationship between society and culture heralds the triumph of signifying culture. Are consumer goods used as cultural signs in a free-association manner by individuals to produce an expressive effect within a social field in which the old coordinates are rapidly disappearing, or can taste still be

Reprinted with permission of Sage Publications Ltd from *Theory, Culture & Society* 4(1) 1987: 55–70.

adequately 'read', socially recognized and mapped onto the class structure? Does taste still 'classify' the classifier? Does the claim for a movement beyond fashion merely represent a move within, not beyond the game, being instead a new move, a position within the social field of lifestyles and consumption practices which can be correlated to the class structure?

This chapter is an attempt to develop a perspective which goes beyond the view that lifestyle and consumption are totally manipulated products of a mass society, and the opposite position which seeks to preserve the field of lifestyles and consumption, or at least a particular aspect of it (e.g. sport), as an autonomous playful space beyond determination. An attempt will also be made to argue that the 'no rules only choices' view (celebrated by some as a significant movement towards the break up of the old hierarchies of fashion, style and taste in favour of an egalitarian and tolerant acceptance of differences, and the acknowledgement of the right of individuals to enjoy whatever popular pleasures they desire without encouraging prudery or moral censure) does not signify anything as dramatic as the implosion of the social space but should be regarded merely as a new move within it. A perspective informed by the work of Pierre Bourdieu will be developed to argue that the new conception of lifestyle can best be understood in relation to the habitus of the new petite bourgeoisie, who, as an expanding class fraction centrally concerned with the production and dissemination of consumer culture imagery and information, is concerned to expand and legitimate its own particular dispositions and lifestyle. It does so within a social field in which its views are resisted and contested and within, in Britain especially, an economic climate and political culture in which the virtues of the traditional petite bourgeoisie have undergone a revival. Nevertheless it would seem to be useful to ask questions about consumer culture not only in terms of the engineering of demand resulting from the efficiencies of mass production or the logic of capitalism, but to discover which particular groups, strata, or class fractions are most closely involved in symbol production and, in particular, in producing the images and information celebrating style and lifestyles. What follows is very much a schematic account, written at a high level of generality, and acknowledges that these questions can ultimately only be answered by empirical analyses which take into account the specificity of particular societies.

Consumer culture

To use the term consumer culture is to emphasize that the world of goods and their principles of structuration are central to the understanding of contemporary society. This involves a dual focus: first, on the cultural dimension of the economy, the symbolization and use of material goods as 'communicators' not just utilities; and second, on the economy of cultural goods, the market principles of supply, demand, capital accumulation, competition, and monopolization which operates *within* the spheres of lifestyles, cultural goods and commodities.

Turning first to consumer culture it is apparent that the emphasis in some popular and academic circles on the materialism of contemporary consumer societies is far from unproblematic. From an anthropological perspective (Sahlins, 1974, 1976; Douglas and Isherwood, 1978; Leiss, 1983) material goods and their production, exchange and consumption are to be understood within a cultural matrix. Elwert (1984) too has referred to the 'embedded economy' to draw attention to the cultural preconditions of economic life. The movement away from regarding goods merely as utilities, having a use-value and an exchange value which can be related to some fixed system of human needs, has also occurred within neo-Marxism. Baudrillard (1975, 1981) has been particularly important in this context, especially his theorization of the commodity-sign. For Baudrillard the essential feature of the movement towards the mass production of commodities is that the obliteration of the original 'natural' use-value of goods by the dominance of exchange-value under capitalism has resulted in the commodity becoming a sign in the Saussurean sense, with its meaning arbitrarily determined by its position in a self-referential system of signifiers. Consumption, then, must not be understood as the consumption of use-values, a material utility, but primarily as the consumption of signs. It is this refusal of the referent, which is replaced by an unstable field of floating signifiers, which has led Kroker (1985) to describe Baudrillard as 'the last and best of the Marxists'. For Kroker, Baudrillard has pushed the logic of the commodity form as far as it will go until it releases 'the referential illusion' at its heart: the nihilism Nietzsche diagnosed is presented as the completion of the logic of capitalism.

It is this dominance of the commodity as sign which has led some neo-Marxists to emphasize the crucial role of culture in the reproduction of contemporary capitalism. Jameson (1981: 131), for example, writes that culture is 'the very element of consumer society itself; no society has ever been saturated with signs and images like this one'. Advertising and the display of goods in the 'dream-worlds' (Benjamin, 1982; Williams, 1982) of department stores and city centres plays upon the logic of the commodity-sign to transgress formerly sealed-apart meanings and create unusual and novel juxtapositions which effectively rename goods. Mundane and everyday consumer goods become associated with luxury, exotica, beauty and romance with their original or functional 'use' increasingly difficult to decipher. In his more recent writings Baudrillard (1983) has drawn attention to the key role of the electronic mass media in late-capitalist society. Television produces a surfeit of images and information which threatens our sense of reality. The triumph of signifying culture leads to a simulational world in which the proliferation of signs and images has effaced the distinction between the real and the imaginary. For Baudrillard (1983: 148) this means that 'we live everywhere already in an "aesthetic" hallucination of reality'. The 'death of the social, the loss of the real, leads to a *nostalgia* for the real: a fascination with and desperate search for real people, real values, real sex' (Kroker, 1985: 80). Consumer culture for Baudrillard is effectively a postmodern culture, a depthless culture in which all values have become transvalued and art has triumphed over reality.

The concern with lifestyle, with the stylization of life, suggests that the practices of consumption, the planning, purchase and display of consumer goods and experiences in everyday life cannot be understood merely via conceptions of exchange-value and instrumental rational calculation. The instrumental and expressive dimensions should not be regarded as exclusive either/or polarities, rather they can be conceived as a balance which consumer culture brings together. It is therefore possible to speak of a calculating hedonism, a calculus of the stylistic effect and an emotional economy on the one hand, and an aestheticization of the instrumental or functional rational dimension via the promotion of an aestheticizing distancing on the other. Rather than unreflexively adopting a lifestyle, through tradition or habit, the new heroes of consumer culture make lifestyle a life project and display their individuality and sense of style in the particularity of the assemblage of goods, clothes, practices, experiences, appearance and bodily dispositions, they design together into a lifestyle. The modern individual within consumer culture is made conscious that he speaks not only with his clothes, but with his home, furnishings, decoration, car and other activities which are to be read and classified in terms of the presence and absence of taste. The preoccupation with customizing a lifestyle and a stylistic self-consciousness are not just to be found among the young and the affluent; consumer culture publicity suggests that we all have room for self-improvement and self-expression whatever our age or class origins. This is the world of men and women who quest for the new and the latest in relationships and experiences, who have a sense of adventure and take risks to explore life's options to the full, who are conscious they have only one life to live and must work hard to enjoy, experience and express it (Winship, 1983; Featherstone and Hepworth, 1983).

Against the view of a grey conformist mass culture in which individuals' use of goods conform to the purposes which have been dreamed up by the advertisers, it has often been pointed out that the meaning and use of consumer goods, the de-coding process, is complex and problematic. Raymond Williams (1961: 312), for example, has argued that cross-class uniformities in housing, dress and leisure are not significant in understanding the class structure. Rather different classes have different ways of life and views of the nature of social relationships which form a matrix within which consumption takes place. It should also be noted that the uniformities progressively decline with (a) changes in technical capacity which allow greater product variety and differentiation to be built into production runs, and (b) increasing market fragmentation.

Effectively individuals increasingly consume different products. This, coupled with the tendency for more diffuse, ambiguous lifestyle imagery in advertising noted by Leiss (1983), encourages a variety of readings of messages (which increasingly use modernist and even postmodernist formats: a sales-pitch which educates and flatters at the same time). Consequently the consumer culture is apparently able to come nearer to delivering the individuality and differences it has always promised.

The tendency for consumer culture to differentiate, to encourage the play of difference, must be tempered by the observation that differences must be socially recognized and legitimated: total otherness like total individuality is in danger of being unrecognizable. Simmel's (Frisby, 1985) observation that fashion embodies the contradictory tendencies of imitation and differentiation and his assumption that the dynamic of fashion is such that its popularity and expansion lead to its own destruction, suggest that we need to examine more closely the social processes which structure taste in consumer goods and lifestyles, and raise the question of whether the concern for style and individuality itself reflect more the predispositions of a particular class fraction concerned with legitimating its own particular constellation of tastes as the *tastes* of the social, rather than the actual social itself. To do so we must still place the emphasis upon the production of distinctive tastes in lifestyles and consumer goods, but move down from the high level of generality which emphasizes the social and cultural process, the logic of capitalism, which can be regarded as having pushed lifestyle to the fore, to a consideration of the production of lifestyle tastes within a structured social space in which various groups, classes and class fractions struggle and compete to impose their own particular tastes as *the* legitimate tastes, and to thereby, where necessary, name and rename, classify and reclassify, order and reorder the field. This points towards an examination of the economy of cultural goods and lifestyles by adopting an approach which draws on the work of Pierre Bourdieu.

Bibliography

Baudrillard, Jean (1975) *The Mirror of Production*. St Louis: Telos Press.
Baudrillard, Jean (1981) *Towards a Critique of the Political Economy of the Sign*. St Louis: Telos Press.
Baudrillard, Jean (1983) *Simulations*. New York: Semiotext(e).
Bauman, Zygmunt (1985) 'On the origins of civilisation: a historical note', *Theory, Culture & Society*, 1 (3).
Benjamin, W. (1982) *Das Passagen-Werk*, 2 vols. Frankfurt: Suhrkamp.
Bourdieu, Pierre (1971) 'Intellectual field and creative project', in M. Young (ed.), *Knowledge and Control*. Stanford: Collier-Macmillan.
Bourdieu, Pierre (1980) 'The production of belief: contribution to an economy of symbolic goods', *Media, Culture and Society*, 2 (3): 261.
Bourdieu, Pierre (1983) 'Conference introductif'. Paris: INSEP.
Bourdieu, Pierre (1984) *Distinction*, trans. R. Nice. London: RKP.
Douglas, M. and Isherwood, B. (1978) *The World of Goods*. Harmondsworth: Penguin.

Elias, N. and Scotson, J. (1965) *The Established and the Outsider*. London: Cass.

Elwert, G. (1984) 'Markets, veniality and the moral economy', University of Bielefeld, mimeo.

Ewen, E. and Ewen, S. (1982) *Channels of Desire*. New York: McGraw-Hill.

Featherstone, M. (1982) 'The body in consumer culture', *Theory, Culture & Society*, 1 (2).

Featherstone, M. (1986) 'Postmodern culture?'. Paper presented at the 11th World Congress of Sociology, New Delhi.

Featherstone, M. (1987) 'Leisure, symbolic power and the life course', in J. Horne, D. Jary and A. Tomlinson (eds), *Sport, Leisure and Social Relations*, Sociological Review Monograph. London: Routledge and Kegan Paul.

Featherstone, M. and Hepworth, M. (1983) 'The midlifestyle of George and Lynne', *Theory, Culture & Society*, 1 (3).

Frisby, D. (1985) 'Georg Simmel, first sociologist of modernity', *Theory, Culture & Society*, 2 (3).

Jameson, F. (1981)'Reification and mass culture', *Social Text*, 1 (1).

Kroker, A. (1985) 'Baudrillard's Marx', *Theory, Culture & Society*, 2 (3).

Leiss, W. (1983) 'The icons of the market-place', *Theory, Culture & Society*, 1 (3).

Martin, B. (1981) *A Sociology of Contemporary Cultural Change*. Oxford: Blackwell.

Rojek, C. (1985) *Capitalism and Leisure Theory*. Tavistock.

Sahlins, M. (1974) *Stone Age Economics*. Tavistock.

Sahlins, M. (1976) *Cultural and Practical Reason*. Chicago, IL: Chicago University Press.

Sobel, E. (1982) *Lifestyle*. London: Academic Press.

Vaughan, M. (1986) 'Intellectual power and the powerlessness of the intellectuals', *Theory, Culture & Society*, 3 (3).

Weber, Max (1968) *Economy and Society*, 3 vols. Bedminster Press.

Williams, Raymond (1961) *The Long Revolution*. Harmondsworth: Penguin.

Williams, Rosalind (1982) *Dream Worlds*. Berkeley: California University Press.

Winship, J. (1983) 'Options for the way you live now or a magazine for superwomen?', *Theory, Culture & Society*, 1 (3).

Wouters, C. (1986) 'Formalisation and informalisation: changing tension balances in civilizing processes', *Theory, Culture & Society*, 3 (2).

The technological environment

Clearly technological change has had, and will continue to have, profound consequences across a vast range of different spheres. Within organizations, developments in information technology, in communications and in technologically driven product and process (manufacturing) innovations are just three of the most obvious examples of technological impact. There are many others. It would be impossible and inappropriate to attempt a comprehensive overview of key current and future developments. In this section, therefore, we have chosen to include just two chapters which we think present some stimulating ideas about the impact and management of technological change.

The first of these, 'Towards a new industrial America', is a report from the Commission on Industrial Productivity set up by MIT (the Massachusetts Institute of Technology). While the setting is America, the conclusions have far wider relevance. The authors argue that economic conditions do not fully account for failures and successes in industrial performance. Rather they cite such factors as: outdated strategies, neglect of human resources, failures of cooperation, government and industry working at cross purposes, short-term horizons and technological weaknesses in moving effectively from basic research and innovation to 'downstream' product development and manufacture. In the breadth of its analysis, the chapter underlines the organization-wide implications of successful and productive management of technological change.

The next chapter, 'Time – the next source of competitive advantage', by George Stalk Jr is important, not least because it records some of the unforeseen ways that Japanese corporations are rapidly improving their competitiveness. If offers, as well, one unexpected solution – again being pioneered by the Japanese – to the problem of change. This does not try to anticipate the unexpected through 'weak signals'. Instead it simply reduces development times to such an extent that even if the organization is late in recognizing the change, and only alerted to it by developments emerging from its competitors, it can still be in the market soon after those competitors, often with an improved product or service; and will beat them to the launch of the second and third generations when the major sales, and profits, are to be made!

It describes philosophies which are alien to many Western organizations but which they will need to learn if they are not to be swamped by the rate of advance their Japanese competitors can support.

These two chapters give only a bare indication of the scale of technological change, and the rate at which it now takes place. It should be borne in mind, even so, that many of the most fundamental changes facing society are initiated by the emergence of new technology.

15

Toward a new industrial America

Suzanne Berger, Michael L. Dertouzos,
Richard K. Lester, Robert M. Solow and
Lester C. Thurow

The US economy is a perplexing mix of strengths and weaknesses. It is now in the seventh year of the longest peacetime expansion in this century. Since the early 1980s large numbers of new jobs have been created, and both unemployment and inflation have remained low. American exports have recently surged (helped by a decline in the exchange value of the dollar), and in late 1988 American factories were operating at close to full capacity.

On the negative side, the trade deficit remains formidable (although it is beginning to shrink). In 1988 the US bought about $120 billion more goods and services from other countries than it could sell overseas. The US automobile and steel industries, which once dominated world commerce, have lost market share both at home and abroad, and newer industries are also struggling. The American presence in the consumer-electronics market, for example, has all but disappeared.

There are other disturbing signs that American industry as a whole is not producing as well as it ought to produce or as well as the industries of other nations have learned to produce. Growth in productivity, a crucial indicator of industrial performance, has averaged only slightly more than 1 per cent per year since the early 1970s. Productivity has grown more rapidly in several Western European and Asian nations, and US firms are increasingly perceived to be doing poorly in comparison with their foreign competitors in such key aspects as the cost and quality of their products as well as the speed with which new products are brought to market. In many new fields with broad commercial applications, such as advanced materials and semiconductors, America's best technology may already have been surpassed.

In spite of such disquieting developments, some observers maintain that there is nothing fundamentally wrong with American industry itself. The trade deficit, in this view, is the result not of intrinsic deficiencies in industrial performance but rather of such macroeconomic factors as natural

Reprinted from *Scientific American* 260(6) 1989: 21–9. Copyright © 1989 by Scientific American, Inc.

differences in rates of economic growth among countries, fluctuations in currency-exchange rates and the enormous US budget deficit. Then, too, the rise and fall of industries is said to be a normal part of economic evolution; at any given time a certain number of industries are sure to be in decline while others are growing.

Yet if the unfavorable trends in industrial performance are real (and we believe they are), then the US has reason to worry. Americans must produce well if Americans are to live well. The sluggish growth in US productivity is barely sufficient to sustain an improvement in the nation's standard of living. (Real wage rates have in fact hardly increased since the early 1970s.) That, in itself, would be of concern regardless of what is happening in the rest of the world. As it is, the more dynamic productivity performance of other countries is also resulting in a relative decline in the US standard of living. Moreover, because political and military power depend ultimately on economic vitality, weaknesses in the US production system will inevitably raise doubts about the nation's ability to retain its influence and standing in the world at large.

Late in 1986 the Massachusetts Institute of Technology established the Commission on Industrial Productivity (with funding from the Sloan and Hewlett foundations) to determine whether there actually are pervasive weaknesses in US industrial practices and, if so, to identify their causes and formulate a set of recommendations to counter them. Unlike many observers of contemporary US industry, the commission did not view the problem entirely in macroeconomic terms. We believed that we could best contribute to the understanding of the problem by focusing on the nation's production system: the organizations, the plants, the equipment and the people – from factory workers to senior executives – that combine to conceive, design, develop, produce, market and deliver products.

In keeping with this 'bottom-up' approach, the commission began its task by dividing into eight teams, each of which would examine in detail one of eight manufacturing industries: automobiles; chemicals; commercial aircraft; consumer electronics; machine tools; semiconductors, computers and copiers; steel; and textiles. These industries combined account for 28 per cent of US manufacturing output and about half of the total volume of manufactured goods traded by the US (exports and imports). American firms in each industry were evaluated for what we have come to call productive performance: their efficiency, product quality, innovativeness and adaptability, as well as the speed with which they put new products on the market. Such factors are not explicitly captured in conventional measures of industrial productivity. Altogether, the commission's teams visited more than 200 companies and 150 plant sites and conducted nearly 550 interviews in the US, Europe and Japan.

In choosing to focus on the production system itself, we did not underestimate the importance of the macroeconomic factors that regulate the economy at large; on the contrary, we could not avoid observing their manifestations time and again as the teams proceeded with their work. It is clear that the nation's productive performance problems will not be solved without some improvement in the economic environment. The reason is that investment – meant here broadly to include not only new plants, equipment and public works but also education, training and research and development – is crucial for productivity, and the economic environment largely determines the level of a nation's investment. Indeed, we believe that the highest priority of US economic policy must be to reduce the huge federal budget deficit, which saps the savings from which investment funds are drawn.

Nevertheless, after two years of study, it seems clear to us that current economic conditions do not fully explain the deficiencies in US industrial performance, nor will macroeconomic policy changes suffice to cure them. The relation of poor product quality to US interest rates and tax policies, for example, seems at best tenuous. The economic environment also does not directly affect the speed with which firms identify and respond to changes in the market and to new technological possibilities. Finally, macroeconomics cannot adequately explain why some US businesses thrive in the very same sectors where others are failing, nor why Japanese manufacturing plants in the US have often achieved better results than comparable American plants.

By looking at what actually takes place in industry – from the shop floor to the boardroom – the commission was able to observe recurring patterns of behavior and to draw certain conclusions about the most important micro-level factors that have adversely affected US industrial performance. To do so the commission worked much like a jury: we assessed the large mass of detailed, diverse and sometimes contradictory evidence that the study teams had collected, ultimately reaching a verdict.

The verdict is that US industry indeed shows systematic weaknesses that are hampering the ability of many firms to adapt to a changing international business environment. In particular, the commission observed six such weaknesses: outdated strategies; neglect of human resources; failures of cooperation; technological weaknesses in development and production; government and industry working at cross-purposes; and short time horizons.

The industry studies revealed two types of outdated strategies that are impeding industrial progress today: an overemphasis on mass production of standard commodity goods and an economic and technological parochialism. Both are holdovers from the unique economic environment that prevailed after World War II. For decades after the war US industry was able to flourish by mass producing undifferentiated goods principally for its own markets, which were large, unified and familiar. Because firms in most other countries had to rebuild in economies devastated by the war, they could mount no significant competition and were largely ignored by US industry.

Not only did US producers sell their wares primarily to the domestic market, they also drew their technical expertise almost exclusively from

US factories and laboratories. Such technological parochialism blinded Americans to the growing strength of scientific and technological innovation abroad and hence to the possibility of adapting foreign discoveries. In the 1950s and 1960s, for example, American steel producers lagged behind Japanese and European steelmakers in adopting such new process technologies as the basic oxygen furnace; later they were again slow to adopt continuous casters and such quality-enhancing technologies as vacuum degassing and oxygen injection. The critical error in many of these cases was the failure to recognize the worth of someone else's innovation.

The American industry of the 1950s and 1960s pursued flexibility by hiring and firing workers who had limited skills rather than relying on multiskilled workers. Worker responsibility and input progressively narrowed, and management tended to treat workers as a cost to be controlled, not as an asset to be developed.

Training practices in the US have been consistent with that strategy. Workers often receive limited training while on the job; typically it amounts to watching a colleague at work. Even in firms offering organized training programs, in-plant training is usually short and highly focused on transmitting specific narrow skills for immediate application. In other countries we observed a greater inclination to regard firms as learning institutions, where – through education and training – employees can develop breadth and flexibility in their skills and also acquire a willingness to learn new skills over the long term. In a system based on mass production of standard goods, where cost matters more than quality, the neglect of human resources by companies may have been compatible with good economic performance; today it appears as a major part of the US's productivity problem.

The neglect of human resources in the US actually begins long before young Americans enter the workforce. It is in primary and secondary school that they learn the fundamental skills they will apply throughout life: reading, writing and problem-solving. Yet cross-national research on educational achievement shows American children falling behind children in other societies in mathematics, science and language attainment at an early age and falling farther behind as they progress through the school years. The school system – from kindergarten through high school – is leaving large numbers of its graduates without basic skills. Unless the nation begins to remedy these inadequacies in education, real progress in improving the US's productive performance will remain elusive.

The third recurring weakness of the US production system that emerged from our industry studies is a widespread failure of cooperation within and among companies. In many US firms communication and coordination among departments is often inhibited by steep hierarchical ladders and organizational walls. In addition, labor and management continue to expend valuable resources and energies battling over union organizing.

Suppliers and even customers have also been kept at arm's length by the management of many US companies, in spite of the fact that such vertical linkages can be conduits not only for raw materials and finished products but also for technological innovations and other developments that enhance productivity. These companies are reluctant to share designs, technologies and strategies with either their customers or their suppliers for fear that proprietary information will leak to competitors. Yet by keeping that kind of information to itself, a firm misses the chance to work with its suppliers and customers to improve the products it sells and buys. A similar lack of horizontal linkages – cooperative relations between firms in the same industry segment – has led to a dearth of joint projects in such areas as the setting of common standards and industrial research and development, even when they might have been permitted under the law.

The first commercial videotape recorder was made by the Ampex Corporation in Redwood City, California, but no US firms were willing or able to devote the resources to bring unit costs down for sale to retail customers. Ampex concentrated on high-price, high-performance systems; other US firms abandoned the field altogether. Japanese companies had the financial stamina to sustain low returns on investments while perfecting designs and manufacturing processes. The result is that the Japanese now dominate the consumer video-recording market. Moreover, by capitalizing on the profits, technology and economies of mass production built up in that market, they have begun to encroach on the upscale market as well.

Notwithstanding its spotty performance in the global market in recent years, the US remains the world leader in basic research. Ironically that outstanding success may have diverted attention from 'downstream' technological skills in product and process development and production that become progressively more important as new concepts proceed down the path from the laboratory to the marketplace. Simply put, many US firms have been outperformed in the design and manufacture of reliable, high-quality products.

A survey conducted by the International Motor Vehicle Program (IMVP) at MIT found that, despite recent gains, the number of defects reported in the first three months of use was still almost twice as high for cars produced in American plants in 1986 and 1987 as for those from Japanese plants. The commission's automobile study team also learned that American car builders have recently been taking about five years to carry a new design from the conceptual stage to commercial introduction. In contrast, Japanese manufacturers complete the cycle in three-and-a-half years.

The MIT Commission on Industrial Productivity

Michael L. Dertouzos (Chairman)
  Department of Electrical Engineering
  and Computer Science
  Director, Laboratory for Computer
  Science
Robert M. Solow (Vice-chairman)
  Institute Professor
  Department of Economics
Richard K. Lester (Executive Director)
  Department of Nuclear Engineering
Suzanne Berger
  Head, Department of Political Science
H. Kent Bowen
  Department of Materials Science and
  Engineering
  Codirector, Leaders for
  Manufacturing Program
Don P. Clausing
  Department of Electrical Engineering
  and Computer Science
Eugene E. Covert
  Head, Department of Aeronautics and
  Astronautics
John M. Deutch
  Provost

Merton C. Flemings
  Head, Department of
  Materials Science and
  Engineering
Howard W. Johnson
  Special Faculty Professor of
  Management, Emeritus
  President, Emeritus
  Honorary Chairman, MIT Corporation
Thomas A. Kochan
  Sloan School of Management
Daniel Roos
  Department of Civil Engineering
  Director, Center for Technology,
  Policy and Industrial Development
David H. Staelin
  Department of Electrical Engineering
  and Computer Science
Lester C. Thurow
  Dean, Sloan School of Management
James Wei
  Head, Department of Chemical
  Engineering
Gerald L. Wilson
  Dean, School of Engineering

Members of the Commission on Industrial Productivity were drawn from the faculty of the Massachusetts Institute of Technology. The interdisciplinary group included economists, technologists and experts on organization, management and politics.

Some of the responsibility for the persistent failure to convert technologies quickly into viable, high-quality products lies in the American system of engineering education, which has deemphasized product realization and process engineering since World War II. The professional norms of the American engineering community also assign rather low priority to such essential downstream engineering functions as the testing of product designs, manufacturing and product and process improvements.

Other aspects of the problem can be found in certain practices followed by US industry. For one, many American companies simply do not devote enough attention to the manufacturing process. In a recent comparative study of industrial research and development in Japan and the US, Edwin Mansfield of the University of Pennsylvania found that US companies are still devoting only a third of their R & D expenditures to the improvement of process technology; the other two thirds is allocated to the development of new and improved products. In Japan those proportions in R & D expenditure are reversed.

Many US companies also fail to coordinate product design and the manufacturing process. It has been standard practice for design engineers to end their involvement with a new product once they have conceived its design. They hand over the design to manufacturing engineers, who are then supposed to come up with a process for the product's manufacture. This compartmentalization of tasks has led to serious problems. Product-design groups often neglect manufacturing considerations, making it harder to come up with a manufacturing process.

The Proprinter project of the International Business Machines Corporation is an impressive example of what can be achieved when product designers are brought together with manufacturing engineers and research scientists. Charged with designing a new computer printer that has fewer component parts and no springs or screws (which increase assembly time and decrease reliability), a multidisciplinary IBM design team came up with a product having 60 per cent fewer parts than its predecessor. (Ironically because an individual assembly worker could put the printer together in three-and-a-half minutes, the highly automated and expensive assembly plant that had been built to make it was largely rendered superfluous.)

Multifunctional design teams and an orientation toward simplicity and quality at the design stage have been a long-standing fixture of Japanese industry and have contributed to its comparative advantages in quality and productivity. The IMVP survey showed that Japanese-designed automobiles retain their quality advantage even when they are assembled in American factories, which implies that the Japanese automotive engineers had incorporated quality-enhancing features into the design itself.

American companies also have often lagged behind their overseas competitors in exploiting the potential for continual improvement in the quality and reliability of products and processes. The cumulative effect of successive incremental improvements in and modifications of established products and processes can be very large; it may even outpace efforts to achieve technological breakthroughs.

The federal government deserves part of the blame as well for the technological weaknesses in development and production. Whereas the governments of most other industrial nations have purposefully promoted research and technology for economic development, US policy for science and technology has traditionally focused on basic research. The commercial development and application of new technologies have for the most part been considered to be the responsibility of the private sector.

To be sure, the Department of Defense, the National Aeronautics and Space Administration and other federal agencies have invested heavily in technology development. Indeed, about 46 per cent of all US research and development is sponsored by the Government. Those expenditures are usually in the areas of defense and space activities or in other specific Governmental missions, however. In such cases commercial applications of the resulting technology are considered secondarily, if at all. Furthermore, there are indications that defense R & D, which accounts for almost two thirds of all federal R & D spending, is becoming less relevant to the needs of the civilian market.

More generally the lack of a common agenda between government and industry has produced negative effects across broad stretches of the US economy. Some observers, for instance, have blamed the collapse of the consumer-electronics industry in part on the federal government's failure to enact or implement tariffs and import quotas as well as to amend or enforce anti-dumping and anti-trust laws. Yet while some see the problem as too little government support for key industries, others see it as too much government support for inefficient producers.

The evidence gathered from the commission's industry studies was similarly mixed regarding the charge that too much government intervention, particularly in regulating the environment and occupational safety, has put US companies at a disadvantage in relation to foreign competitors. Where problems have arisen, the fault tended to lie in the nature of the regulatory process rather than in the strictness of the regulations themselves. Indeed, many European countries as well as Japan now have environmental and occupational-safety laws in many areas that are at least as strict as those in the US.

The issue, then, is not simply whether there is too much government or too little. What is clear to the commission, however, is that a lower level of cooperation between government and business exists in the US than it does in the countries of American firms' major foreign competitors and that the frequency with which government and industry find themselves at cross-purposes is a serious obstacle to strategic and organizational change in individual US firms.

American industry has also been handicapped by shrinking time

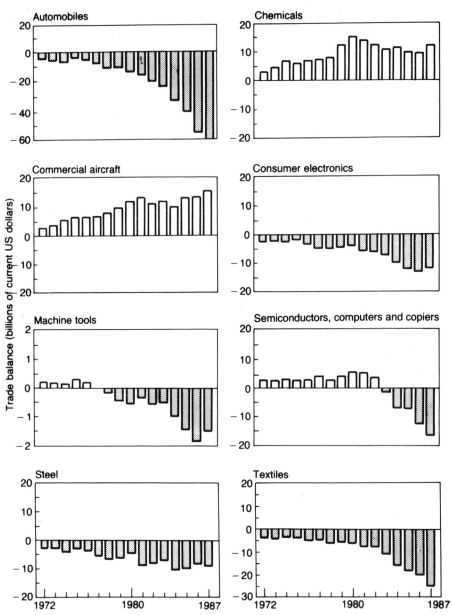

*Balance of trade (the total value of exports less the total value of imports) for
the eight key manufacturing industries studied by the commission reflects the
industries' general condition in the US. A positive balance means that more of
an industry's products are sold overseas than are exported to the US by foreign
rivals; a negative balance implies the converse. An industry's trade balance is
affected by the performance of its firms with respect to product cost and
quality, service and the speed of response to new technological and market
opportunities. Macroeconomic conditions – particularly currency-exchange rates
– can also affect the balance.*

horizons and a growing preoccupation with short-term profits. There have been many recent instances in which US firms have lost market share to overseas competitors despite an early lead in technology or sales, or both. Often these firms effectively cede a potential market by not 'sticking to their knitting'; instead, they diversify into activities that are more profitable in the short run.

The development of the videocassette recorder provides an exemplary case. Video-recording technology was first developed in the US, but the early machines were complex and expensive and suitable only for industrial and professional applications; many years of further development were needed to create low-cost, highly reliable products for the mass-consumer market. No American manufacturer was willing or able to spend the time and money, but several Japanese manufacturers were. The Japanese are now virtually unchallenged as makers of the most important single product in the consumer-electronics market.

Why are US firms less willing than their rivals to live through a period of heavy investment and meager returns in order to build expertise and secure a foothold in a new market? Is it that American managers are incapable of looking as far ahead as their foreign counterparts? Or are they forced by external circumstances to focus on the short term, even though they realize that it is not in their firm's best interest to do so? Or might it be that a short-term focus is actually in the best interest of the firm but not of the US economy as a whole?

Some observers argue that the higher cost of capital in the US compared with its cost in Japan is the overriding reason for the different time horizons of firms in the two countries. Certainly the cost of capital is important, but we think that other factors are also important.

The nature of the institutions that influence the supply of capital may affect investment decisions at least as much as the cost of capital. A large and growing share of the capital of US firms is owned by mutual funds and pension funds, which hold assets in the form of a market basket of securities. The actual equity holders, the clients of the funds, are far removed from managerial decision-making. The fund managers also have no long-term loyalty to the corporations in which they invest and have no representation on their boards. (Indeed, legislation prohibits their participation in corporate planning.)

Although some fund managers do invest for the long term, most turn over their stockholdings rapidly in an effort to maximize the current value of their investment portfolio, since this is the main criterion against which their own performance is judged. Firms respond to this financial environment by maximizing their short-term profit in the belief that investment policies oriented toward the long term will be under-valued by the market and thus leave them vulnerable to a take-over.

At the same time senior executives are also motivated to maintain steady growth in earnings by their own profit-related bonus plans and stock options. At chief executive whose compensation is a strong function

The nature of US securities market has contributed to the short time-horizons of American businesses. Managers of mutual and pension funds, which own a large and growing share of the capital of US firms, tend to turn over their fund's stockholdings rapidly in an effort to maximize the current value of the investment portfolio. Such a strategy undervalues long-term development and investment policies of US firms.

of his or her company's financial performance in the current year will naturally stress short-term results.

Explanations that cite the cost of capital and the sources of financing all tend to depict corporate managers as victims of circumstance, forced by external conditions into a short-term mind-set. Yet Robert H. Hayes and the late William J. Abernathy of the Harvard Business School have argued that executive ranks have come to be dominated by individuals who know too little about their firm's products, markets and production processes and who rely instead on quantifiable short-term financial criteria. These modern executives are more likely to engage in restructuring to bolster profits than to take risks on technological innovation.

As part of its work the commission sought to find not only patterns of weakness in US industry but also patterns of change that are common to successful US firms – firms that are doing well in the international arena. Indeed, we probably learned as much from what such 'best practice' firms are doing right as from what many other US firms are doing wrong.

In particular, we found that successful firms emphasize *simultaneous* improvements in quality, cost and speed of commercialization. Whereas other firms often trade off one dimension of performance against another, only the best companies have made significant improvements in all three. To gauge progress, one common practice among the successful firms is to emphasize competitive benchmarking: comparing the performance of their products and work processes with those of the world leaders. At the Xerox Corporation, for example, quality improved by an order of magnitude over the past decade after the company instituted detailed comparison tests of Xerox copiers and competing Japanese models.

In addition, the best-practice firms we observed are developing closer ties to their customers. These ties enable companies to pick up more detailed signals from the market and thus to respond to different segments of demand. They also increase the likelihood of rapid response to shifts in the market. Even high-volume manufacturers have combined a continuing emphasis on economies of scale with a new flexibility, reflected in shorter production runs, faster product introductions and greater sensitivity to the diverse needs of customers.

Closer and more tightly coordinated relations with suppliers were also observed among the best-practice firms. In some cases, better coordination with suppliers has been achieved through the coercive power of market domination, in others by new forms of cooperation and negotiation. No matter how it comes about, coordination with external firms is crucial in cutting inventories (and thereby costs), in speeding up the flow of products and in reducing defects.

For example, Greenwood Mills, Inc. (a textile company specializing in the production of denim), brought down its inventory radically over two years, even as sales doubled. To achieve those results the company tightened up its own operations and at the same time negotiated new arrangements with suppliers, who now deliver on a just-in-time basis. In exchange, Greenwood Mills halved the number of its suppliers, leaving itself more vulnerable to price hikes but gaining the advantages of closer collaboration.

Most thriving firms in the US have also realized that business strategies based on throwing new hardware at performance problems are unlikely to work. They have instead learned to integrate technology in their manufacturing and marketing strategies and to link them to organizational changes that promote teamwork, training and continuous learning. In the generally depressed domestic apparel industry, firms such as the Model Garment Company and Levi Strauss & Company are succeeding by investing heavily in information technologies that allow them to fill orders very rapidly and reduce inventory levels.

In virtually all successful firms, the trend is toward greater functional integration and lesser organizational stratification, both of which promote quicker product development and increased responsiveness to changing markets. The Ford Motor Company was the first US automobile company to experiment with cross-functional teams to speed the development and introduction of a new model. The product-development team for the Taurus model included representatives from planning, design, engineering, manufacturing and marketing. The specialists worked simultaneously rather than serially.

Flattening steep organizational hierarchies goes hand in hand with dismantling functional barriers. A flatter hierarchy generally enhances organizational flexibility. It also promotes closer relations with customers: a customer with a problem can speak directly with the group that has responsibility for the product instead of having to go through a sales department. In leaner, less hierarchical organizations the number of job categories at each level is reduced, and the responsibilities associated with particular jobs are broadened.

At the Chaparral Steel Company, for instance, there are almost 1000 employees, and yet there are only four job levels. Production workers are responsible for identifying new technologies, training, meeting with customers and maintaining equipment. Foremen and crews install new equipment. Security guards are trained as emergency medical technicians, and they update computer records while on their shift.

An essential ingredient for greater worker responsibility and commitment is continual training. Large companies such as IBM have the resources to train their own workers. Having lower labor turnover, they also have more incentive to invest in training, because they are more likely to capture the benefits of that investment. Smaller companies do tend to draw more heavily on outside institutions for training, but there is often a major internal component as well.

The Kingsbury Machine Tool Corporation once built dedicated equipment for vehicles; it has since successfully converted to building computer-controlled machines and production lines for flexible manufacturing. Under the old regime the primary demand on the workforce was for mechanical skills, but the new product line requires workers with some knowledge of computers. To retrain the employees, the company provided everyone – from janitors to vice presidents – with computers to use at work or at home and offered classes to employees and their families.

Although an increasing number of American companies are recognizing what it takes to be the best in the world, many US firms have not yet realized that they will have to make far-reaching changes in the way they do business. They will need to adopt new ways of thinking about human resources, new ways of organizing their systems of production and new approaches to the management of technology. What distinguishes the best-practice firms from the others in their industries is that they see these innovations not as independent solutions but as a coherent package. Each change for the better reinforces the others, and the entire organization is affected by them.

Of course, today's best practices will surely not remain the best forever. The nature of industrial competition is changing rapidly, and new challenges will undoubtedly emerge. The commission identified three major and pervasive long-term trends that will have broad implications for the future productive performance of US firms.

First, economic activity will continue to become more international. A company's ownership, location, workforce, purchases and sales are all

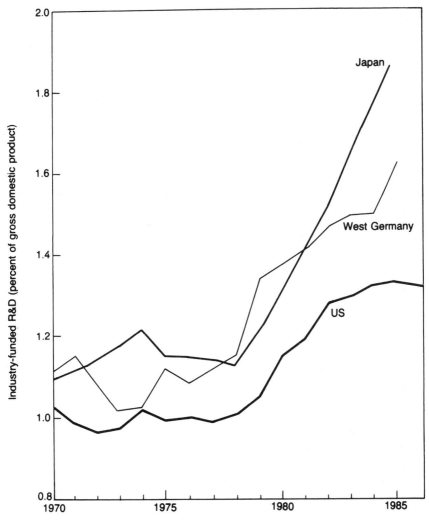

Industry-funded research and development has grown more slowly in the US than in Japan and West Germany. Total spending on R & D as a percentage of gross domestic product, however, is about the same in the three countries, because the difference in industry-funded R & D is made up in the US by federal funding of R & D.

spreading beyond the boundaries of the nation in which it originated. A growing number of countries will acquire the capacity to produce and to export sophisticated goods and services. Many of these emerging economies have labor costs even lower than those of Taiwan and South Korea and far lower than those of the US, Japan and Europe.

Second, partly because of internationalization and partly because of rising incomes around the world, markets for consumer goods and intermediate goods are becoming more sophisticated. Markets are also

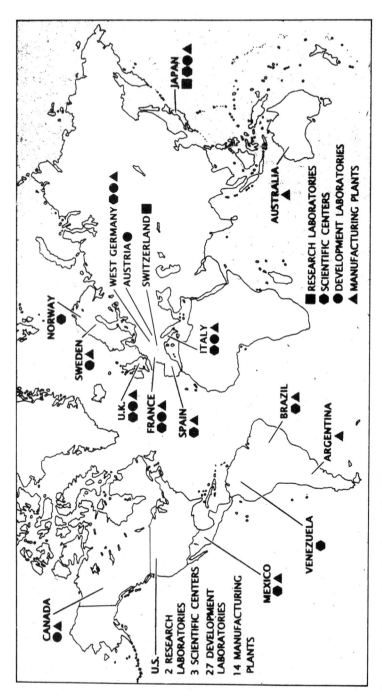

Increasing internationalization of the US economy has led the International Business Machines Corporation to establish numerous research laboratories, scientific centers, development laboratories and manufacturing plants in foreign countries. Such a geographic distribution helps the corporation remain abreast of technological advances throughout the world. IBM also maintains sales offices in more than 100 countries in order to keep in closer contact with its customers.

becoming more segmented and specialized; not everyone is prepared to accept the same product designs and specifications.

Third, we expect the rapid pace of technological change to continue. Particularly rapid progress seems likely in information technology, materials science and engineering, and biotechnology. Information technology has already permeated nearly every facet of the production of goods and delivery of services, and we expect it to affect the business environment in a number of ways in the future.

The obvious implication of these three trends is that US firms will not be able to compete on the basis of cost alone. The future of US industry lies in specialized, high-quality products; standard commodities will be made in the US only if their production is extraordinarily capital-intensive and technologically advanced. At the same time, competition among US, Japanese and European firms in markets for high-value-added products will become increasingly fierce.

Indeed, the convergence of future consumer preferences, market forces and technological opportunities may lead in some industries to the introduction of 'totally flexible' production systems. In such systems custom-tailoring of products to the needs and tastes of individual customers will be combined with the power, precision and economy of modern production technology.

In a market economy such as that of the US, individual firms have the primary responsibility to correct past problems and find ways to compete successfully in the future. Yet for the US to achieve an economy marked by high productivity growth, all sectors – business, government, labor and educational institutions – will need to work together. Based on its study of current weakness and best practices in American industry, as well as its forecast of long-term trends, the commission believes that five inter-connected imperatives should form the core of any such national effort.

First, the US needs to invest more heavily in its future. This means investment not only in tangible factories and machinery but also in research, and above all, in human capital. At the macroeconomic level, as noted earlier, bringing the budget closer into balance should take high priority. In order to encourage firms to develop the necessary outlook for long-term investments, American economic policy should also favor increasing productive investment over private consumption through an approach that combines a more expansionary monetary policy with a fiscal policy that taxes consumption more heavily than savings or invest-ment. Such policies can increase the supply of capital to business. Tax and credit legislation making it harder and more expensive to raise large sums of money for take-overs and buy-outs is additionally needed. Government must also work with industry and academia to ensure not only that invest-ment continues strongly in basic research but also that it expands in the direction of productive manufacturing technologies.

Public resources should be allocated not only to improve the existing economic infrastructure (roads, airports, harbors and the like) but also to invest in new kinds of infrastructure. For example, we think that the time is right for American business and Government to begin developing a national information infrastructure, which would eventually become a network of communication highways as important for tomorrow's business as the current highway network is for today's flow of goods.

The most important investment in the long run is in the nation's schools. A better basic education will be crucial to the technological competence that will be required to raise the productivity of US industry. Without major improvements in primary and secondary schooling, no amount of macroeconomic fine-tuning or technological innovation will yield a rising standard of living.

The second major imperative, closely related to the first, is to develop a new 'economic citizenship' in the workplace. The effective use of modern technology will require people to develop their capabilities for planning, judgment, collaboration and the analysis of complex systems. For that reason learning – particularly through on-the-job training programs – will acquire new importance.

Greater employee involvement and responsibility will be needed to absorb the new production technologies. Companies will no longer be able to treat employees like cogs in a big and impersonal machine. If people are asked to give maximum effort and to accept uncertainty and rapid change, they must be full participants in the enterprise rather than expendable commodities. Just as important as job security is a financial stake in the long-term performance of the firm. We see in this combination of technological and organizational change an unprecedented opportunity to make jobs more satisfying and rewarding for workers at all levels of a firm.

Third, the US needs to make a major commitment to mastering the new fundamentals of manufacturing. Manufacturing, as we use the term here, encompasses a great deal more than what happens on a production line. It includes designing and developing products as well as planning, marketing, selling and servicing them. Global competition, changing markets and modern technologies are transforming virtually every phase of the production system.

Managers who are detached from the details of production will lose the competitive battle to managers who know their business intimately. Manufacturability, reliability and low cost should be built into products at the earliest possible stages of design. Innovation must be applied to process development as intensively and creatively as it is now applied to product development. Corporate management and financial institutions must work together to develop indicators that better reflect how well companies are actually doing in developing, producing and marketing their products than do short-term financial measures such as quarterly earnings. New measures might include indicators of quality, productivity, product-development time and time to market.

Fourth, Americans should strive to combine cooperation and

individualism. The nation's culture has traditionally emphasized individualism, often at the expense of cooperation. Yet in the best US companies (as in other societies), group solidarity, a feeling of community and a recognition of interdependence have led to important economic advantages.

To this end, steep organizational hierarchies, with their rigidity and compartmentalization, should be replaced with substantially flatter organizational structures that provide incentives for communication and cooperation among different corporate departments. Companies should put less emphasis on legalistic and often adversarial contractual agreements; they should promote business relations based on mutual trust, common goals and the prospect of continuing transactions over the long run. Management must also accept workers and their representatives as legitimate partners in the innovation process. Both individual and group efforts need recognition and reward.

Americans should think of cooperation among economic entities as a way of overcoming the defects of the market, which often undersupplies collective factors essential to economic success. Cooperative efforts can take the form of research consortiums, joint business ventures, partnerships with Government and standard-setting committees. (To be sure, such arrangements might lead producers to combine forces in order to exploit the consumer. Now and in the future, competition from imports will no doubt provide some protection from domestic monopolies. Still, a little vigilance would help too.)

Fifth, to compete successfully in a world that is becoming more international and more competitive, Americans must expand their outlook beyond their own boundaries. They must gain knowledge of other languages, cultures, market customs, tastes, legal systems and regulations; they will need to develop a new set of international sensitivities.

Cost considerations will increasingly dictate whether materials and components are best procured at home or abroad. It follows that not only a company's marketing division but also its purchasing agents and production managers will have to be knowledgeable about global conditions. Shopping internationally should go beyond the buying of raw materials and off-the-shelf products to the adoption of effective practices and technologies – wherever they happen to be found.

Americans need to understand that the world they live in has changed. The effortless economic superiority that the US enjoyed in the aftermath of World War II has gone. Strong economic cultures now exist across both the Atlantic and Pacific oceans. The US has much to learn from the rest of the world. Indeed, the rest of the world will force changes in some of the most cherished American operating procedures and assumptions, if the US is to continue to have a standard of living second to none. What Americans must do is determined decreasingly by what they wish to do and increasingly by the best practices of others.

Implementing these five imperatives will not be easy. In many cases, fundamental changes in attitude will be necessary. Just accepting the need for a sense of common purpose – a shared national goal – may require the biggest attitudinal change of all. The commission believes that if industry, government and the educational system in this country unite in steadfast pursuit of these basic imperatives the next generation of Americans will live in a nation moving into the twenty-first century with the same dynamism and strength that made it a world leader a generation ago.

Bibliography

Dertouzos, M. L., Lester, R. K., Solow, R. M. and The MIT Commission on Industrial Productivity (1989) *Made in America: Regaining the Productive Edge*. Cambridge, MA: MIT Press.

16

Time – the next source of competitive advantage

George Stalk Jr

Like competition itself, competitive advantage is a constantly moving target. For any company in any industry, the key is not to get stuck with a single simple notion of its source of advantage. The best competitors, the most successful ones, know how to keep moving and always stay on the cutting edge.

Today, *time* is on the cutting edge. The ways leading companies manage time – in production, in new product development and introduction, in sales and distribution – represent the most powerful new sources of competitive advantage. Though certain Western companies are pursuing these advantages, Japanese experience and practice provide the most instructive examples – not because they are necessarily unique but because they best illustrate the evolutionary stages through which leading companies have advanced.

In the period immediately following World War II, Japanese companies used their low labor costs to gain entry to various industries. As wage rates rose and technology became more significant, the Japanese shifted first to scale-based strategies and then to focused factories to achieve advantage. The advent of just-in-time production brought with it a move to flexible factories, as leading Japanese companies sought both low cost and great variety in the market. Cutting-edge Japanese companies today are capitalizing on time as a critical source of competitive advantage: shortening the planning loop in the product development cycle and trimming process time in the factory – managing time the way most companies manage costs, quality, or inventory.

In fact, as a strategic weapon, time is the equivalent of money, productivity, quality, even innovation. Managing time has enabled top Japanese companies not only to reduce their costs but also to offer broad product lines, cover more market segments, and upgrade the technological sophistication of their products. These companies are time-based competitors.

Reprinted from *Harvard Business Review*, July/August 1988: 41–51. Copyright © 1988 by the President and Fellows of Harvard College.

From low wages to variety wars

Since 1945, Japanese competitors have shifted their strategic focus at least four times. These early adaptations were straightforward; the shift to time-based competitive advantage is not nearly so obvious. It does, however, represent a logical evolution from the earlier stages.

In the immediate aftermath of World War II, with their economy devastated and the world around them in a shambles, the Japanese concentrated on achieving competitive advantage through low labor costs. Since Japan's workers were still productive and the yen was devalued by 98.8 per cent against the dollar, its labor costs were extraordinarily competitive with those of the West's developed economies.

Hungry for foreign exchange, the Japanese government encouraged companies to make the most of their one edge by targeting industries with high labor content: textiles, shipbuilding, and steel – businesses where the low labor rates more than offset low productivity rates. As a result, Japanese companies took market share from their Western competition.

But this situation did not last long. Rising wages, caused by high inflation, combined with fixed exchange rates to erode the advantage. In many industries, manufacturers could not improve their productivity fast enough to offset escalating labor costs. By the early 1960s, for instance, the textile companies – comprising Japan's largest industry – were hard-pressed. Having lost their competitive edge in world markets, they spiraled downward, first losing share, then volume, then profits, and finally position and prestige. While the problem was most severe for the textile business, the rest of Japanese industry suffered as well.

The only course was adaptation: in the early 1960s, the Japanese shifted their strategy, using capital investment to boost workforce productivity. They inaugurated the era of scale-based strategies, achieving high productivity and low costs by building the largest and most capital-intensive facilities that were technologically feasible. Japanese shipbuilders, for example, revolutionized the industry in their effort to raise labor productivity. Adapting fabrication techniques from mass production processes and using automatic and semi-automatic equipment, they constructed vessels in modules. The approach produced two advantages for the Japanese. It drove up their own productivity and simultaneously erected a high capital-investment barrier to others looking to compete in the business.

The search for ways to achieve even higher productivity and lower costs continued, however. And in the mid-1960s, it led top Japanese companies to a new source of competitive advantage – the focused factory. Focused competitors manufactured products either made nowhere else in the world, or located in the high-volume segment of a market, often in the heart of their Western competitors' product lines. Focusing of production allowed the Japanese to remain smaller than established broad-line producers, while still achieving higher production and lower costs – giving them great competitive power.

Variety of manufactured products

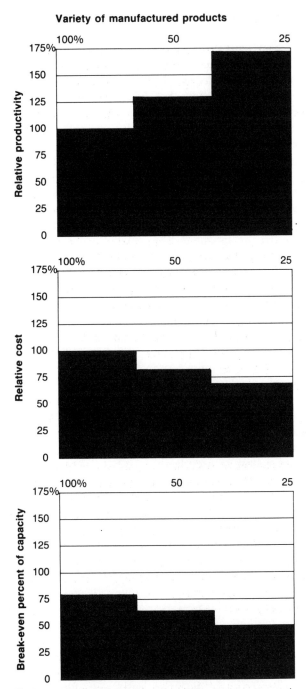

Cutting variety yields higher productivity, lower costs, and reduced break-even points.

Figure 1 *The benefits of focus*

Factory costs are very sensitive to the variety of goods a plant produces. Reduction of the product-line variety by half, for example, raises productivity by 30 per cent, cuts costs 17 per cent and substantially lowers the break-even point. Cutting the product line in half again boosts productivity by 75 per cent, slashes costs 30 per cent, and diminishes the break-even point to below 50 per cent. (See Figure 1.)

In industries like bearings, where competition was fierce in the late 1960s, the Japanese fielded product lines with one-half to one-quarter the variety of their Western competitors. Targeting the high-volume segments of the bearing business – bearings for automobile applications was one – the Japanese used the low costs of their highly productive focused factories to undercut the prices of Western competitors.

SKF was one victim. With factories scattered throughout Europe, each geared to a broad product line for the local market, the Swedish company was a big target for the Japanese. SKF reacted by trying to avoid direct competition with the Japanese: it added higher margin products to serve specialized applications. But SKF did not simultaneously drop any low-margin products, thereby complicating its plant operations and adding to production costs. In effect, SKF provided a cost umbrella for the Japanese. As long as they operated beneath it, the Japanese could expand their product line and move into more varied applications.

Avoiding price competition by moving into higher margin products is called margin retreat – a common response to stepped-up competition that eventually leads to corporate suicide. As a company retreats, its costs rise as do its prices, thus 'subsidizing' an aggressive competitor's expansion into the vacated position. The retreating company's revenue base stops growing and may eventually shrink to the point where it can no longer support the fixed cost of the operation. Retrenchment, restructuring, and further shrinkage follow in a cycle that leads to inevitable extinction.

SKF avoided this fate by adopting the Japanese strategy. After a review of its factories, the company focused each on those products it was best suited to manufacture. If a product did not fit a particular factory, it was either placed in another, more suitable plant, or dropped altogether. This strategy not only halted SKF's retreat but also beat back the Japanese advance.

At the same time, however, leading Japanese manufacturers began to move toward a new source of competitive advantage – the flexible factory. Two developments drove this move. First, as they expanded and penetrated more markets, their narrow product lines began to pinch, limiting their ability to grow. Second, with growth limited, the economics of the focus strategy presented them with an unattractive choice: either reduce variety further or accept the higher costs of broader product lines.

In manufacturing, costs fall into two categories: those that respond to volume or scale and those that are driven by variety. Scale-related costs decline as volume increases, usually falling 15 per cent to 25 per cent per unit each time volume doubles. Variety-related costs, on the other hand,

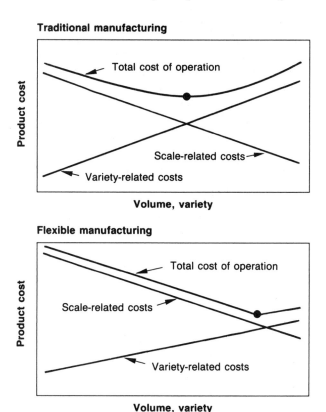

Figure 2 *The advantage of flexible manufacturing*

reflect the costs of complexity in manufacturing: set-up, materials handling, inventory, and many of the overhead costs of a factory. In most
cases, as variety increases, costs increase, usually at a rate of 20 per cent
to 35 per cent per unit each time variety doubles.

The sum of the scale- and variety-related costs represents the total cost
of manufacturing. With effort, managers can determine the optimum cost
point for their factories – the point where the combination of volume and
variety yields the lowest total manufacturing cost for a particular plant.
When markets are good, companies tend to edge toward increased variety
in search of higher volumes, even though this will mean increased costs.
When times are tough, companies pare their product lines, cutting variety
to reduce costs.

In a flexible factory system, variety-driven costs start lower and increase
more slowly as variety grows. Scale costs remain unchanged. Thus the
optimum cost point for a flexible factory occurs at a higher volume and
with greater variety than for a traditional factory. A gap emerges between
the costs of the flexible and the traditional factory – a cost variety gap
that represents the competitive advantage of flexible production. Very

simply, a flexible factory enjoys more variety with lower total costs than traditional factories, which are still forced to make the trade-off between scale and variety. (See Figure 2.)

Yanmar Diesel illustrates how this process works. In 1973, with the Japanese economy in recession, Yanmar Diesel was mired in red ink. Worse, there was no promise that once the recession had passed, the existing strategy and program would guarantee real improvement in the company's condition.

As a Toyota supplier, Yanmar Diesel was familiar with the automaker's flexible manufacturing system. Moreover, Yanmar was impressed with the automaker's ability to weather the recession without losing money. Yanmar decided to install the Toyota procedure in its own two factories. The changeover took less than five years and produced dramatic results: manufacturing costs declined 40 per cent to 60 per cent, depending on the product; factory break-even points dropped 80 per cent to 50 per cent; total manufacturing labor productivity improved by more than 100 per cent.

But it was Yanmar's newfound capability in product variety that signaled the arrival of a unique strategic edge: during the restructuring Yanmar more than quadrupled its product line. With focused factories, Yanmar could have doubled productivity in such a short time only by reducing the breadth of the product line by 75 per cent. The Toyota system made Yanmar's factories more flexible, reducing costs and producing a greater variety of products.

As its inventor, Taiichi Ohno, said, the Toyota production system was 'born of the need to make many types of automobiles, in small quantities with the same manufacturing process.' With its emphasis on just-in-time production, total quality control, employee decision-making on the factory floor, and close supplier relations, the Toyota system gave the many Japanese manufacturers who adopted it in the mid-1970s a distinct competitive advantage.

A comparison of a US company with a Japanese competitor in the manufacture of a particular automotive suspension component illustrates the nature and extent of the Japanese advantage. The US company bases its strategy on scale and focus: it produces 10 million units per year – making it the world's largest producer – and offers only eleven types of finished parts. The Japanese company's strategy, on the other hand, is to exploit flexibility. It is both smaller and less focused: it manufactures only 3.5 million units per year but has thirty-eight types of finished parts.

With one-third the scale and more than three times the product variety, the Japanese company also boasts total labor productivity that is half again that of its American competitor. Moreover, the unit cost of the Japanese manufacturer is less than half that of the US company. But interestingly, the productivity of the Japanese direct laborers is not as high as that of the US workers, a reflection of the difference in scale. The Japanese advantage comes from the productivity of the overhead

Table 1 *Flexible manufacturing's productivity edge (Automobile suspension component)*

	US competitor	Japanese competitor
Annual volume	10M	3.5M
Employees		
Direct	107	50
Indirect	135	7
Total	242	57
Annual units/employee	43,100	61,400
Types of finished parts	11	38
Unit cost for comparable part (index)	$100	$49

(1987 figures)

employees: with one-third the volume and three times the variety, the Japanese company has only one-eighteenth the overhead employees. (See Table 1.)

In the late 1970s, Japanese companies exploited flexible manufacturing to the point that a new competitive thrust emerged – the variety war. A classic example of a variety war was the battle that erupted between Honda and Yamaha for supremacy in the motorcycle market, a struggle popularly known in Japanese business circles as the H-Y War. Yamaha ignited the H-Y War in 1981 when it announced the opening of a new factory which would make it the world's largest motorcycle manufacturer, a prestigious position held by Honda. But Honda had been concentrating its corporate resources on the automobile business and away from its motorcycle operation. Now, faced with Yamaha's overt and public challenge, Honda chose to counter-attack.

Honda launched its response with the war cry, 'Yamaha wo tsubusu!' ('We will crush, squash, slaughter Yamaha!'). In the no-holds-barred battle that ensued, Honda cut prices, flooded distribution channels, and boosted advertising expenditures. Most important – and most impressive to consumers – Honda also rapidly increased the rate of change in its product line, using variety to bury Yamaha. At the start of the war, Honda had sixty models of motorcycles. Over the next eighteen months, Honda introduced or replaced 113 models, effectively turning over its entire product line twice. Yamaha also began the war with sixty models; it was able to manage only thirty-seven changes in its product line during those eighteen months.

Honda's new product introductions devastated Yamaha. First, Honda succeeded in making motorcycle design a matter of fashion, where newness and freshness were important attributes for consumers. Second, Honda raised the technological sophistication of its products, introducing four-valve engines, composites, direct drive, and other new features. Next to a Honda, Yamaha products looked old, unattractive, and out of date.

Demand for Yamaha products dried up; in a desperate effort to move them, dealers were forced to price them below cost. But even that did not work. At the most intense point in the H-Y War, Yamaha had more than twelve months of inventory in its dealers' showrooms. Finally Yamaha surrendered. In a public statement, Yamaha President Eguchi announced, 'We want to end the H-Y War. It is our fault. Of course there will be competition in the future but it will be based on a mutual recognition of our respective positions.'

Honda did not go unscathed either. The company's sales and service network was severely disrupted, requiring additional investment before it returned to a stable footing. However, so decisive was its victory that Honda effectively had as much time as it wanted to recover. It had emphatically defended its title as the world's largest motorcycle producer and done so in a way that warned Suzuki and Kawasaki not to challenge that leadership. Variety had won the war.

Time-based competitive advantage

The strength of variety as a competitive weapon raises an interesting question. How could Japanese companies accommodate such rapid rates of change? In Honda's case, there could be only three possible answers. The company did one of the following:

1 Began the development of more than 100 new models 10 to 15 years before the attack.
2 Authorized a sudden, massive spending surge to develop and manufacture products on a crash basis.
3 Used structurally different methods to develop, manufacture, and introduce new products.

In fact, what Honda and other variety-driven competitors pioneered was time-based competitiveness. They managed structural changes that enabled their operations to execute their processes much faster. As a consequence, time became their new source of competitive advantage.

While time is a basic business performance variable, management seldom monitors its consumption explicitly – almost never with the same precision accorded sales and costs. Yet time is a more critical competitive yardstick than traditional financial measurements.

Today's new-generation companies compete with flexible manufacturing and rapid-response systems, expanding variety and increasing innovation. A company that builds its strategy on this cycle is a more powerful competitor than one with a traditional strategy based on low wages, scale, or focus. These older, cost-based strategies require managers to do whatever is necessary to drive down costs: move production to or source from a low-wage country: build new facilities or consolidate old plants to gain economies of scale; or focus operations down to the most economic subset of activities. These tactics reduce costs but at the expense of responsiveness.

In contrast, strategies based on the cycle of flexible manufacturing, rapid response, expanding variety, and increasing innovation are time based. Factories are close to the customers they serve. Organization structures enable fast responses rather than low costs and control. Companies concentrate on reducing if not eliminating delays and using their response advantages to attract the most profitable customers.

Many – but certainly not all – of today's time-based competitors are Japanese. Some of them are Sony, Matsushita, Sharp, Toyota, Hitachi, NEC, Toshiba, Honda, and Hino; time-based Western companies include Benetton, The Limited, Federal Express, Domino's Pizza, Wilson Art, and McDonald's. For these leading competitors, time has become the overarching measurement of performance. By reducing the consumption of time in every aspect of the business, these companies also reduce costs, improve quality, and stay close to their customers.

Breaking the planning loop

Companies are systems; time connects all the parts. The most powerful competitors understand this axiom and are breaking the debilitating loop that strangles much of traditional manufacturing planning.

Traditional manufacturing requires long lead times to resolve conflicts between various jobs or activities that require the same resources. The long lead times, in turn, require sales forecasts to guide planning. But sales forecasts are inevitably wrong; by definition they are guesses, however informed. Naturally, as lead times lengthen, the accuracy of sales forecasts declines. With more forecasting errors, inventories balloon and the need for safety stocks at all levels increases. Errors in forecasting also mean more unscheduled jobs that have to be expedited, thereby crowding out scheduled jobs. The need for longer lead times grows even greater and the planning loop expands even more, driving up costs, increasing delays, and creating system inefficiencies.

Managers who find themselves trapped in the planning loop often respond by asking for better forecasts and longer lead times. In other words, they treat the symptoms and worsen the problem. The only way to break the planning loop is to reduce the consumption of time throughout the system; that will, in turn, cut the need for lead time, for estimates, for safety stocks, and all the rest. After all, if a company could ever drive its lead time all the way to zero, it would have to forecast only the next day's sales. While that idea of course is unrealistic, successful time-based competitors in Japan and in the West have kept their lead times from growing and some have even reduced them, thereby diminishing the planning loop's damaging effects.

Thirty years ago, Jay W. Forrester of MIT published a pioneering

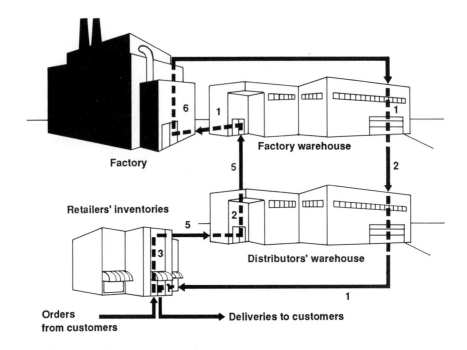

Figure 3   *Time in the planning loop (in weeks)*

article in *Harvard Business Review*, 'Industrial Dynamics: A Major Breakthrough for Decision Makers' (July–August 1958), which established a model of time's impact on an organization's performance. Using 'industrial dynamics' – a concept originally developed for ship-board fire control systems – Forrester tracked the effects of time delays and decision rates within a simple business system consisting of a factory, a factory warehouse, a distributor's inventory, and retailers' inventories. The numbers in Figure 3 are the delays in the flow of information or product, measured in weeks. In this example, the orders accumulate at the retailer for three weeks, are in the mail for half a week, are delayed at the distributor for two weeks, go back into the mail for another half a week, and need eight weeks for processing at the factory and its warehouse. Then the finished product begins it journey back to the retailer. The cycle takes nineteen weeks.

The system in this example is very stable – as long as retail demand is stable or as long as forecasts are accurate nineteen weeks into the future. But if unexpected changes occur, the system must respond. The chart, also taken from the Forrester article, shows what happens to this system when a simple change takes place: demand goes up 10 per cent, then flat-tens. Acting on new forecasts and seeking to cut delivery delays, the factory first responds by ramping up production 40 per cent. When management realizes – too late – that it has overshot the mark, it cuts

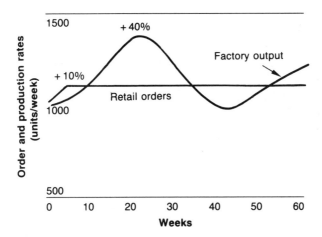

Figure 4 *Unexpected change distorts the system*

production 30 per cent. Too late again it learns that it has overcorrected. This ramping up and cutting back continue until finally the system stabilizes, more than a year after the initial 10 per cent increase.

What distorts the system so badly is time: the lengthy delay between the event that creates the new demand and the time when the factory finally receives the information. The longer that delay, the more distorted is the view of the market. Those distortions reverberate throughout the system, producing disruption, waste, and inefficiency.

These distortions plague business today. To escape them, companies have a choice: they can produce to forecast or they can reduce the time delays in the flow of information and product through the system. The traditional solution is to produce to forecast. The new approach is to reduce time consumption.

Because time flows throughout the system, focusing on time-based competitive performance results in improvements across the board. Companies generally become time-based competitors by first correcting their manufacturing techniques, then fixing sales and distribution, and finally adjusting their approach to innovation. Ultimately, it becomes the basis for a company's overall strategy.

Time-based manufacturing

In general, time-based manufacturing policies and practices differ from those of traditional manufacturing along three key dimensions: length of production runs, organization of process components, and complexity of scheduling procedures.

When it comes to lot size, for instance, traditional factories attempt to maximize production runs while time-based manufacturers try to shorten their production runs as much as possible. In fact, many Japanese companies aim for run lengths of a single unit. The thinking behind this is as simple as it is fundamental to competitive success: reduced run lengths mean more frequent production of the complete mix of products and faster response to customers' demands.

Factory layout also contributes to time-based competitive advantage. Traditional factories are usually organized by process technology centers. For example, metal goods manufacturers organize their factories into shearing, punching, and braking departments; electronic assemblers have stuffing, wave soldering, assembly, testing, and packing departments. Parts move from one process technology center to the next. Each step consumes valuable time: parts sit, waiting to move; then move; then wait to be used in the next step. In a traditional manufacturing system products usually receive value for only 0.05 per cent to 2.5 per cent of the time that they are in the factory. The rest of the time products sit waiting for something to happen.

Time-based factories, however, are organized by product. To minimize handling and moving of parts, the manufacturing functions for a component or a product are as close together as possible. Parts move from one activity to the next with little or no delay. Because the production process eliminates the need to pile and repile parts, they flow quickly and efficiently through the factory.

In traditional factories, scheduling is also a source of delay and waste. Most traditional factories use central scheduling that requires sophisticated materials resource planning and shop-floor control systems. Even though these systems are advanced, they still waste time: work orders usually flow to the factory floor on a monthly or weekly basis. In the meantime, parts can sit idle.

In time-based factories, local scheduling enables employees to make more production control decisions on the factory floor, without the time-consuming loop back to management for approval. Moreover, the combination of the product-oriented layout of the factory and local scheduling makes the total production process run more smoothly. Once a part starts through the production run, many of the requirements between manufacturing steps are purely automatic and require no intermediate scheduling.

These differences between traditional and time-based factories add up. Flexible factories enjoy big advantages in both productivity and time: labor productivity in time-based factories can be as much as 200 per cent higher than in conventional plants; time-based factories can respond eight to ten times faster than traditional factories. Flexible production means significant improvements in labor and net-asset productivity, These, in turn, yield reductions of up to 20 per cent in overall costs and increases in growth for much less investment.

Toyota offers a dramatic example of the kinds of improvements that leading time-based competitors are making. Dissatisfied with the response time of a supplier, Toyota went to work. It took the supplier fifteen days to turn out a component after arrival of the raw materials at its factory. The first step was to cut lot sizes, reducing response time to six days. Next Toyota streamlined the factory layout, reducing the number of inventory holding points. The response time fell to three days. Finally Toyota eliminated all work-in-progress inventories at the supplier's plant. New response time: one day.

Toyota, of course, is not alone in improving manufacturing response times. Matsushita cut the time needed to make washing machines from 360 hours to just 2, Honda slashed its motorcycle fabricating time by 80 per cent; in North America, companies making motor controllers and electrical components for unit air conditioners have improved their manufacturing response time by 90 per cent.

Time-based sales and distribution

A manufacturer's next challenge is to avoid dissipation of factory performance improvements in other parts of the organization. In Jay Forrester's example of the planning loop, the factory and its warehouse accounted for roughly one-half of the system's time. In actuality today, the factory accounts for one-third to one-half of the total time – often the most 'visible' portion of time. But other parts of the system are just as important, if less apparent. For example, in the Forrester system, sales and distribution consume as much or more time than manufacturing.

What Forrester modeled, the Japanese experienced. By the late 1970s, leading Japanese companies were finding that inefficient sales and distribution operations undercut the benefits of their flexible manufacturing systems. Toyota, which at that time was divided into two separate companies, Toyota Motor Manufacturing and Toyota Motor Sales, again makes this point. Toyota Motor Manufacturing could manufacture a car in less than two days. But Toyota Motor Sales needed from fifteen to twenty-six days to close the sale, transmit the order to the factory, get the order scheduled, and deliver the car to the customer. By the late 1970s, the cost-conscious, competition-minded engineers at Toyota Manufacturing were angry at their counterparts at Toyota Motor Sales, who were frittering away the advantage gained in the production process. The sales and distribution function was generating 20 per cent to 30 per cent of a car's cost to the customer – more than it cost Toyota to manufacture the car!

Finally, in 1982 Toyota moved decisively to remedy the problem. The company merged Toyota Motor Manufacturing and Toyota Motor Sales. The company announced that it wanted to become 'more market driven'. While Toyota assured the public that the reorganization only returned it to its original configuration in the 1950s, within eighteen months all the Toyota Motor Sales directors retired. Their jobs were left vacant or filled by executives from Toyota Motor Manufacturing.

The company wasted no time in implementing a plan to cut delays in sales and distribution, reduce costs, and improve customer service. The old system, Toyota found, had handled customer orders in batches. Orders and other crucial information would accumulate at one step of the sales and distribution process before dispatch to the next level, which wasted time and generated extra costs.

To speed the flow of information, Toyota had to reduce the size of the information batches. The solution came from a company-developed computer system that tied its salespeople directly to the factory scheduling operation. This link bypassed several levels of the sales and distribution function and enabled the modified system to operate with very small batches of orders.

Toyota expected this new approach to cut the sales and distribution cycle time in half – from four to six weeks to just two to three weeks across Japan. (For the Tokyo and Osaka regions, which account for roughly two-thirds of Japan's population, the goal was to reduce cycle time to just two days.) But by 1987 Toyota had reduced system responsiveness to eight days, including the time required to make the car. In the Forrester example, this achievement is equivalent to cutting the nineteen-week cycle to six weeks. The results were predictable: shorter sales forecasts, lower costs, happier customers.

Time-based innovation

A company that can bring out new products three times faster than its competitors enjoys a huge advantage. Today, in one industry after another, Japanese manufacturers are doing just that to their Western competition:

- In projection television, Japanese producers can develop a new television in one-third the time required by US manufacturers.
- In custom plastic injection molds, Japanese companies can develop the molds in one-third the time of US competitors and at one-third the cost.
- In autos, Japanese companies can develop new products in half the time – and with half as many people – as the US and German competition.

To accomplish their fast-paced innovations, leading Japanese manufacturers have introduced a series of organizational techniques that precisely parallel their approach to flexible manufacturing:

- In manufacturing, the Japanese stress short production runs and small lot sizes. In innovation, they favor smaller increments of improvement in new products, but introduce them more often – versus the Western approach of more significant improvements made less often.
- In the organization of product development work, the Japanese use

factory cells that are cross-functional teams. Most Western new product development activity is carried out by functional centers.
- In the scheduling of work, Japanese factories stress local responsibility, just as product development scheduling is decentralized. The Western approach to both requires plodding centralized scheduling, plotting, and tracking.

The effects of this time-based advantage are devastating; quite simply, American companies are losing leadership of technology and innovation – supposedly this country's source of long-term advantage.

Unless US companies reduce their new product development and introduction cycles from thirty-six to forty-eight months to twelve to eighteen months, Japanese manufacturers will easily out-innovate and outperform them. Taking the initiative in innovation will require even faster cycle times.

Residential air conditioners illustrate the Japanese ability to introduce more technological innovation in smaller increments – and how in just a few years these improvements add up to remarkably superior products. The Japanese introduce innovations in air conditioners four times faster than their American competitors; in technological sophistication the Japanese products are seven to ten years ahead of US products.

Look at the changes in Mitsubishi Electric's three-horsepower heat pump between 1975 and 1985. From 1975 to 1979, the company did nothing to the product except change the sheet metal work, partly to improve efficiency but mostly to reduce materials costs. In 1979, the technological sophistication of the product was roughly equal to that of the US competition. From this point on, the Japanese first established, and then widened the lead.

In 1980, Mitsubishi introduced its first major improvement: a new product that used integrated circuits to control the air-conditioning cycle. One year later, the company replaced the integrated circuits with microprocessors and added two important innovations to increase consumer demand. The first was 'quick connect' freon lines. On the old product (and on the US product) freon lines were made from copper tubing and cut to length, bent, soldered together, purged, and filled with freon – an operation requiring great skill to produce a reliable air conditioner. The Japanese substituted quick-connect freon lines – precharged hoses that simply clicked together. The second innovation was simplified wiring. On the old product (and still today on the US product) the unit had six color-coded wires to connect. The advent of microprocessors made possible a two-wire connection with neutral polarity.

These two changes did not improve the energy-efficiency ratio of the product; nor were they intended to. Rather, the point was to fabricate a unit that would be simpler to install and more reliable, thereby broadening distribution and increasing demand. Because of these innovations, white-goods outlets could sell the new product, and local contractors could easily install it.

In 1982, Mitsubishi introduced a new version of the air conditioner featuring technological advances related to performance. A high-efficiency rotary compressor replaced the outdated reciprocating compressor. The condensing unit had louvered fins and inner fin tubes for better heat transfer. Because the balance of the system changed, all the electronics had to change. As a result, the energy-efficiency ratio improved markedly.

In 1983, Mitsubishi added sensors to the unit and more computing power, expanding the electronic control of the cycle and again improving the energy-efficiency ratio.

In 1984, Mitsubishi came out with another version of the product, this time with an inverter that made possible an even higher energy-efficiency ratio. The inverter, which requires additional electronics for the unit, allows unparalleled control over the speed of the electric motor, dramatically boosting the appliance's efficiency.

Using time-based innovations, Mitsubishi transformed its air conditioner. The changes came incrementally and steadily. Overall they gave Mitsubishi – and other Japanese companies on the same track – the position of technological leadership in the global residential air-conditioning industry.

In 1985, a US air-conditioner manufacturer was just debating whether to use integrated circuits in its residential heat pump. In view of its four- to five-year product development cycle, it could not have introduced the innovation until 1989 or 1990 – putting the American company ten years behind the Japanese. Faced with this situation, the US air-conditioner company followed the example of many US manufacturers that have lost the lead in technology and innovation: it decided to source its air conditioners and components from its Japanese competition.

Time-based strategy

The possibility of establishing a response time advantage opens new avenues for constructing winning competitive strategies. At most companies, strategic choices are limited to three options:

1 Seeking coexistence with competitors. This choice is seldom stable, since competitors refuse to cooperate and stay put.
2 Retreating in the face of competitors. Many companies choose this course; the business press fills its pages with accounts of companies retreating by consolidating plants, focusing their operations, outsourcing, divesting businesses, pulling out of markets, or moving upscale.
3 Attacking, either directly or indirectly. The direct attack involves the classic confrontation – cut price and add capacity, creating head-on competition. Indirect attack requires surprise. Competitors either do not understand the strategies being used against them or they do understand but cannot respond – sometimes because of the speed of the attack, sometimes because of their inability to mount a response.

Of the three options, only an attack creates the opportunity for real growth. Direct attack demands superior resources; it is always expensive and potentially disastrous. Indirect attack promises the most gain for the least cost. Time-based strategy offers a powerful new approach for successful indirect attacks against larger, established competitors.

Consider the remarkable example of Atlas Door, a ten-year-old US company. It has grown at an average annual rate of 15 per cent in an industry with an overall annual growth rate of less than 5 per cent. In recent years, its pretax earnings were 20 per cent of sales, about five times the industry average. Atlas is debt free. In its tenth year the company achieved the number one competitive position in its industry.

The company's product: industrial doors. It is a product with almost infinite variety, involving limitless choices of width and height and material. Because of the importance of variety, inventory is almost useless in meeting customer orders; most doors can be manufactured only after the order has been placed.

Historically, the industry had needed almost four months to respond to an order for a door that was out of stock or customized. Atlas' strategic advantage was time: it could respond in weeks to any order. It had structured its order-entry, engineering, manufacturing, and logistics systems to move information and products quickly and reliably.

First, Atlas built just-in-time factories. These are fairly simple in concept. They require extra tooling and machinery to reduce changeover times and a fabrication process organized by product and scheduled to start and complete all of the parts at the same time. But even the performance of the factory – critical to the company's overall responsiveness – still only accounted for two-and-a-half weeks of the completed product delivery cycle.

Second, Atlas compressed time at the front end of the system, where the order first entered and was processed. Traditionally, when customers, distributors, or salespeople called a door manufacturer with a request for a price and delivery, they would have to wait more than a week for a response. If the desired door was not in stock, not in the schedule, or not even engineered, the supplier's organization would waste even more time, pushing the search for an answer around the system.

Recognizing the opportunity to cut deeply into the time expenditure in this part of the system, Atlas first streamlined, then automated its entire order-entry, engineering, pricing, and scheduling processes. Today Atlas can price and schedule 95 per cent of its incoming orders while the callers are still on the telephone. It can quickly engineer new special orders because it has preserved on computer the design and production data of all previous special orders – which drastically reduces the amount of re-engineering necessary.

Third, Atlas tightly controlled logistics so that it always shipped only fully complete orders to construction sites. Orders require many components. Gathering all of them at the factory and making sure that they are with the correct order can be a time-consuming task. It is even more time-consuming, however, to get the correct parts to the job site *after* they have missed the initial shipment. Atlas developed a system to track the parts in production and the purchased parts for each order, ensuring arrival of all necessary parts at the shipping dock in time – a just-in-time logistics operation.

When Atlas started operations, distributors were uninterested in its product. The established distributors already carried the door line of a larger competitor; they saw no reason to switch suppliers except, perhaps, for a major price concession. But as a start-up, Atlas was too small to compete on price alone. Instead, it positioned itself as the door supplier of last resort, the company people came to if the established supplier could not deliver or missed a key date.

Of course, with industry lead times of almost four months, some calls inevitably came to Atlas. And when it did get a call, Atlas commanded a higher price because of its faster delivery. Atlas not only got a higher price but its time-based processes also yielded lower costs: it thus enjoyed the best of both worlds.

In ten short years, the company replaced the leading door suppliers in 80 per cent of the distributors in the country. With its strategic advantage the company could be selective, becoming the house supplier for only the strongest distributors.

In the wake of this indirect attack, the established competitors have not responded effectively. The conventional view is that Atlas is a 'garage shop operator' that cannot sustain its growth: competitors expect the company's performance to degrade to the industry average as it grows larger. But this response – or non-response – only reflects a fundamental lack of understanding of time as the source of competitive advantage. The extra delay in responding only adds to the insurmountable lead the indirect time-based attack has created. While the traditional companies track costs and size, the new competitor derives advantage from time, staying on the cutting edge, leaving its rivals behind.

SECTION 3

DEVELOPING STRATEGY

This final section returns to some of the key themes first set out at the beginning of the book. In particular it addresses the process of moving towards 'creating and managing' the future through strategic planning.

The first two chapters examine how two of the leading exponents of sophisticate ! planning, Royal Dutch/Shell and ICI, set about developing their strategies. Both are in similar fields, oil/chemical process industries, where investments have to be recouped not just over years, but decades; so it is unsurprising that they both adopt long time-scales in their planning processes. In particular, both are among the few organizations which make practical use of scenarios in their long-range planning.

Indeed, as described in the first chapter, 'Scenarios: shooting the rapids' by Pierre Wack, Royal Dutch/Shell use these as the central focus of their whole strategy process. In effect three alternative, complementary scenarios, *become* the corporate strategy. Depending upon which of the many alternative futures emerges at the detailed level, the company selects the most appropriate response already documented in one of these scenarios.

In the case of ICI, as described in the second chapter, 'Strategic leadership through corporate planning at ICI', by Alan I.H. Pink, scenarios are used as the (long-term) input to a more conventional planning process. Thus, alternative – but not complementary – scenarios are constructed to describe the long-term (10 or more years) future. Of these, (contrary to the most rigorous use of scenarios), just one is selected; to be developed as the conventional, single strand, forecast to which the usual corporate-planning processes are then applied.

Comparison between the two approaches is enlightening as illustration of how scenarios may, in different ways, contribute to long-range planning; and, more importantly, of how long-range planning in general may be conducted, to allow for the uncertainties which emerge over such long time-scales.

The third chapter, 'Strategic planning – which style do you need?', by Bernard Taylor, offers an overview of a range of different approaches to strategic planning, each reflecting a different level of sophistication and indeed a different philosophy about the nature and role of the strategic-planning process. It usefully overviews the diversity of strategic-planning approaches within organizations, and, as the author argues, offers managers one way of 'locating' and assessing the strategic planning undertaken in their own organizations.

As a footnote, but an important one, corporate strategy should also be tempered by an organization's responsibilities *to* its external environment. An organization may have a wide range of stakeholders, few of whom will be satisfied by the simple provision of maximum profits. A number of these stakeholders, especially those in the community at large, look to the organization to live up to certain values – often summarized as 'service to the community'.

This naturally leads to the concept of ethics in management: conventionally not a key issue for management but one which has increasingly come to the fore in the teaching of management schools. It is a complex subject but we believe we can do no better than let Sir Adrian Cadbury have the last word in the final chapter, 'Ethical managers make their own rules'.

17

Scenarios: shooting the rapids

Pierre Wack

I recently discussed scenario analysis with a well-known futurist. After I had listened to his presentation of a set of six scenarios, he asked me what I thought. 'It was beautifully written, if complex,' I replied. When pressed, I admitted that is was 'impenetrable.' I added, 'The managers who hear it won't know what to do with it.' To which the consultant responded, 'That is not really my concern. I simply lay out the possibilities for them. It is up to the managers to know what they should do. I can't possibly tell them.'

This small illustration points up the key problem with scenario planning: the interface of scenarios and decision-makers is ignored or neglected. By interface, I mean the point at which the scenario really touches a chord in the manager's mind – the moment at which it has real meaning for him or her. The fact that those with the responsibility for preparing the scenarios do not feel any responsibility for the interface is the main reason that – despite the logical appeal scenarios should have for managers disenchanted with forecasts – scenario planning has been scarcely developed.

Scenarios that merely quantify alternative outcomes of obvious uncertainties never inspire a management team's enthusiasm, even if all the alternatives are plausible. Most executives do not like to face such alternatives. They yearn for some kind of 'definiteness' when dealing with the uncertainty that is the business environment, even if they have had their fingers burned for relying on past forecasts.

The same managers who can easily decide between different courses of action when they are in control often become unstuck when confronted with alternative futures they can't control and don't really understand. The reason is partly historical: many managers developed their skills in the 1950s and 1960s, an era characterized by an unusually high level of economic predictability. Being competent then meant knowing the right answer; it was considered incompetent or unprofessional to say, 'Things could go this way – or that.'

In truth, scenarios are often popular with middle managers who do not have to make awesome, final decisions. It is really top managers – who have ultimate responsibility for a company's long-term strategy – who

Reprinted from *Harvard Business Review*, Nov/Dec 1985: 139–50. Copyright © 1985 by the President and Fellows of Harvard College.

find scenarios unhelpful. Most have risen to the top of large organizations based on their good judgment. They are proud of that judgment and trust it; their faith in it is one of their key motivations. The usual scenario analysis confronts them with raw uncertainties on which they cannot exercise their judgment. Because they cannot use what they consider to be their best quality, they often say, 'Why bother with all that scenario stuff? We'll go on as before.' Top management's desire for a framework in which to exercise good judgment is so strong that many executives continue to rely on forecasts, even though they know that forecasts often miss critical turning points in the business environment and even when they have been hurt by poor forecasts before.

What distinguishes Shell's decision scenarios from the first-generation analyses delineated in my earlier article is not primarily technical; it is a different philosophy, having to do with management perceptions and judgment.[1] The technicalities of decision scenarios derive from that philosophy. Almost by definition, scanning the business environment and crystallizing the findings in a set of scenarios means dealing with a world outside the corporation: for example, the evolution of demand, supply, prices, technology, competition, business cycle changes, and so forth. But this is only a half-truth and dangerous because there is another half. Because the raw materials of scenarios are made from this stuff of 'outer space,' it is not realized that more is needed: scenarios must come alive in 'inner space,' the manager's microcosm where choices are played out and judgment exercised.

Scenarios deal with two worlds: the world of facts and the world of perceptions. They explore for facts but they aim at perceptions inside the heads of decision-makers. Their purpose is to gather and transform information of strategic significance into fresh perceptions. This transformation process is not trivial – more often than not it does not happen. When it works it is a creative experience that generates a heartfelt 'Aha!' from your managers and leads to strategic insights beyond the mind's previous reach.

I have found that getting to that management 'Aha!' is the real challenge of scenario analysis. It does not simply leap at you when you've presented all the possible alternatives, no matter how eloquent your expression or how beautifully drawn your charts. It happens when your message reaches the microcosms of decision-makers, obliges them to question their assumptions about how their business world works, and leads them to change and reorganize their inner models of reality.

Setting out

Scenario analysis demands first that managers understand the forces driving their business systems rather than rely on forecasts or alternatives (that is, someone else's understanding and judgment crystallized in a figure that then becomes a substitute for thinking). Using scenarios is as different from relying on forecasts as judo is from boxing: you want to use outside forces to your competitive advantage and make them work for you so that two plus two equals five and even more. You will find little or no power by merely accepting expert information about an outcome like the future price of oil or the future level of demand; power comes with an understanding of the forces behind the outcome. Scenarios must help decision-makers develop their own feel for the nature of the system, the forces at work within it, the uncertainties that underlie the alternative scenarios, and the concepts useful for interpreting key data.

Scenarios structure the future into predetermined and uncertain elements (see Figure 1). The foundation of decision scenarios lies in exploration and expansion of the predetermined elements: events already in the pipeline whose consequences have yet to unfold, interdependencies within the system (surprises often arise from interconnectedness), breaks in trends, or the 'impossible.' Decision scenarios rule out impossible developments; they deny much more than they affirm.

I will now take a risk and describe a ten-year-old scenario analysis. It is a risk because the scenario's subject is the business cycle, and no subject threatens to bore the reader in quite the same way as a business cycle that has passed. Even so, the discussion is important because:

1 We may be near the top of the business cycle, and a recession with serious implications could begin, given the fragility of the world economy. It troubles me that so few companies have analyzed the implications for them of economic developments outside the range of surprise-free possibility. Macroeconomists may discuss contingencies but managers do not.
2 The scenario analysis I presented in the first article* was somewhat atypical. It dealt with an economic disruption of a magnitude we do not often encounter. Moreover, we believed the disruption was a predetermined factor; uncertain were the reactions to it.

The following example deals with more typical cyclical fluctuations. We presented it in May 1975, when the world was nearly at the bottom of the worst recession since World War II.

Analyzing the predetermined elements

When the oil shock of 1973–4 made the dreams – and nightmares – described in the scenarios discussed in my first article* come true, managers at Shell (like managers everywhere) redirected their attention to the short term, focusing on economic growth, oil demand, inflation, interest rates, and their sensitive relationship with OPEC suppliers. In

---

* In the previous issue of *The Harvard Business Review* [ed.]

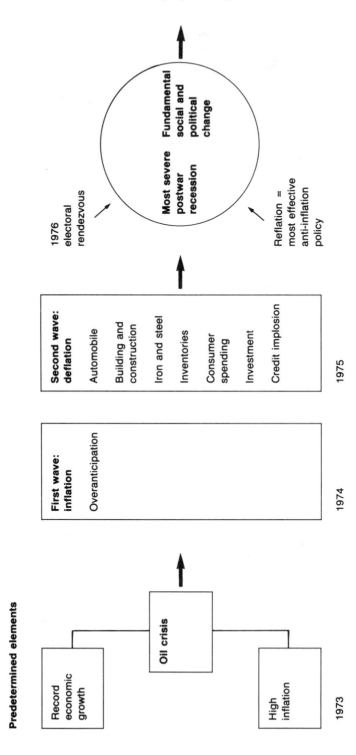

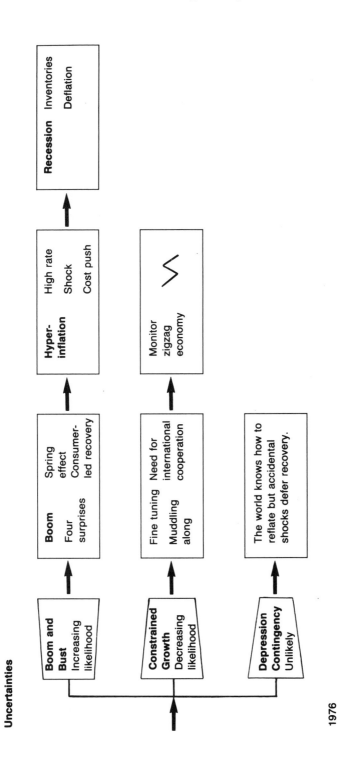

Figure 1 *Global framework (1975)*

1975, we addressed their concerns by developing medium-term scenarios for the rapids. The predetermined elements of these scenarios were:

The first wave – inflation   Like a large rock dropped in a lake, the 1973 oil price increase generated a series of waves, beginning with inflation, which was higher than simple cost-through-the-system arithmetic would indicate (on average, only 3 per cent or 4 per cent). Booming world economies were already out of balance prior to the oil shock and affected by high inflation. Furthermore, the enormous publicity surrounding the oil price increase (coming as it did with production cuts and selective embargoes) caused major economic actors – trade unions, entrepreneurs, and consumers – to overanticipate the actual inflationary impact. Such overreaction added fuel to the fire, accelerating the rate of inflation.

The second wave – deflation   From mid-1974, a contraction in demand to well below production capacity followed. The extra cash outflow to OPEC acted like an external excise tax on consumer demand of some $60 billion each year – or 2.5 per cent of OECD economies. Government anti-inflation policies contributed to pushing demand far below production potential. Economic dominoes fell one by one as:

- The automobile industry, always on the margin of discretionary spending and vulnerable to both the real increase in gasoline prices and the 'oil link' in the consumer's mind, suffered an immediate decline, with extensive multiplier effects through the balance of the economy.
- Building and construction, also a powerful engine of economic activity, fell some six months later as government anti-inflation policies caused a credit crunch.
- The world iron and steel industry remained an island of continuing high activity for nine months after the oil shock. It was propped up by a backlog of orders (from shipyards, for instance) plus some stock building. Large orders from the communist world contributed toward keeping it buoyant longer than other sectors. Eventually, however, the decline in the automobile and construction industries had a domino effect on the iron and steel industry.

Two other actions deepened the recession. First, companies drastically ran down inventories. The imposition of credit controls in the face of shrinking demand and the expectation of a fall in prices guaranteed a drastic drop in inventories. When inventories are reduced by eight days, it is equivalent to forgoing six months of 5 per cent economic growth; inventories in many segments were reduced by more than eight days. Next, consumer spending, long the stable engine of OECD economies, took a nosedive. For the first time since recovery started in the early 1950s, consumers stopped buying, increased savings, and began to worry about what the future might hold. The resulting recession was the most severe since World War II (see Table 1).

Table 1 *Decline in industrial production measured from previous cyclical peak*

	USA	Europe	Japan
Recession, first quarter, 1975	− 14%	− 9%	− 19%
Previous postwar recessions	− 7%	− 2%	− 2%

Electoral rendezvous The governments of Japan, Germany, and the United States would each face the electorate in 1976. If the truism applies that people vote with their pocketbooks, then presiding over a recession is an invitation to defeat at the polls. The incentives for incumbent governments to go for growth were thus overwhelming.

Reflation in the pipeline Not only were politicians anticipating the 1976 elections, but they were also keenly aware that much of the hardship borne in 1975 was unnecessary and self-inflicted – the deflation was too harsh. With excess capacity so widespread, governments could safely reflate and expanding output could reduce unit prices and further curb inflation. Such reflation would largely be self-financing through taxation on increasing income, sales, and profits, and lowered costs for unemployment benefits.

Long-term unemployment was becoming evident as a social problem. Unemployment falls most heavily on the young. Few governments could afford to do nothing about the prospect of a third graduating class moving from the classroom to the welfare rolls.

All these predetermined elements combined to make it virtually certain that governments would attempt to reflate.

Reaching the rapids

We spent much time developing the predetermined elements and understanding the recent past. To recapitulate, managers will only accept scenarios when their common, predetermined elements enter and unfold in their minds. We call this process 'rooting' because scenarios on their own – that is, as mere description of alternative courses of events – would be effective and alive in the minds of managers as long as a tree without roots. I have seen many scenarios suffer this fate.

That economies would reflate was largely predetermined. What was unknown in the spring of 1975 was the timing and nature of the recovery. To illuminate the forces driving the further development of the system and its critical uncertainties, we designed two scenarios of recovery:

The 'Boom and Bust' scenario foresaw a vigorous recovery that contained the seeds of its own destruction.

The 'Constrained Growth' scenario projected a kind of 'muddling-through' recovery that would differ fundamentally from earlier business cycle recoveries.

We also considered the possibility that reflation would not happen; our 'Depression Contingency' scenario seemed so improbable, however, that we did not think it relevant for planning. The three possibilities are arrayed in Figure 1.

Boom and bust: a series of surprises

Boom and Bust described an economic world more characteristic of the 1950s than the 1960s. Cycles of greater amplitude and shorter duration would develop. We believed that the longer the recovery was deferred, the more likely this scenario – as governments turned to panic measures to reflate their economies.

First surprise – rapid recovery   Rather than tepid, the recovery would be swift, strong, and forceful, as some economies like that of the United States would grow by 11 per cent or 12 per cent in eighteen months. Such growth would be as if an economy the size of Britain's were to appear all at once on the world map. Such a rebound would not imply spectacular achievements; it would only reflect the depth of the 1973–5 dent in the economy – a coiled-spring effect.

Second surprise – oil-intensive recovery   Reports of OPEC's death, we believed, were premature. Even though news of energy savings might persuade governments that Western conservation measures could negate OPEC's negotiating strength, such a boast could not stand up to analysis. Reduced oil consumption resulted not from a fundamental change in behavior but mainly from the recession, which had cut both industrial and consumer demand. A boom in 1976 or 1977 would allow most consumers to revert to previous patterns of behavior and consumption. Economic growth in 1976–7 would have to be fueled by a rise in energy demand, particularly for oil (see Figure 2).

Third surprise – booming US oil imports   The upsurge in US oil imports would easily put to rest talk about 'Project Independence,' President Gerald Ford's import-reduction targets, and alternative energy projects. Our estimates indicated that in such a scenario US imports would rise by 2.5 million barrels per day in 1976 (more than Britain's total imports or Kuwait's current exports), with a further increase of 2 million barrels per day in 1977 (in aggregate, more than Britain's total energy consumption).

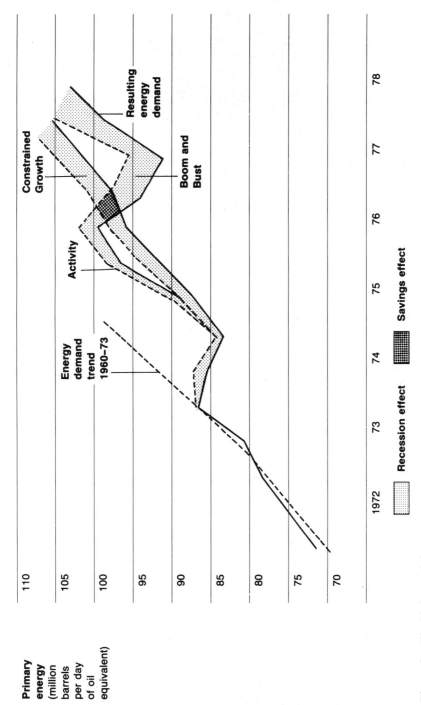

Figure 2 *World demand for energy*

Because we believed that a normal recovery would be equivalent to the sudden creation of a new economic nation, we could now add that the new nation would be almost totally dependent on Middle East oil. Consumer countries would once again be trapped.

Fourth surprise – stagnant alternative energies   Countries would find that alternative energy programs consisted largely of empty words and paper tigers. Most nuclear plants operated well below design capacity, and many had been deferred or canceled. Little had been done in the coal sector. The OECD nations were not meeting their target forecasts for coal production. The world had come far from the crash programs of the dark days of the oil embargo. Alternative energies could do little to relieve consumer countries' continued dependence on Middle East oil.

The bust – a second recession   High inflation – approaching hyperinflation in many of the weaker OECD nations – threatened a sustained recovery. Rates that would exceed the highest levels of 1974–5 by a further 5 per cent would become politically and socially intolerable, signaling to governments that the boom was getting out of control. Their reaction would be to reapply deflationary measures, including credit restrictions, higher interest rates, oil import controls, and limits on oil consumption. Just as the recovery would be surprisingly rapid, so the downturn could be sharp. Inventories would play an important role: stock building, starting from the depths of the current recession, would promote growth in production during the upswing. But as liquidity disappeared in the face of strong deflationary measures, stocks would be run down rapidly, making the downturn that much sharper.

How probably was the Boom and Bust scenario? Because it held out dramatic implications for all sectors of the world economy and oil in particular, we found it hard to give equal attention to the other scenario. Even so, in 1975, we still considered it less probable than its alternative, Constrained Growth. While we made no forecasts about the start of a boom, we were willing to assume that the longer the recovery took to get under way, the more likely the Boom and Bust scenario would occur.

Constrained growth: a new economic world

Everything in the Boom and Bust scenario was normal; the 'surprises' were typical of business cycles. The Constrained Growth scenario was built on a more genuine surprise: recovery would be slower and more halting than any upturn of the post-World War II era.

The internal logic of this scenario was that the high-growth trend of the past twenty-five years had come to an end – not only because of the oil shock and the eclipse of the Bretton Woods monetary order, but also because the very success of the postwar economies brought with it limitations on continued vigorous growth. Along with unprecedented economic growth had come unprecedented expectations for higher standards of living and more impressive social welfare programs. High expectations produced a new economic rigidity as governments were locked into a continual round of tax increases to pay for these social programs. Moreover, industrialized countries now were slower to change and adjust to surprises – whether an oil crisis or new competitors like Japan and the industrializing countries of Southeast Asia.

Constrained growth would characterize the first years of this new economic world in which all the engines of growth – consumption, international trade, government spending, and investment – would work with less power.

Investment was emphasized as a change that we called a lasting 'technological recession.' From the end of World War II until the early 1970s, the best new technology in basic industries could, on its own merit, outcompete existing technology. A new steel plant, for example, was more economical than an existing one per ton of capacity; new cement and paper plants, new refineries and tankers, and new power generation plants were regularly more efficient than the previous technology. Beginning in the early 1970s, however, such technological progress could not beat rising costs. It was now cheaper to acquire existing capacity than it was to order new capacity.

For perhaps ten to fifteen years, the unit capital and operating costs of almost all new plants in basic industries would exceed the costs of existing equipment. That would obviously discourage new investment in industries that had been the engine of postwar economic growth and accentuate inflationary pressure. We analyzed the other engines of growth: government spending would result in budget deficits and more rigidity; consumer spending would be changed by the maturation in the life cycle of a large range of consumer durables; and international trade would be characterized by accumulating imbalances and frictions.

The overall conclusion was that the prospects for economic growth would be well below past achievements. This confirmed one of our long-term scenarios introduced in 1974: we would enter – by means of this constrained growth period – a completely new 'world of internal contradictions': a world of low economic growth that would stand in stark contrast to the booming economies of the past twenty-five years.

Reaching shore

Let me give one final example of how global scenarios are used to bring focus to particular issues or projects. Scenarios are like cherry trees: their fruit grows neither on the trunk nor on the large boughs but rather on the small branches. The tree needs the trunk and boughs to grow the small branches.

The global scenarios I have described correspond to the tree's trunk; the country scenarios developed by the national Shell operating companies can be likened to boughs. They account for the predetermined and uncertain elements peculiar to their countries. The fruits are picked from the small branches. These are the scenarios that focus on a particular strategic issue, market, or investment.

One such set of focused scenarios has to do with the demand for OPEC oil – as opposed to oil received from other sources. Because OPEC oil is the balancing factor in the world energy system, its fluctuations reflect cyclical economic fluctuations – but amplified several times. A decline in economic activity translates into a larger decline in world oil consumption, which then translates into a much larger decline in OPEC oil demand. The reasons are: first, energy-intensive industries (like cement and steel) are more than proportionately affected in a recession; second, alternative energy sources are usually cheaper than oil; and third, OPEC oil, unlike domestic oil, has to be paid in foreign exchange.

In a recovery, a small rise in world energy demand would translate into larger rises in oil demand and even larger rises in OPEC oil demand. In the Boom and Bust scenario, for example, a 13 per cent increase in world energy demand in the first two years of a recovery would translate into a 23 per cent increase in world oil demand and a 34 per cent increase in OPEC oil demand. How would this demand match available supply? OPEC's oil production fluctuates in a narrow band between two danger zones (see Figure 3). Technical production capabilities and political willingness to produce determine the upper band, which is dangerous for oil-consuming countries; the threshold of 'OPEC dissatisfaction' is shown in the lower band, which is dangerous for oil-producing countries because the solidarity and discipline of OPEC come under severe stress.

As an illustration, we made two simulations (shown in Figure 3). The demand changes implicit in a normal boom starting in late 1975 would become manifest in the winter of 1976–7, when supply would be tight and prices under severe pressure. A boom starting in late 1976 would be less dangerous.

Looking back at the trip

In the recovery of 1976–8, economies developed mainly along the lines foreseen in the Constrained Growth scenario. We were indeed introduced to the world of internal contradictions. What had been the floor for long-term economic growth expectations before 1973 now became the ceiling. Many Shell managers recognized they were entering an era of slower growth and hedged their business plans accordingly. When the 1980s demanded leanness and restructuring, Shell was ready because it had begun the regimen early. That Shell saw this new world earlier than most could be seen by comparing the various energy forecasts made at the time. Shell consistently projected one of the lowest energy growth paths for the 1980s.

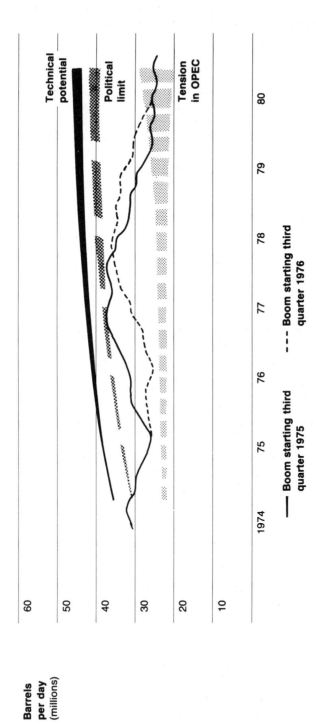

Figure 3 *OPEC production boundaries*

Scenarios serve two main purposes. The first is protective: anticipating and understanding risk. The second is entrepreneurial: discovering strategic options of which you were previously unaware. This latter purpose is in the long run more important. But while the more dramatic and (for Shell) dangerous of the two scenarios – Boom and Bust – did not occur, the exercise proved useful enough to our managers that medium-term scenarios were prepared every year thereafter while in the rapids. As C. W. MacMahon of the Bank of England has succinctly observed: 'No time is as usefully wasted as that spent guarding against disasters that do not in the event occur.'

Reflections in twilight

I have found that scenarios can effectively organize a variety of seemingly unrelated economic, technological, competitive, political, and societal information and translate it into a framework for judgment – in a way that no model could do.

Decision scenarios acknowledge uncertainty and aim at structuring and understanding it – but not by merely crisscrossing variables and producing dozens or hundreds of outcomes. Instead, they create a few alternative and internally consistent pathways into the future. They are not a group of quasi-forecasts, one of which may be right. Decision scenarios describe different worlds, not just different outcomes in the same world. Never more than four (or it becomes unmanageable for most decision-makers), the ideal number is one plus two; that is, first the surprise-free view (showing explicitly why and where it is fragile) and then two other worlds or different ways of seeing the world that focus on the critical uncertainties.

The point to repeat, is not so much to have one scenario that 'gets it right' as to have a set of scenarios that illuminates the major forces driving the system, their interrelationships, and the critical uncertainties. The users can then sharpen their focus on key environmental questions, aided by new concepts and a richer language system through which they exchange ideas and data.

A design that includes three scenarios describing alternative outcomes along a single dimension is dangerous because many managers cannot resist the temptation to identify the middle scenario as a baseline. A scheme based on two scenarios raises a similar risk if one is easily seen as optimistic and the other pessimistic. Managers then intuitively believe that reality must be somewhere in between. They 'split the difference' to arrive at an answer not very different from a single-line forecast.

Experience shows that decision scenarios focus on critical uncertainties that are often very different from those that seemed obvious to managers at the beginning of the process. Despite this focus on uncertainty, decision scenarios do not paralyze managers. Rather, the deeper understanding of the risks that is gained often makes the decision-maker capable of confronting apparently greater risk.

You can test the value of scenarios by asking two questions:

1 What do they leave out? In five to ten years, managers must not be able to say that the scenario did not warn them of important events that subsequently happened.
2 Do they lead to action? If scenarios do not push managers to do something other than that indicated by past experience, they are nothing more than interesting speculation.

It is impossible to develop a set of decision scenarios without knowledge of managers' deepest concerns – something we did not fully appreciate when we developed our scenarios in the 1970s. We were lucky, however; our managers' concerns turned out to be precisely what we were studying. Later, we developed interview techniques to find out what was on their minds and to illuminate the existing decision framework. Today, the interview is one of the first steps taken when Shell starts a scenario exercise.

The decision scenarios I have described were global, or macroscenarios. To analyze particular aspects of a business, you develop focused scenarios that are custom tailored around a certain strategic issue, market, or investment. But you cannot start with a narrow focus because you will likely miss key things (or dimensions), or else you may cast the scenarios in the wrong way. You must wide-angle first to capture the big picture and then zoom in on the details.

We have found that scenarios are most effective when combined with:

Strategic vision You should have a clear, structured view of what you want your company to be, which precedes your view of what you want your company to do (investing, divesting, penetrating new markets, and so forth).

Option planning In most planning approaches, strategies are put forward on a single line and options – if there are any – are merely straw men. This is even more dangerous than single-line forecasting. Option planning, in which all options are put forward on a neutral mode, is practiced at both the business unit and corporate levels.

The purpose of a combined approach is option generation (see Figure 4). If the scenario process does not bring out strategic options previously unconsidered by managers, then it has been sterile.

The gentle art of reperceiving

Companies differ greatly in their effectiveness and speed in transforming the potential of scientific research into new products and processes. In times of rapid change, their effectiveness and speed in identifying and

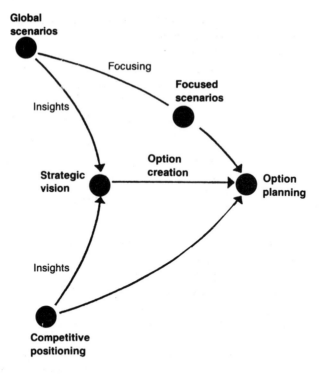

Figure 4   *Generating management options*

transforming information of strategic significance into strategic initiatives differ just as much.

Today, however, such a capacity is critical. Unless companies are careful, novel information outside the span of managerial expectations may not penetrate the core of decision-makers' minds, where possible futures are rehearsed and judgment exercised.

Historical examples abound. After concluding the non-aggression pact with Hitler in 1939, Stalin was so convinced the Germans would not attack as early as 1941 – and certainly not without an ultimatum – that he ignored eighty-four warnings to the contrary. According to Barton Whaley, the warnings about Operation Barbarossa included communications from Richard Sorge, a Soviet spy in the German embassy in Tokyo, and Winston Churchill; the withdrawal of German merchant shipping from Soviet ports; and evacuation of German dependents from Moscow.[2]

Or consider the case of Pearl Harbor. 'Noise,' the massive volume of signals, impeded understanding of what was to come. As Roberta Wohlstetter points out, 'To discriminate significant sounds against this backdrop of noise, one has to be listening for something or for one of several things. . . . One needs not only an ear but a *variety of hypotheses* that guide observation'[3] (emphasis added). Indeed, the Japanese commander of the Pearl Harbor attack, Mitsuo Fuchida, surprised at having achieved surprise, asked, 'Had these Americans never heard of Port Arthur?' (the event preceding the Russo-Japanese War of 1904 – and famous in Japan – when the Japanese navy destroyed the Russian Pacific fleet at anchor in Port Arthur in a surprise attack).

Similar business cases are not as well documented. I have observed some: the French steel industry's handling of the 'FOS project' near Marseilles; the tanker market before and after the first oil shock; petrochemical investments in Europe in the 1970s; and a large US automobile manufacturer's misinterpretation and dismissal of Japanese competition during a good part of the 1970s.

In each case, a number of executives – not just one individual – made decisions. Their inappropriate behavior extended over several months or even years – it was not just a one-time error. Problems resulted from a crisis of perception rather than from poor strategic reasoning. These decision-makers' strategies made sense and indeed were sometimes brilliant – within the context of their limited worldview.

In times of rapid change, a crisis of perception (that is, the inability to see an emerging novel reality by being locked inside obsolete assumptions) often causes strategic failure, particularly in large, well-run companies. Opportunities missed because managers did not recognize them in time are clearly more important than failures, which are visible to all. As Peter Drucker said, 'The greatest danger in times of turbulence is not the turbulence; it is to act with yesterday's logic.'

Central to decision scenarios – indeed the basis for their success or failure – is the microcosm of the decision-makers: their inner model of reality, their set of assumptions that structure their understanding of the unfolding business environment and the factors critical to success. A manager's inner model never mirrors reality; it is always a construct. It deals with complexity by focusing on what really matters. It is a superior simplification of reality – the more so, the wider a manager's span of responsibility is.

During stable times, the mental model of a successful decision-maker and unfolding reality match. Some adjustment and fine tuning will do. Decision scenarios have little or no leverage.

In times of rapid change and increased complexity, however, the manager's mental model becomes a dangerously mixed bag: rich detail and understanding can coexist with dubious assumptions, selective inattention to alternative ways of interpreting evidence, and illusory projections. In these times, the scenario approach has leverage and can make a difference.

In today's world, a management microcosm shaped by the past and sustained by the usual types of forecasts is inherently suspect and inade-quate. Yet it is extremely difficult for managers to break out of their worldview while operating within it. When they are committed to a certain way of framing an issue, it is difficult for them to see solutions that lie outside this framework.

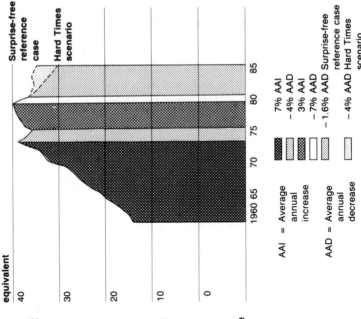

Million barrels per day of oil equivalent

40

30

20

10

0

1960 65   70   75   80   85

Surprise-free reference case

Hard Times scenario

▨	7% AAI	
▥	–4% AAD	
☐	3% AAI	
▤	–7% AAD	
	–1.6% AAD	Surprise-free reference case
▦	–4% AAD	Hard Times scenario

AAI = Average annual increase

AAD = Average annual decrease

Figure A   OECD oil consumption

As any adult knows, a magician cannot produce a rabbit unless it is already in (or very near) his hat. In the same way, surprises in the business environment almost never emerge without warning. To understand the warnings, managers must be able to look at available evidence in alternative ways. Otherwise, they can be badly misled by apparently valid facts if that is all they see, or they do not interpret them in different ways.

After the second oil shock, a 'scenario for the rapids' covering the medium term 1980–5 introduced a notion at odds with prevailing wisdom. Called a 'high savings case,' it alerted management to 'the possibility that consumers themselves would produce a surprise in the form of a much more rapid decrease in energy and oil intensity than that assumed for the reference case.' This would mean a further drop of 6 million barrels per day in the demand for OPEC oil.

At the time, there was little hard evidence to support the case. There is always a lag in the impact on demand of a price rise. Furthermore, there was great uncertainty about the oil market and anxiety about further supplies. The outbreak of the Iran–Iraq war increased anxiety about supplies from the Middle East. Both oil consumers and oil companies tried to increase their stocks of oil; customers' orders were strong; and industry forecasts as well as the 'feel of the market' all pointed towards sustained demand. The mood of the industry leaned towards expansion: 1980–1 saw an enormous increase in drilling activity and feverish competition to secure term contracts for the supply of crude. The problems of the oil industry were obviously on the supply side, not on the demand side.

In March 1981, the new 1981–5 scenarios for the rapids stated that 'last year's conservation surprise can no longer be regarded merely as a contingency.' We also introduced a new scenario, 'Hard Times,' that foresaw an economic recession deeper than most observers expected, an oil conservation surprise (drawn from the remarkable analysis by Aart Beijdorff), and societal change that would significantly affect both economic behavior and oil demand.

Under the Hard Times scenario, the combined effect of these three elements could lead to a totally different – and much lower – level of oil demand (see Figure A) than from the first oil shock – even though the immediate impact on GNP, balance of payment of OECD, and so on was surprisingly similar.

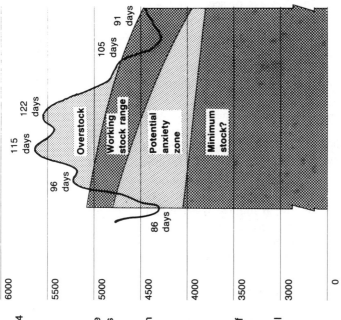

Figure B *Free world stocks*

We called the likelihood of there being a real conservation surprise a 'rabbit in the hat.' Moreover, we were increasingly convinced that at least the two ears of our particular 'rabbit' were already visible. First, less than one-sixth of the 1973–4 crude oil price increase had been passed on to final consumers because of the cushioning effect of refining and transport costs and of various taxes in the selling price of the total products barrel. This time, however, more than half of the crude price rise would be felt by final consumers, a change that suggested consumers' reactions would be non-linear.

Second, a radical change in consumers' perceptions seemed likely to reinforce this growing price leverage. Few people had believed in the reality of an oil crisis after 1973–4; now the popular concensus seemed to be that the upward price trend was irreversible. This change in attitude, combined with the normal effect of a large price increase, could reawaken previously dormant price elasticity from the first oil shock.

Finally, we believed that the oil industry and OPEC were being fooled by the demand statistics, which reflected not real demand or actual consumption but deliveries only. Stock building at the consumer level as well as at the oil company level was abnormally high (see Figure B).

It is now clear that much of the oil industry in 1980–1 overestimated future demand. In such a context, a company can make a lot of money selling weeks of unnecessary stocks before prices erode. It may be just a coincidence, but Shell companies' reduction in oil stocks through 1981 was much greater and earlier than that for the commercial stocks of the industry as a whole, even though Shell stocks at the beginning of the year (in terms of days' supply of current demand) were already well below the average.

The Hard Times scenario used a new hypothesis to analyze demand behavior and thereby alerted decision-makers to the possibility of a major discontinuity in future oil demand. We saw more than the conventional consensus view of the industry mainly because we had been looking for alternative ways of seeing our world. A new strategic option emerged that encouraged us to go against the mainstream of the oil industry.

Figure 5 *Seeing 'rabbits in the hat'*

By presenting other ways of seeing the world, decision scenarios allow managers to break out of a one-eyed view. Scenarios give managers something very precious: the ability to reperceive reality. In a turbulent business environment, there is more to see than managers normally perceive. Highly relevant information goes unnoticed because, being locked into one way of looking, managers fail to see its significance (see Figure 5).

It has been my repeated experience that the perceptions that emerge when the disciplined approach of scenario analysis is practiced are richer and often critically different from the previous implicit view. The scenario process of converting information into fresh perceptions has something of a 'breeder effect': it generates energy, much more energy than has been consumed in time and effort during the process.

A mere high or low around a baseline can never achieve a conceptual reframing. The reperception of reality and the discovery of strategic openings that follow the breaking of the manager's assumptions (many of which are so taken for granted that the manager no longer is aware of them) are, after all, the essence of entrepreneurship. Scenario planning aims to rediscover the original entrepreneurial power of foresight in contexts of change, complexity, and uncertainty. It is precisely in these contexts – not in stable times – that the real opportunities lie to gain competitive advantage through strategy.

Notes

The illustrations are reprinted with the kind permission of Shell International Petroleum Company. I would like to acknowledge the original contributions of my former colleagues and members of Group Planning. G. A. Wagner, A. Benard, K. Swart, and J. C. Davidson get special thanks because they were instrumental in launching the concept. My conceptualization of scenario analysis has benefitted greatly from discussion with my former Harvard Business School colleagues, in particular Bruce Scott and David Bell. This chapter would not have been written without Norman Duncan and Peggy Evans. It expresses one or two things I have learned; it does not necessarily represent Shell's current planning views or practices.

1. Pierre Wack, 'Scenarios: uncharted waters ahead', *Harvard Business Review*, September–October 1985: 72.
2. Barton Whaley, *Codeword Barbarossa* (Cambridge, MA: MIT Press, 1973).
3. Roberta Wohlstetter, *Pearl Harbor: Warning and Decision* (Stanford, CA: Stanford University Press, 1962).

18

Strategic leadership through corporate planning at ICI

Alan I.H. Pink

'The Executive Team are the Planners.' This is a statement made whenever a member of the Planning Department discusses Corporate Planning at ICI. It is not a disclaimer, nor is it a sign of excessive modesty, but it is a statement of the fundamental philosophy which lies at the heart of both ICI's strategic planning process and the way it operates in practice.

The Chairman and the Executive Directors exert clear strategic leadership on the ICI Group. The role of Planning Department, with appropriate essential key inputs from Finance Department, is to support the Executive Team in its strategic role and to facilitate the strategic dialogue between the Executive Team and the units through whom corporate strategy must largely be implemented.

The role of the Executive Directors in strategic planning has not always been as it is today and we are, therefore, in a good position to see the advantages which flow from our current organization. Some background will help to put this in context (Turner, 1984).

The challenge

ICI is large and complex. It currently makes an annual profit of over £1bn from sales in excess of £10bn, manufactures products in forty countries and sells to virtually all of the world's markets through its own sales offices in over sixty territories. It has a vast multiplicity of businesses ranging from pharmaceuticals to petrochemicals, all based on exploiting chemical, biological and related sciences and engineering. ICI is the most diverse and international of all the major world chemical companies.

The challenge is, on the one hand, to free business managers to develop individual businesses competitively and profitably whilst, on the other, directing the Group and managing the complex portfolio to achieve coherence and integration. This objective is captured succinctly by the statement 'the whole should be greater than the sum of the parts'. To this

Reprinted by permission of Pergamon Press PLC from *Long Range Planning* 21(1) 1988: 18–25.

end the style of the direction and management of the Group has changed
substantially over the last six years.

Changing gear

In 1980 ICI declared losses in two quarters, and reluctantly cut its divi-
dend for the first time since the 1930s. The exceptional drop in performance was due to a combination of factors – world recession following
the oil shocks of the 1970s, particular weakness in the UK economy, high
domestic inflation and an overvalued currency supported by oil, which
was penal to a major exporter like ICI. The difficult situation in the external economic environment was exacerbated by the fact that ICI, in the
late 1970s, had invested heavily for further growth, particularly in plastics
and petrochemicals. This growth did not materialize and in the early
1980s capacity surpluses world-wide caused intense competitive pressure
and a resultant squeeze on profit margins.

In the short term massive restructuring took place across the chemical
industry in Europe, but the particular circumstances of the United
Kingdom meant that ICI had to improve its cost-base more rapidly than
its competitors. Manpower in the United Kingdom was reduced by almost
30 per cent in five years and many older production units were closed.
The intended capacity *expansions* of the late 1970s became effective
modern low cost *replacement* plants. As a result, and helped by a range
of portfolio exchanges, ICI was put into a strong competitive position and
was poised to benefit from the improving economic conditions in the
second half of the 1980s.

These moves were urgent and successful, albeit painful, reactions to a
profits crisis. In addition, a major reassessment of both the short-term performance objectives and the long-term strategy of the ICI Group was also
clearly necessary. Part of the recovery plan called for a reappraisal of the
role of the Executive Directors in planning for, directing and managing the
company. The financial budgeting and monitoring processes were also
completely restructured and formed a key part of the overall new approach.

One major change was to delegate profit and operating responsibility
for business units clearly and unambiguously to the level of management
immediately below the Main Board. This left a smaller team of Executive
Directors – reduced from fourteen to now only eight – free to concentrate
on Group financial performance and corporate direction as a whole,
without having personal profit accountability for the individual parts of
the company worldwide. Executive Directors thus ceased to advocate for
particular spheres of influence and started working as a more closely knit
team to develop a shared vision for the ICI Group. They became better
placed to determine where to take ICI as a whole and to decide objectively
about the allocation of resources to the individual units in a way which
best meets the corporate aims.

The problems faced by ICI in the early 1980s have already been defined broadly. They led to an urgent need to:

- Increase profit
- Improve profitability
- Achieve consistent improvement in performance.

This had to be done against the background of key issues faced by the chemical industry:

- Lower growth
- Overcapacity in commodity chemicals
- Greater competitive pressures
- More rapid change/more uncertainty

and particular issues faced by ICI:

- Overdependence on slow-growing UK economy
- Collapse of UK customer-base
- For historical reasons, major involvement in sectors with most over-capacity
- Overvaluation of sterling
- Poor relative labour productivity.

The broad strategy was set, therefore, to achieve two major thrusts. These were to improve *competitiveness*, in terms both of costs and of the ability to add value, and to *change Group shape* in respect of both products and territorial spread.

In the case of products the aim was to move the balance away from the cyclicality and competitive vulnerability of commodity chemicals, particularly where these were exposed to foreign currency fluctuations, towards differentiated, high value-added, effect (speciality) chemicals. In the basic chemicals businesses in Europe the thrust was to achieve the maximum cost efficiencies of scale and concentration, whilst also adding value in the product chain in differentiated sectors of the market. The effect businesses to be emphasized included pharmaceuticals, agro-chemicals, seeds, advanced materials, electronics, polyurethanes, films, explosives, colours and speciality chemicals. All of these were judged to have good growth prospects and potential for further development.

In the case of territories the emphasis was to increase business outside the slow-growing UK market towards the higher growth United States, Japan and selected less developed countries, especially on the Pacific Rim.

ICI thus embarked upon a major and strategic problem-solving phase in which existing businesses had a key part to play alongside central initiatives directed at macrorestructuring, generation of new businesses and achievement of targeted acquisitions. The last five years have seen the major problems largely solved and the need today is to build successfully on the solid base which has been established. Table 1 and Figures 1 and 2 illustrate in different ways the considerable changes achieved in the ICI

Table 1   *ICI performance*

	1982	1986
Return on chemical sales (%)	5	10.5
Return on assets (%)	7	19
Earnings per share (pence 1986)	29	92

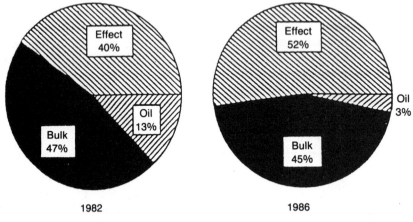

Figure 1   *Product shape*

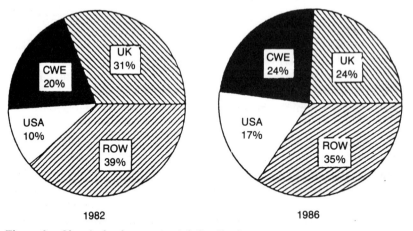

Figure 2   *Chemical sales: territorial distribution*

Group between 1982 and 1986. The overall objective now is to move
forward aggressively and to achieve sustained growth in earnings through
time.

Against this objective the broad strategic thrusts on competitiveness and
Group shape are still relevant. They are required now, less in the sense
of urgent problem-solving, but more to encourage a continuous evolution
of appropriate competitive strategies for existing businesses and for

developing new vehicles to bring ICI's core innovative skills to an ever-changing market. Blended together and applied to a mix of old and new, they are the means of sustaining the momentum of growth, renewal and more growth, through time. This strategic intent will be achieved only if the processes throughout the ICI Group enable and encourage good decision-taking by the level appropriate to the decision.

The strategic process

The strategic processes introduced in the early 1980s have been developed and refined to achieve a tightly integrated strategic planning and financial budgeting process which aims:

- to give the Executive Team the ability to steer the Group;
- to retain the necessary financial control at the ICI Centre;
- to delegate as much responsibility and freedom of action as possible to Chief Executives of operating units.

The need is to ensure that individual businesses and territories are following strategies which are consistent with Group strategy and that the implementation is broadly following the intended path on the required timescale. This means that at the heart of the process is the agreement by the Executive Team of a strategy for a unit, followed by subsequent monitoring of financial and strategic performance within the context of the agreed strategy.

At any time each unit has an agreed strategy to which it must work. There is no fixed pattern for a fundamental review of strategy, but a review will be called for if, from the perspective of the Executive Team, the strategy is clearly becoming untenable or if the Chief Executive Officer (CEO) of the unit believes he must offer different options.

The strategy review is carried out against a common economic background using central assumptions. It must provide an assessment of the range of strategic options available to the unit over a ten-year planning horizon (and for some business units a longer view is also appropriate), and should evaluate these against the background of ICI Group strategic aims.

When a preferred strategy is agreed it provides a framework in which the CEO can operate and it commits ICI Group resources in principle to the strategy. It also establishes definitive milestones against which to measure progress of implementation of the strategy.

Table 2 summarizes the process in practice. The milestones cover a ten-year period, being more detailed and precise in the early years and less so later on. They are a mixture of quantitative and qualitative critical factors which provide reference points for the annual evaluation of budgets. They also act through time as key markers against which to test whether performance is meeting requirements or significantly and persistently falling short, indicating the need for strategy to be reappraised.

Table 2 *Business strategy review: the process in practice*

- Strategy paper and background review documents produced by businesses in consultation with planning and other Millbank functions
- Papers circulated by business director with covering letter highlighting key issues. Single brief prepared by corporate functions
- Presentation by CEO to Executive Team
- Initial feedback after discussion by Executive Team: minutes issued by secretary's department
- Summary of issues, preferred strategy and milestones prepared by planning department and business
- Strategy summary and milestones submitted for main board approval

At any time the add-up of the business strategies indicates what the ICI Group as a whole will achieve if the businesses are successful in the execution of their strategies. The add-up may or may not match the aspirations that the Executive Team have for the ICI Group to achieve sustained growth of earnings and to be strongly competitive in its performance. In order to test this the Executive Team divorces itself from day-to-day activities and retreats, at least once a year, for two days to Hever Castle in Kent to reflect on both Group strategy and its implementation.

During these discussions corporate objectives are reviewed and the totality of business projections is tested for credibility, adjusted as appropriate, and the resulting overall forecast performance is compared against the corporate objectives. The total resources required to fund existing strategies are reviewed against available resources and the impact through time on company financial ratios is assessed. In other words the strategy loop is closed and the Executive Team tests whether the totality is credible, acceptable and can be financed. It also identifies the need for additional initiatives which may be either offensive or defensive.

Also during these Hever discussions, the business portfolio is reviewed to judge its strength, to identify problems and to seek ways to eradicate weaknesses. The deployment of the company's resources across the portfolio is assessed critically to ensure that the strong and profitable businesses are being adequately funded for maximum growth and that the poorer businesses are receiving minimum cash until their future is clear.

To help the process a simple broad, four-way categorization of businesses is used. The categories are Strong, Ongoing/Cash-generating, Problem and New. Table 3 shows the characteristics and objectives for businesses in each sector. For the businesses in the ICI portfolio we have found this essentially qualitative approach to be more appropriate than such techniques as the Boston Consultancy Group Growth/Share matrix or the Shell Directional Policy matrix. The factors incorporated on the axes of those matrices, relating to industry sector prospects and our own competitive position within the industry, receive considerable attention.

Table 3 *Selectivity overview: characterization and objectives*

Ongoing cash	Strong
Profitable cash-generator but with no major growth prospects – Run for long-term cash, increasing contribution by improving profits through limited selective investment directed at increasing efficiency of existing operations in preference to expansion	Strong and growing profit contributor based on good competitive position in growing good quality market – Stimulate innovation and invest to sustain profitable growth and to increase total size of this sector
Problem	**New**
Inadequate profitability and cash generation – Turn around, divest or close down	New business with the potential of being 'strong' but meanwhile relatively high cash requirement with relatively high-risk – Nurture; then select and invest sufficient resources and management attention in chosen businesses to develop 'strong' positions

However, the process by which the Executive Team assesses the appropriate categorization for individual businesses, and then moves on from there to approve a specific strategy, embraces a wider range of relevant judgement factors including the Group corporate goals and objectives.

This approach is a particular example of a strongly fulfilled general determination that techniques should be kept in perspective as tools and should not become potential substitutes for applying business experience and judgement. Further in line with this general thesis the business categorization is not a mechanical fixed classification. It is a dynamic process with businesses moving between categories if this is justified by a strategy review.

A problem business, for example, which can develop a convincing and financially rewarding strategy to turn itself around, within a reasonable period, into a good cash business or perhaps eventually into a strong business, will get reasonable support through its time of crisis. There are some outstanding cases of successful turnarounds probably best exemplified by ICI's Polyurethanes business and its Fibres business. The corporate use of this selectivity quadrant is broad and units are encouraged to apply the same kind of categorization to their subportfolios. Many do and some elaborate the four categories into subgroupings to define more accurately the strategic issues facing the businesses.

The categorization is simple, but the Executive Team finds it has provided it with a clearer overview of the portfolio and enabled it to arrive more quickly at decisions to encourage Chief Executives to divest poorly performing businesses with little recovery potential or, at the very least to limit resources until prospects improve. Similarly the Executive Team can ensure it is channelling sufficient resources into strong businesses and that enough 'patient' money is being devoted to the long-term development of new businesses without unduly straining current Group profitability.

The Executive Team believe they are now better placed to manage the diverse portfolio effectively, to direct resources towards making the maximum contribution to sustained growth of earnings and also objectively to assess management performance. The use of the categorization model down the organization is contributing to an upgrading of strategic thinking throughout the Group. It is helping the management to focus more consciously on the need to be selective in their use of resources and to apply strategically differentiated criteria in their business decisions. The quality of the strategic debate around the Group is sharper and is still improving against a heightened appreciation of the corporate direction.

Corporate strategy *does* make the difference

The iteration between the review of the whole Group strategy at Hever and the review of individual strategies with CEOs, coupled with the launching of central strategic initiatives aimed at improving the performance of the whole, provides the process for ensuring that, in spite of its diversity and complexity, the ICI Group moves forward coherently and proactively under positive strategic direction.

There are always critical decisions to be taken on the relative importance to be given to strategic and financial control of individual businesses. Some companies go unequivocally for one or the other. The ICI Executive seeks to balance the two so that in difficult times financial targets are met as closely as possible whilst key strategic initiatives are preserved. This is a very appropriate, but difficult, style of management which requires a considerable understanding by the Executive Team of the individual business issues and of the strategic parameters which are key to the future competitive success of the business. As will be seen later Planning Department has a role in highlighting key issues relevant to any debate with strategic implications. This does not set a restrictive agenda and additions are made by the Executive Team or by the responsible CEO, but it is expected to provide the core focus for the dialogue.

This role, together with the Department's formal and informal involvement in the total strategy process, will be seen to be at the heart of the contribution made by Corporate Planning at ICI towards the pursuit of corporate strategy. To quote Michael Porter (1987) 'Corporate Strategy is what makes the whole add up to more than the sum of its business unit parts', and it is one of the factors which will ensure that ICI's future performance exceeds that of a diversified conglomerate.

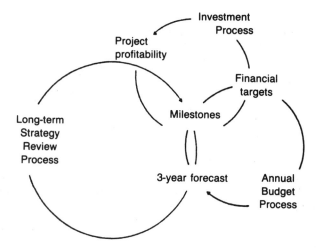

Figure 3   *Interaction of strategy, budget and investment processes*

The budget process

Each year the Executive Team, as a group, assisted primarily by Finance Department and also with input from Planning, reviews the budgets of all the main units for the next three years with each CEO in what is known colloquially as 'hell fortnight'. This is the key instrument of financial control and the agreed budget becomes a contract between the Executive Team and the Chief Executive of the unit.

At the budget review the Executive Team tests briefly whether the unit is proceeding along its agreed strategic path and whether the milestones are being passed. This provides an essential interlinking between the strategy process and the budget process (see Figure 3). The performance of a CEO against his agreed profit and cash budgets is subsequently monitored quarterly to ensure business performance is on target. If it is not the CEO must take corrective action or persuade the Executive Team that dispensation is justified. It is under these circumstances that the debate will centre on whether to continue to incur costs on following longer term strategic goals.

Once a CEO has a budget agreed in the context of an established strategy the approval of capital investment subsequently falls naturally into the overall process, as illustrated in Figure 3.

Where the cost of a planned project or acquisition falls within the sanction of authority delegated to a CEO, he can approve it provided he will still meet his profit and cash budgets. Where the cost exceeds his delegated authority, the CEO presents for consideration by the Executive Team a short paper outlining the case and the way the proposal fits the approved business strategy and the agreed budgets. Unless there are exceptional reasons for believing the business has moved off course there is no recycling of the strategic issues. The debate with the CEO, which is usually quite short, focuses on the market, technical and financial aspects of the proposal. The purpose is to establish whether the project is robust and of a quality which justifies the commitment of the requested capital. This is the final step in ensuring that financial resources are put to fully beneficial uses consistent with the Group meeting its profitability targets.

The result – integrated and interactive

Overall this adds up to a tightly knit process for corporate planning, business strategic planning, financial budgeting and strategic/financial control. As with all things it is capable of further improvement and refinement, but we believe that the broad pattern gives the necessary insights and stimulates the right debate between the Executive Team and those running the individual businesses. The major interaction is between these, but Planning Department, along with Finance Department, have a key constructive and facilitating role to play and it is worth describing in some detail what this is.

Role of corporate planning department

The key elements of the role of Corporate Planning Department can be summarized as follows:

- Provocation and catalysis of Executive Team strategic thinking, identifying Group strategic issues and possible new initiatives.
- Management and development of the strategic planning process.
- Acting as custodian of the Group strategy, proposing options on Group objectives and milestones for achievement.
- Provision of strategic framework for discussion between Executive Team and business and territorial units.
- Provision of world-wide economic assumptions for planning and budgeting, and continuous assessment of the implications of economic trends on Group strategy.
- Assisting units to put strategy proposals in corporate context.
- Assisting Executive Team in highlighting key issues for debate in units' strategy or project proposals.
- Assisting units in recording strategy summaries and developing appropriate milestones.
- Assisting Executive Team in assessing units' budgets for progress against strategic objectives and achievement of milestones.
- Early identification of problems for the Group and its customers.
- Monitoring competitors and interpreting their strategies.
- Seeking out opportunities for the Group and ways to exploit them.
- Assessment of strategic relevance and value of potential acquisition targets.

- Making proposals for resolution of business-related organizational issues.
- Supporting the Executive Team in presenting and explaining Group strategy inside and outside the Group.
- Acting as a forceful advocate of strategic planning throughout the Group.

This role involves working for the Executive Team on one hand, with implications of a critique of the units' performance, whilst on the other hand working with the units themselves. This is a difficult dual role and can be carried out only by planners who are respected for their views and for the practical contribution they can make to thinking at both levels, whilst most importantly being, and being seen to be, honest. On many occasions a planner prematurely receives information, which used inappropriately would be unhelpful to the unit. The whole Department recognizes that they would not get a second opportunity to break this trust.

The Executive Team helps to guard the impartiality of Planning Department. The principle that briefs, which are written for the Executive Team about a unit's proposal, are also discussed with and received by the unit, helps to keep the process 'open'.

Three or four longer-term scenarios are considered by the Executive Team each year and they select the scenario to be used for planning purposes. The other scenarios are used to set the boundaries of upside and downside on the forecasts and to assist in judging whether the balance of probability lies above or below the planning assumptions. The scenarios are kept updated and are used as background for all strategy and budget projections.

A macroeconomic model of the Group is maintained which gives the ability to test the effect of different economic growth rates and varying exchange rates on financial performance. The economic work is given a long-term dimension by a 'Futures' capability which projects social and technical trends. The purpose is to raise the Group's eyes above current horizons to try to spot trends and even discontinuities in markets and technology and to encourage use of this insight in identifying threats to existing business and also new opportunities of high potential.

Planning is a department with a graduate strength of twenty, divided into two mainstreams: a Planning Group and an Economics and External Studies Group. The former works largely internally on the corporate and business strategies and the latter is mostly involved with assessing the external environment. These skills must be integrated and information about the economic environment, the health of customer industries, competitor performance and major strategic thrusts of competitors is brought to bear on both ICI corporate strategy and the evaluation of individual business options. For many tasks, mixed discipline teams of people from across the Department are formed to provide the strongest possible blend of skills.

To assist integration within the Planning Department and also with other departments (principally Finance and the Acquisitions Team), a unified data-base of internal and external data has been generated. Manipulation and clear display of these data are critical to their value in improving decision-taking. To this end a third group of Planning Department has been established to manage Information Technology (IT), in the ICI corporate headquarters.

The IT skills are developing very rapidly and a suite of models and displays is being created which will transform the capability to test interactively various options and events. Such a system needs to be tightly managed, but provides a powerful new tool in support of strategic thinking and dimensions to communication.

Planning in a nutshell

The description of ICI's planning and budgeting processes and the role of Corporate Planning has covered many of the key characteristics of the way the company operates. It may be helpful to summarize these operational characteristics and add one or two more.

- An Executive Team with a strong strategic planning role.
- A concise and precise statement of agreed strategies for units, with achievement milestones.
- Short-term profit and cash budgets for units set using the strategic milestones to provide a linkage with their long-term strategies.
- Close working between Corporate Planning Department and Finance Department.
- A simple, flexible, action-oriented, portfolio management tool.
- A quantitative vision of the Group ten years ahead with assessment of availability and allocation of resources.
- A process for setting corporate objectives and milestones and for identifying potential short-comings in the corporate achievement.
- Strategic identification and justification for acquisitions
- Understanding of both customer industries and trends in society to provide early warning of changes or even discontinuities in ICI businesses.
- Interpretation of competitor strategies.
- Identification of territorial shifts and opportunities.
- Ensuring changes in business shape are reflected by changes in employee skills and organizational structures.
- Strategies for maintaining excellence in innovative skills central to competitive success in present and future business.

A corporate planning process with characteristics as diverse as these presents a challenging role to Planning Department to keep the various threads appropriately connected. The disparate issues must be sufficiently related to allow individual decisions, whilst at the same time they must be sufficiently separate to allow discrete decisions without over complicated debate on each and every subject. Planning Department, therefore, has a major role in ordering and allocating priority to issues and in helping to sort wood from trees.

Overall this adds up to a job which is difficult, challenging and hectic, but which is also stimulating and exciting for all concerned. A staff role, yes, but one which is involved, proactive and above all *additive*.

References

Porter, Michael (1987) 'From competitive advantage to corporate strategy', *Harvard Business Review*, 65 (3): 43–59.
Turner, Graham, (1984) 'ICI becomes proactive', *Long Range Planning*, 17 (6): 12–16.

19

Strategic planning – which style do you need?

Bernard Taylor

Over the past decade the practice of corporate planning has matured and developed in response to pressures from inside and outside the business. What started out as a unique system based on a simple model of problem-solving and decision-making, has evolved into a broad range of philosophies and techniques which are designed to help the executive to build an organization which is adaptable and responsive in a rapidly changing environment.

Each style of planning has a philosophy, a 'school' of adherents, and a range of techniques which have been tested in practice. And each can provide management with a sensible approach to changing the orientation of a business.

A small or medium-size firm may adopt only one of these styles – typically a system controlling the allocation of resources, or a framework for generating strategies for new ventures. However, in the large corporation such as General Electric USA, or Shell International, most or all of these approaches will be present. The philosophies and techniques are largely compatible and complementary. The main styles or modes of planning which have emerged in recent years are as follows:

1 Central Control System. The view of planning as a system for acquiring and allocating resources.
2 Framework for Innovation. The idea that planning should provide a framework for the generation of new products and new processes and the entry into new markets and new businesses.
3 Strategic Management. The notion that planning should be concerned not just with formulating strategies but with developing the commitment, the skills and the talents required to implement the strategies.
4 Political Planning. The perspective which sees planning as a process for resolving conflicts between interest groups and organizations inside and outside the business.
5 Futures Research. The concept of planning as exploring and creating the future. Futurists believe that the future cannot be forecast,

Reprinted by permission of Pergamon Press PLC from *Long Range Planning* 17(3) 1984: 51–62.

therefore decision-makers should consciously assess the uncertainties, then develop and work towards a vision of the future.

Corporate planning has a central role in the management of the modern corporation. It provides a practical approach to changing the way an enterprise is managed. For planning to succeed, however, it needs to be seen not just as a set of techniques, but as part of a coherent programme of change.

This chapter describes five basic approaches to corporate planning. Each represents an important school of thought in management thinking and practice. Each view has a large body of supporters, both academics and practitioners, and each offers a coherent philosophy and a range of practical systems and techniques for implementing them.

In determining their approach to planning, the chief executive and his planning staff need to examine the different methodologies which are available to discover which system best meets their needs. They should then adapt the approach to suit their own organization. For corporate planning systems do not come ready-made. They have to be tailor-made to fit each enterprise. The decision is important because typically it takes two or three years to introduce a particular planning approach, and if it is to be effective it requires wholehearted commitment from both the board and from operating management.

In any large organization of course it is likely that several different planning approaches will be present at any one time. And in one part of the business, planning is likely to move through various phases – with the management adopting different planning philosophies at different stages in the development of the firm. Corporate planning, like other managerial activities, is a process which grows and evolves – and sometimes has major setbacks and needs to be re-launched. It is my hope that this chapter will help the reader to assess the state of planning in his own organization and to suggest areas where the activity may be strengthened or improved. It is rare to find an enterprise where all the available planning approaches are being employed equally effectively.

Table 1 sets out the five main views of planning in broad outline under four headings:

1 The focus – the main objective or purpose.
2 Important ideas – the characteristic view or philosophy of planning.
3 The elements – the key steps or stages in the process.
4 The techniques – some of the techniques which are widely used.

As with any classification system, the categories are not water-tight but they do represent quite distinct traditions in current thinking and practice.[1]

Table 1   *Strategic planning: five basic approaches*

	Central control system	Framework for innovation	Strategic management	Political planning	Futures research
The focus	Allocation and control of resources	Developing new business	Managing organizational change	Mobilizing power and influence	Exploring the future
Important ideas	A rational decision-making and control process	A vehicle for commercializing innovation	A community with common values and culture	Interest groups and organizations competing for resources	A management with a real awareness of future uncertainty
The elements	1 Specific objectives 2 A balanced portfolio of investments 3 Action programmes and budgets 4 Monitoring and control	1 Commitment to innovation 2 Funds for new development 3 Strategies for corporate development 4 Organizing project teams and action programmes	1 Organization development 2 Staff development 3 Organization structure 4 Management systems	1 Monitoring and forecasting social and political trends 2 Assessing the impact on the firm 3 Organizing and implementing action programmes	1 Developing alternative futures 2 Assessing social and economic impact 3 Defining key decisions
The techniques	1 SWOT analysis 2 Business portfolio analysis 3 Gap analysis 4 Extrapolative forecasting 5 Extended budgeting	Programmes for: 1 Divestment 2 Diversification 3 Acquisition 4 New product development 5 Market penetration and development	Group work on: 1 Stakeholder analysis 2 SWOT analysis 3 Portfolio analysis etc.	1 Public affairs 2 Civic affairs 3 Employee communication 4 Social issue analysis 5 Country risk analysis 6 Media relations	1 Scenarios 2 Delphi studies 3 Cross impact analysis 4 Trend analysis 5 Computer simulation 6 Contingency planning

Planning as a central control system

From the beginning, one of the main drives behind the development of corporate planning has been the desire of top management to have a better control over the allocation of capital and other key resources.

The philosophy

The philosophy of planning and control is fundamental to management. Early thinkers on management, like Henri Fayol, described the management process in terms of: 'planning, command, co-ordination and control'. An analogy is often made with an army or another hierarchical organization, where decisions are taken at the top, instructions are passed down through the enterprise and the leaders get back information which enables them to measure actual results against the plan.

The business enterprise is also frequently compared with a machine which can be regulated by an engineering control system. Automatic control systems such as the domestic thermostat contain certain basic elements: a sensor, a standard of performance, a collator, which compares actual performance with the standard, and an actor, which takes action to make up any deficiency in performance or to change the standard.

Writers and practitioners on planning have seen corporate planning as a comprehensive control system which could be used to regulate the operations of a whole firm – a logical extension of departmental control systems such as stock control, sales control, and production control. They were also attracted by the idea of the business as a total system with an integrated information and control system.

It is perhaps natural that accountants should have seen corporate planning as an adjunct to the budgetary control system. There is, however, an important distinction to be drawn between strategic planning and management control – though they are obviously related. Strategic planning includes, for example, choosing company objectives, planning the organizational structure, setting policies for personnel, finance, marketing and research, choosing new product lines, acquiring a new division and deciding on non-routine capital expenditures. Management control is concerned with formulating budgets, determining staff levels, formulating personnel, marketing and research programmes, deciding on routine capital expenditures, measuring, appraising and improving management performance etc.[2]

The processes

The rise of corporate planning in the 1960s coincided with a period of diversification and international expansion in large companies. In many cases these same firms were divided into product divisions which were designated as profit centres or cost centres. Divisional general managers were appointed and each was instructed to manage his division as if it were an independent business. Unfortunately, some of these executives took the instruction too literally and top management saw their subordinates riding off in all directions. Corporate planning was seized upon as a technique which might enable the main board to re-establish some control over the situation. Traditional budgeting systems proved woefully inadequate to the task of controlling a multidivisional business – particularly when the divisional managers usually formed a majority in the main board and sat in judgement on their own capital projects.[3]

The solution commonly adopted was:

1 To re-structure the board so as to reduce the power of the divisional managers by bringing in heads of functional departments, non-executive directors, and others who could form a board representing the whole corporation rather than specific local interests.
2 Requiring the divisions to put forward Divisional Strategies. This enabled the top management and the central staff groups to debate various options for each product group before divisional plans became embedded in detailed project plans as 'the one true way to go'.

The corporate staff groups (finance, personnel, manufacturing, etc.) and the planners themselves, are involved in the corporate planning process through:

1 preparing the planning guidelines for divisions;
2 reviewing divisional strategies and plans;
3 advising the board or an executive committee in approving the plans; and
4 monitoring divisional performance against the plans.

The problems

The close association between planning and financial control has led to all kinds of problems. In particular there has been a tendency:

1 to confuse strategic planning with extended budgeting;
2 to produce three-year or five-year plans simply by extrapolating or pushing forward the present operations;
3 to prepare company plans by merely consolidating the operational plans of divisions and subsidiaries;
4 to stress the numbers rather than the quality of the thinking.

This still goes on. It is common to find corporate plans which consist of comprehensive and detailed operational plans and budgets – without any discussion objectives, organization structure or alternative strategies.

Another problem with the five-year plan and budget is that it can easily degenerate into a sterile but time-consuming routine. Corporate planning has provided many examples of this: highly structured planning systems which required many man-hours to build and maintain – and resulted in plans which were 'wrong to three points of decimals'.

Nevertheless, the resource allocation process is at the core of most planning systems, and the operational plan and budget is the basic planning document. Other 'qualitative' and 'informal' approaches to planning have been developed to compensate for its inflexibility and its narrow scope.

Planning as a framework for innovation

One powerful reason, then, for the growth of business planning was the need to establish a central steering mechanism for the direction and coordination of large, diverse, multinational operations. An equally strong and opposite motivation was the desire to promote initiative at the local level – in particular to prevent centralization and bureaucracy from stifling creativity and innovation.

Over time the need for continuous change and innovation has become accepted by many leading businessmen and writers on business as an article of faith. To quote Peter Drucker, the businessman's philosopher:

> In a world buffeted by change, faced daily with new threats to its safety, the only way to conserve is by innovating. The only stability possible is stability in motion.[4]

The implications of this philosophy were spelled out for businessmen, politicians and public health officials by John Gardner, the former US Secretary of Health Education and Welfare in his best-selling book *Self-Renewal*. He wrote:

> A society whose maturing consists simply of acquiring more firmly established ways of doing things is headed for the graveyard – even if it learns to do these things with greater and greater skill. In the ever-renewing society what matures is a system or framework within which continuous innovation, renewal and rebirth can occur.[5]

For a competitive business this process of self-renewal is fundamental to survival. In the short term a management can make profits by mortgaging the future – and many managements are tempted to do this in the present crisis. But in a rapidly changing situation, unless there is continual re-investment in staff training, market development, new products, and up-to-date equipment, companies are likely to find themselves overtaken by their competitors. As the Boston Consulting Group consultants concluded in their enquiry into the failure of the British motorcycle industry:

> The result of the British industry's historic focus on short-term profitability has been low profits and now losses in the long term. The long-term result of the Japanese industry's historic focus on market share and volume, often at the expense of short-term profitability, has been the precise opposite: high and secure profitability.[6]

This process of entrepreneurship has long been acknowledged as a central function of the businessman. It involves:

- identifying a market opportunity,
- developing a product to match it,
- raising the necessary finance and matching the risk to the opportunity,
- mobilizing the staff and the other resources necessary to provide the required service,
- producing and distributing the product at a profit.

To quote Donald Schon:

> The firm defines itself as a vehicle for carrying out a special kind of process. It defines itself through its engagement in entrepreneurship, the launching of new ventures, or in commercializing what comes out of development. The principal figure in the firm becomes the manager of the corporate entrepreneurial process; and the question is this: what are the potentials in development for new commercial ventures.[7]

In a one-man business the owner can be his own entrepreneur, but in a large corporation this process has to be formalized and systematized. To quote Peter Drucker again:

> Every one of the great business builders we know of – from the Medici to the founders of the Bank of England down to Thomas Watson in our days – had a definite idea, a clear 'theory of business' which informed his actions and decisions. Indeed a clear simple and penetrating 'theory of the business' rather than 'intuition' characterizes the truly successful entrepreneur, the man who not only amasses a large fortune but builds an organization that can endure and grow long after he is gone.
>
> But the individual entrepreneur does not need to analyse his concepts and to explain his 'theory of business' to others, let alone spell out the details. He is in one person thinker, analyst and executor. Business enterprise, however, requires that entrepreneurship be systematized, spelled out as a discipline and organized as work.[8]

In many corporations strategic planning is regarded as a form of 'organized entrepreneurship'. Patrick Haggerty, the former Chairman of Texas Instruments, described their planning system as a 'framework for innovation'. He said:

> Self-renewal at Texas Instruments begins with deliberate, planned innovation in each of the basic areas of industrial life – creating, making and marketing. With our long range planning system we attempt to manage this innovation so as to provide a continuing stimulus to the company's growth.

The management of corporate development

Most management systems are concerned with operational problems. Operational plans start with the present situation and push it forward – in terms of sales quotas, production targets, stock levels, budgets etc. The horizon is typically one year, occasionally two years – or perhaps three to five years for a specific product or facility. Other management systems – performance appraisal, salaries and incentives, promotions and career development – also help to focus managers' ideas on the short-term. A major problem for the large corporation is how to persuade staff to spend some of their time thinking and planning for new products, new markets, new production and administrative processes and maybe entirely new kinds of businesses – joint ventures, mergers and acquisitions, new social and political initiatives.

How, for a start, can top management produce a strategy and a programme for the development of the business? Typically, this involves the formation of *ad hoc* groups which report directly to the Board; project teams, venture groups, a diversification task force, a group to deal with acquisitions or international expansion, etc. In the present recession we have also seen task forces formed to look at closures, divestments, rationalization and organizational re-structuring.

The challenge is to develop a 'vision of success' for the total enterprise and its parts and then to produce action plans, budgets and timetables to realize the vision.

The techniques which are in common use provide broad frameworks for discussion and analysis. For example:

Gap analysis describes the planning tasks by identifying the gap between the company's objectives and its likely achievement in terms of profits, sales, cash flow, etc. Management is invited to:

(a) set an objective – in quantitative terms – e.g. rate of return on investment or market share;
(b) forecast the 'momentum' line for the present business assuming no major changes;
(c) plan to fill the gap with projects for increased efficiency, expansion and diversification.

SWOT analysis provides a series of check-lists for auditing the company's strengths and weaknesses, and the opportunities and threats in the business environment. The business is assessed against leading competitors in world markets in terms of its technology, market position, financial base, production efficiency, management and organization. The opportunities and threats are considered in the light of trends in the environment – economic, sociopolitical, technological and competitive. Then the two analyses are compared to see what are the market opportunities which match the firm's resources, what new resources are required, etc.

Business portfolio analysis – the process of funds allocation (i.e. allocation of both fixed and working capital) is frequently discussed on the basis of a matrix showing the pattern of businesses in the company's 'portfolio'. Many large companies have their own matrix or screen, typically displaying on one scale the prospects for the industry and on the other the strength of the company's market position. The criteria for the industry's attractiveness might include: growth potential, expected changes in markets and in technology, the strength of competition from existing competitors and possible newcomers, and government and environmental constraints. The analysis of one's own company strengths requires a comparison with leading competitors in terms of market share, production capability, relative costs, technical expertise, patent position, marketing, distribution and service and government support.

PIMS (Profit Impact of Market Strategy) – the PIMS database which was set up originally by General Electric, USA, is derived from around a thousand 'businesses' in the USA and Western Europe over a period of up to ten years. The programme collects 300 items of information about each business and attempts to discover which factors have most effect on profitability (return on investment), e.g. market share, product quality, marketing expenditure, capital investment vs sales, etc. The database is used primarily by holding companies in assessing the performance of divisions and subsidiaries and in making decisions about investment and divestment.

In practice, the majority of managers find the task of strategic planning difficult and they require a good deal of help. This is partly a matter of temperament. Operating managers tend to be chosen for their ability to get things done and it has been well said that 'A man of action, forced into a state of thought, is unhappy until he can get out of it.' It is largely the size and complexity of the task – to try to plan for the long-term development of the total enterprise in all its dimensions. It is also the problem of planning with little solid information in a situation of great uncertainty where all the elements interact. Inevitably, the manager has to rely on his judgement and imagination much more than he does in operational management.

Faced with these practical difficulties in generating new strategies, leading companies such as General Electric in the USA and Philips in Europe have started to think not just in terms of strategic planning but in terms of strategic management, i.e. changing the whole management system.

Strategic management

This increasingly popular approach takes the view that policy-making is a learning process and strategic planning is the specific activity through which the members of an organization learn to adapt to radical changes in the external environment.

The philosophy

Consider the changes which are taking place and their impact on human institutions – fluctuations in supply and demand, the advent of new technologies, the appearance of social and political movements, the rise and fall of governments. . . . All these trends are rendering established institutions and traditional ways of thinking and acting obsolete. In a rapidly changing world, organizations must adapt or go under. To quote Donald Schon:

> Our society and all of its institutions are in continuing processes of transformation . . . we must learn to understand, guide, influence and manage these transformations . . .
> We must invent and develop institutions which are 'learning systems' – systems capable of bringing about their own transformations.[9]

This is the theory of natural selection again: the view that organizations must adapt or be replaced by others which are better suited to their environment.

How then can we build institutions which learn to adapt to their environment? Is it possible to develop management's ability to cope with change? Can we help organizations or teams of people to set objectives, to be more aware of the changes taking place around them, and to develop their own plans for the future? Can management learn to do this on a continuing basis?

Those who support the view of planning as part of a process of social change usually reject the theory that planning is a logical search for solutions, a cognitive decision-making process which establishes the area of search and certain performance criteria, collects and analyses data, assesses alternatives and makes an optical choice. We are after all dealing not with inert objects but with people who have their own ideas, beliefs and motivations.[10]

In place of this model of planning as rational and sequential, behavioural scientists frequently present it as a trial-and-error process. Managers and administrators are encouraged to adopt an experimental approach. Not looking for comprehensive solutions or great leaps forward but attempting to engineer incremental changes with the top managers and their advisers not moving too far ahead of the group.[11]

The approach

This 'behavioural' view of planning is more human, less comprehensive, more easily related to the organizations which we all know and work in:

1 Planning is seen as a *process* through which individuals and teams can learn to cope with an unpredictable and rapidly changing environment. The fact that a forecast or a plan turns out to be wrong is therefore not an indication that the management is incompetent or that planning is not feasible, but rather as confirmation that we are living in an uncertain world and we need to reassess our situation continually. However, we should learn by experience and our involvement in forecasting, strategy-making, planning, programming and budgeting should help us get a better 'feel' for the trends in the environment and should improve

the organization's capacity to respond to them.

2 Planning is seen as one element in a wider programme of organizational change. This may involve many other measures.

   (a) *Moves affecting individual managers:* retiring or retraining existing managers, recruiting new managers, promoting and developing staff for new roles.

   (b) *Changes in organization structure:* these might include, for example:

      i dividing the company into semi-autonomous units such as product divisions;

      ii establishing new groupings to coordinate policy by geographical regions, by product groups or by strategic business units (i.e. parts of the organization which have a common business strategy); or

      iii re-organizing the board and revising the capital investment procedures to strengthen the role of the board as a policy-making body.

   (c) *Changes in management systems:*

      i changing the procedures for staff appraisal, promotion and payment, to encourage management to give a higher priority to new company-wide programmes, e.g. social responsibility, new business development or staff development;

      ii the introduction of improved information systems for finance, manpower and production;

      iii the development of planning and control systems to focus management attention on cash flow, productivity, planning for manpower, etc.;

      iv the provision of new procedures for environmental assessment to give managers a better understanding of the external trends which are likely to affect their business.

3 In adopting the organizational learning mode of planning, the planner takes on the role of a 'change agent'. His task is not merely to produce a product 'the plan', but rather to intervene in 'the process', i.e. to work with management at various levels to help them to define their problems and to produce new programmes directed at changing the orientation of the organization to fit new circumstances.

   Sometimes, the firm is engaged in a slow evolution. Occasionally there is a major crisis. Often the problem is to help a management team to adjust to some kind of radical change or discontinuity:

   (a) the integration and rationalization of several companies into a larger, divisionalized operation, following a programme of diversification or a series of mergers;

   (b) the closure or sale of a number of businesses, and the slimming down of central staff functions following a reduction in demand or expropriation by government;

   (c) developing the capacity to design, sell and manage total systems or turn-key projects as opposed to selling individual products to developing countries or the communist world;

(d) the introduction of a sea-change in technology such as containerization in shipping or the use of micro-processors and fibre optics in telecommunications.

One of the problems with the 'organizational learning' approach is that these radical changes occur infrequently in the life of an individual firm. It is therefore difficult for a manager to gain experience of closures and divestments, or mergers and acquisitions, within one company, except in a large multidivisional business. In cases of radical change, therefore, it is often necessary for top management to bring in consultants or to recruit managers from outside the company who have acquired the relevant experience in other businesses.

4 However, the strategic planner who adopts a social learning approach does not act merely as a change agent intervening as and when required to carry out an attitude study, diagnose an organizational problem, to improve working relationships between individuals and departments. He is concerned to develop the competence of management teams in various parts of the organization to take a 'strategic' view of their businesses, to identify the key issues for decisions and to take the action which they regard as necessary for the survival and growth of the enterprise.

This usually involves:

  i taking a comprehensive and realistic view of the organization from various perspectives – the world market, competitors, long-term trends in technology and in society;

 ii assessing in comparative terms the business' overall performance – its levels of costs, productivity, product quality, price, customer service;

iii considering feasible alternative futures for the organization – making established activities more efficient and more productive, developing new technologies and building new businesses.

Planning as a political process

A fourth approach to planning consists of a kind of realpolitik – a view which says that planning is essentially concerned not with logic, innovation or learning but with *power*. Planning after all is a process which allocates resources. Planning decisions affect people's lives. Planning determines where investments are made and where businesses stop investing; where jobs are created and where employees are made redundant; which new projects go forward and which existing projects are terminated. Dividends, wages and salaries, promotion and advancement, recognition and status – this is what planning is about.

The philosophy

The supporters of this idea share the view that life is a struggle for survival, a continual battle between competing groups.

In the political analyst's eyes, society is made up of organizations and interest groups which are continually competing for support from the public, from politicians and from other decision-makers in public and private organizations. Various groups in society are engaged in a struggle for power. Sometimes the opposing lines are drawn up according to social level in a type of class conflict. On other occasions, or on other issues, they may be arranged by nationality, by religious creed, by race or by sex.

Each political party or pressure group also consists of warring factions all clamouring for the attention of those in power. The business, too, is seen not as a homogeneous unit, a hierarchy led by the board, or a single culture with a common purpose. Instead the firm is conceived as a model or miniature of society itself in which department vies with department, region with region and product division with product division to gain a greater share of the firm's resources and the power which goes with them.

A major danger with this political game is that it can take everyone's eyes off the business of creating wealth. In their own interests and in the interests of society, managers and employees should be mainly concerned with building businesses: introducing new products, increasing productivity and expanding markets at home and abroad. If the political battle inside and outside the firm becomes too intense, then the energies of business leaders and trade union officials can become absorbed in continual in-fighting and negotiation. Too much effort is spent in dividing the cake and too little time is left for the battle to keep ahead of international competition.

The changing political environment

Nevertheless, the businessman has much to learn from politicians, trade unionists and the leaders of political pressure groups when it comes to influencing public opinion and using the media.

Management's authority is continually being challenged by trade unions and groups of workers, by government agencies and by pressure groups acting on behalf of consumers, conservationists, women's liberation and various ethnic minorities. Inside and outside the business the objectives, strategies and plans of management are being questioned. Groups of employees, local politicians and social action groups are rejecting or vetoing the plans of management, demanding the right to be informed or consulted – or to participate in the planning process.

These interest groups are in practice asking: 'Whose objectives?', 'Whose plans?' They oppose the idea of unilateral planning by management and claim the right to employee participation or public participation. Trade unions, committees of shop stewards and action committees working on behalf of local communities are also putting forward their own alternative plans and requesting government assistance in putting their case.

The process of planning in the political arena needs to be studied by management. A number of elements are clear.

1 *Group action.* Planning in the public arena takes place largely *between* organizations and the groups which are most successful are those which are well organized. In many cases businesses must forget their traditional animosities in working for their common good – to influence government, or to make a case when challenged by social action groups.

2 *Influence and coercion.* In the public arena it is rarely possible for one party to control the activities of another. Each group has to operate by influence and persuasion; and occasionally by threatening sanctions.

3 *Communications.* It becomes essential, therefore, for management to put their case in plain terms to company staff at all levels, to local communities, to particular interest groups, to national governments and to the general public.

4 *Building networks.* Another central activity of the top management team is to deal with the external relations or foreign policy of the firm. This means carrying on a diplomatic campaign. Maintaining liaison within professional and industrial associations, making contacts with political and social interest groups and forming alliances within the industries and in the regions where the business operates.

5 *Liaison with the media.* Continuing contact with the press, radio and television is vital. Demonstrations, protests, marches, petitions – these are the stock-in-trade of the political activist. Industry has to be prepared to put its case like other interest groups through policy statements, manifestos, national conferences, surveys and reports.

6 *Contacts with governments.* Links with government bodies need to be established on a continuing basis, directly in the case of a large firm, indirectly via a trade association for a smaller business. In either case it is essential to know how decisions will be made, who are the decision-makers, and who will influence the decisions. Also it is necessary to identify key social and political issues which are important to the company, to put forward proposals which are constructive and politically feasible – if possible speaking not just for one firm but on behalf of a sector or subsector of industry, or a region.

7 *Contact with trade unions.* Employee organizations need to be studied in the same way as government agencies, to determine the political strength of various groups, the framework of regulations and practices, the arrangements for electing officials, the ambitions and policies of various individuals, etc.

Also it is necessary to establish communications with trade union officials outside the process of wage bargaining, if possible in normal times so that an effective relationship can become established without the pressure of a crisis.

Futures research

The futures movement grew up in the late 1960s but planning in terms of 'alternative futures' only became fashionable in large companies in the late 1970s.[12] Managers in business and administrators in government are now using scenarios and other futures research techniques to try to cope with what they perceive as discontinuities. The year of the oil crisis, 1974, is seen as a watershed marking the end of an era of relative stability and affluence and the beginning of a period of turbulence and economic stagnation. In this new environment a number of trends – political, social, economic and technological – seem to be gathering momentum and interacting to create a business environment which is highly volatile.

Scenario planning

As management witnessed successive plans being rendered obsolete by unforeseen changes, they began to doubt the value of traditional forecasting and planning techniques based on extrapolation and budgeting and looked for other approaches better suited to a complex and turbulent environment. They were also convinced of the need to expand their planning and forecasting procedures to cover not only economic and market trends but also social and political changes which might be reflected in legislation and in the activities of trade unions and social pressure groups.

The result was a spate of experiments in the use of modern forecasting techniques: Delphi Studies, Cross Impact Analyses, Trend Impact Analyses, etc. Also there was an increase in the use of simple financial models aimed at examining the sensitivity of company plans to changes in assumptions, about prices, levels of sales, costs of raw materials, wages and salaries, interest rates, etc. And companies began to make tentative contingency plans – confidentially and informally to provide for major risks such as a strike, action by a social pressure group, a change of government, a new piece of legislation, the shortage or non-availability of a key raw material or component, or a substantial delay in the construction of a new facility.

However, the most impressive of these changes in planning techniques has been the increasing use of scenarios. In the late 1960s, Herman Kahn and Anthony Wiener defined scenarios as: 'hypothetical sequences of events constructed for the purpose of focusing attention on causal processes and decision points'.[13] As used in business, scenarios usually take the form of 'qualitative descriptions of the situation of a company, an industry, a nation or a region at some specified time in the future'.[14]

Coping with an uncertain environment

Scenario planning has been criticized on the grounds that it is 'a practice without a discipline'; that scenarios lack the exactness of traditional economic forecasting techniques, and there is no proof of their effectiveness. On the other hand, it is the very precision and the bogus authority of conventional approaches to forecasting which has led operating managers and those involved in forecasting to search for other methods which reflect the real uncertainty in the environment. The supporters of scenarios assert that 'it is better to be approximately right than precisely wrong'. To quote Alvin Toffler:

> Linear extrapolation, otherwise known as straight-line thinking is extremely useful and it can tell us many important things. But it works best between revolutionary periods, not in them.[15]

Scenarios are not intended to predict the future. They are designed to help executives deal with a highly uncertain environment: to assist the executive who is used to extrapolative forecasting and budgeting in coping with the unexpected.

Scenarios are not supposed to provide an accurate picture of the future: they are designed to challenge the imagination; to encourage managers to plan, not just for the most likely future but also for other alternative futures which are less likely.

Scenario planning should help managers to be more flexible in various ways.

1 Environmental scanning. It should stimulate managers to scan the business environment for 'weak signals', especially social and political changes, which might foreshadow a crisis.
2 Robust plans. It should encourage executives to produce plans which are 'robust', i.e. which may not be optimal but would keep the business profitable under a wide range of conditions.
3 Contingency planning. It should prompt managers to be prepared for contingencies, e.g. strikes, revolutions or a slump in demand.
4 Awareness of risk. It should make decision-makers more realistic about the risk to their business, social, political, technological and competitive, and persuade them to minimize the risk to the business from overdependence on any one source – a customer group, a technology, a range of products, a national or regional market.
5 Concern with flexibility. Scenario planning also invites businessmen to consider the advantages of building flexibility into their operations, i.e.:
   ● designing facilities which can be used in different ways;
   ● training staff for a broad range of tasks;
   ● consciously carrying 'slack resources' (skilled staff, extra stocks, back-up generators, etc.) in case of a crisis or a new opportunity;
   ● diversifying one's operations so as to have businesses, suppliers, production facilities, stockholding or computers in more than one country or region.

A possible danger of scenarios planning is that managers may become too preoccupied with uncertainty and risk – which is inseparable from business. As a result, they may play safe whilst their less sophisticated competitors are taking new initiatives, accepting or ignoring the risks and capitalizing on opportunities for profit and growth.

Planning without information

Futures research is a way of helping managers to think creatively about the future. This is especially important in a business where a technology, a market or the sociopolitical situation is changing quickly. In such an environment, the management have little useful information. They are planning in a vacuum. Often there is no historical data, the technology could develop in several directions; the market may not exist – the regulatory framework may not yet have been developed. Today, a surprisingly large number of businesses face this type of situation in relation to new technologies; biotechnology, cable television, telecommunications, the next generation of computers, etc. and also in international markets such as Brazil, Mexico, Nigeria, Hong Kong and the Middle East. In these cases the only sensible way of 'planning' seems to be in terms of alternative futures.

The construction of scenarios

The writing of scenarios typically involves using a number of futures research techniques. For example, the approach recommended by the General Electric Company shown in Table 2, includes the use of a Delphi Study, Trend Analysis, Trend Extrapolation, Trend Impact Analysis and Cross Impact Analysis.

A number of the techniques most commonly used in the development of scenarios are listed below.

1 Trend analysis. This involves scanning and analysing publications and other sources of information on a regular basis to plot long-term trends.
2 Computer simulations. This entails building a computer model of an enterprise or an industry and making projections on different assumptions.
3 Decision analysis. Using this technique, the analyst creates a 'road map' of decisions relating to a particular issue or project. At each step he plots the alternatives available to the 'decision-maker', the estimated payoff or loss for each course of action and the probability of success or failure.

   The technique is useful to determine the broad dimensions of a decision and as a means of keeping various options open. In analysing real decisions, however, the range of alternatives available is often far too wide for a planner to carry out a comprehensive quantitative analysis.
4 Sensitivity analysis. One of the commonest ways to explore alternative futures is by analysing the sensitivity of a plan to variations in the

Table 2 *Constructing scenarios for an industrial sector (General Electric USA)*

1 Prepare background
    Assess environmental factors – social, regulatory, technological, economic and competitive
    Develop crude 'systems' model of the industry

2 Select critical indicators
    Key indicators (trends)
    Future events affecting key indicators (literature search)
    Delphi panel to evaluate industry's future

3 Establish past behaviour for each indicator
    Historical performance
    Reasons for past behaviour of each trend
    Delphi questionnaire

4 Verify potential future events
    Delphi panel
    Past trends, future events, impact/probability, future trends
    Assumptions for forecasts, rationale for future trends

5 Forecast each indicator
    Range of future values for each indicator
    Results from literature search and Delphi study
    Trend Impact Analysis and Cross Impact Analysis

6 Write scenarios
    Guidelines for strategic business units
    Annual revision

Based on: Rochelle O'Connor, *Planning Under Uncertainty*, Conference Board, New York, p. 8 (1978)

assumptions. For this purpose it is helpful to have access to a simple computer model. Thus the planner can produce an operating statement, a cash flow analysis or a balance sheet based on different assumptions about investments, sales, costs, prices, interest rates, etc. Many companies require their subsidiaries or divisions to explore the effects of a 10 or 15 per cent increase or decrease in the major assumptions underpinning any major new project.

5 Delphi study. This is a systematic way of carrying out a poll among experts. The experts are asked a series of questions, usually concerning the likelihood of certain events taking place. Then the results are fed back to the panel and they are asked a further set of questions.

Experience to date suggests that the technique is valuable in eliciting the opinion of specialists on a narrow subject such as the probability of a breakthrough in a particular technology which they know well. It seems to be less useful in exploring social and political issues which are much less structured and where there are fewer experts. However, General Electric (USA) have used this technique to explore likely trends in population, employment, education, etc.

6 Impact analysis. This implies setting up a matrix of events which are likely to affect other events (Cross Impact Analysis) or exploring the various impacts that a particular trend may have (Trend Impact Analysis). These techniques involve weighing the likely effects and then assessing which are the most important and the most urgent.

Summary

In the modern business corporation today strategic planning is a widespread and highly diverse activity.

1 Conventional budgeting is being supplemented by a 'funds allocation' procedure based on a systematic evaluation of each business, its general environment, its competitive situation, and its strategy for the future. Also, instead of operating as a simple financial holding company, the top management of multi-industry, multinational businesses are setting out to manage their investments as a 'portfolio of businesses'.

2 It is being recognized that the process of corporate development – improving the competitive performance of existing businesses, generating new products, penetrating new markets, expanding internationally and creating or acquiring new businesses – is a prime task of top management and needs to be fostered and managed with separate budgets, plans, project teams, task forces, etc.

3 Executives who have tried to implement these kinds of changes have found that it is often not enough to set demanding targets, and ask for new strategies. It is a major problem to recruit and train managers who have the capacity to 'think strategically'. Usually a team of managers needs to work together over a period of time. They have to develop a new information system which relates to strategic issues rather than operational problems. Often the organization structure has to be changed to pull out the separate businesses, or to coordinate strategies internationally in world-wide product divisions. The way managers are appraised and rewarded also needs to be adjusted to demonstrate that the development of new strategies and new businesses is just as important as the achievement of this year's targets.

4 The managements of most large business corporations now find themselves in a continual dialogue with governments, international agencies, trade unions, social pressure groups and the media. To handle this sociopolitical area they now have public affairs' departments and external consultants who monitor social trends, forecast emerging sociopolitical issues and formulate action programmes to safeguard the interests of the business and to help to contribute to the solution of social problems, such as unemployment and the decline of city centres.

5 In businesses which have to cope with a great deal of uncertainty, e.g. in new and growing technologies, in countries which are politically unstable, or in fluctuating international markets, managers have been

forced to 'plan' in terms of alternative futures using simulations, scenarios and contingency plans rather than traditional forecasting based on extrapolation.

Dealing with crises

The strategic planning processes all take time to put into operation. But what about the firm which is in crisis? Often the company which is in a turnaround situation is there because its top management have not been able to think strategically, to anticipate international competition or the appearance of a new technology, and to develop new products or enter new markets in good time.

Their most urgent need is usually to improve the cash flow and buy time by closing loss-making businesses, cutting overheads, reducing staff, selling off assets, etc. But the next step should be to produce a strategy for the future, and to buy or build new businesses. It is interesting to note that in these crisis situations, top managers in such firms as Fisons, the Burton Group, Scandinavian Airlines and Electrolux have discovered that strategic thinking or strategic management is extremely effective without the usual apparatus of five-year planning, portfolio analysis, scenarios, etc.

Notes

1. For a list of the publications in each of these schools of thought see: B. Taylor, 'New dimensions in corporate planning', *Long Range Planning*, December (1976).
2. Robert N. Anthony, *Planning and Control Systems – A Framework for Analysis*, p. 67, Harvard University, Boston (1965).
3. Joseph Bower, *Managing the Resource Allocation Process*, p. 54, Harvard (1970).
4. Peter F. Drucker, *Landmarks of Tomorrow* (1959).
5. John W. Gardner, *Self-Renewal – The Individual and the Innovative Society*, p. 5, Harper & Row, New York (1963).
6. Boston Consulting Group, *Strategic Alternatives for the British Motorcycle Industry* (2 vols.), Department of Industry, HMSO, London (1975).
7. Donald A. Schon, *Beyond the Stable State*, p. 67, Temple Smith, London (1971).
8. Peter F. Drucker, 'Entrepreneurship in business enterprise', *Journal of Business Policy*, 1 (1), Autumn (1970).
9. Donald A. Schon, *Beyond the Stable State*, p. 30, Temple Smith, London (1971).
10. Donald N. Michael, *On Learning to Plan and Planning to Learn*, p. 19, Jossey-Bass (1973).
11. J. Friedman, 'The future of comprehensive urban planning: a critique', *Public Administration Review*, 31 (3): 325 (1971).
12. See Rochelle O'Connor, *Planning Under Uncertainty: Multiple Scenarios and Contingency Planning*, Conference Board, New York (1978).
13. Herman Kahn and Anthony Wiener, *The Year 2000*, p. 6, Macmillan, New York (1967).
14. Recent scenarios developed in the UK cover, for example: the British economy, unemployment, supply and demand for energy, banking, the chemical industry, television, the world pharmaceutical industry and the future for Japan.
15. *Choosing Our Environment: Can We Anticipate the Future?* Senate Committee Report, Washington (1976).

20

Ethical managers make their own rules

Sir Adrian Cadbury

In 1900 Queen Victoria sent a decorative tin with a bar of chocolate inside to all of her soldiers who were serving in South Africa. These tins still turn up today, often complete with their contents, a tribute to the collecting instinct. At the time, the order faced my grandfather with an ethical dilemma. He owned and ran the second-largest chocolate company in Britain, so he was trying harder and the order meant additional work for the factory. Yet he was deeply and publicly opposed to the Anglo-Boer War. He resolved the dilemma by accepting the order, but carrying it out at cost. He therefore made no profit out of what he saw as an unjust war, his employees benefitted from the additional work, the soldiers received their royal present, and I am still sent the tins.

My grandfather was able to resolve the conflict between the decision best for his business and his personal code of ethics because he and his family owned the firm which bore their name. Certainly his dilemma would have been more acute if he had had to take into account the interests of outside shareholders, many of whom would no doubt have been in favor both of the war and of profiting from it. But even so, not all my grandfather's ethical dilemmas could be as straightforwardly resolved.

So strongly did my grandfather feel about the South African War that he acquired and financed the only British newspaper which opposed it. He was also against gambling, however, and so he tried to run the paper without any references to horse racing. The effect on the newspaper's circulation was such that he had to choose between his ethical beliefs. He decided, in the end, that it was more important that the paper's voice be heard as widely as possible than that gambling should thereby receive some mild encouragement. The decision was doubtless a relief to those working on the paper and to its readers.

The way that my grandfather settled these two clashes of principle brings out some practical points about ethics and business decisions. In the first place, the possibility that ethical and commercial considerations will conflict has always faced those who run companies. It is not a new

Reprinted from *Harvard Business Review*, Sept/Oct 1987: 69–73. Copyright © 1987 by the President and Fellows of Harvard College.

problem. The difference now is that a more widespread and critical interest is being taken in our decisions and in the ethical judgments which lie behind them.

Secondly, as the newspaper example demonstrates, ethical signposts do not always point in the same direction. My grandfather had to choose between opposing a war and condoning gambling. The rule that it is best to tell the truth often runs up against the rule that we should not hurt people's feeling unnecessarily. There is no simple, universal formula for solving ethical problems. We have to choose from our own codes of conduct, whichever rules are appropriate to the case in hand; the outcome of those choices makes us who we are.

Lastly, while it is hard enough to resolve dilemmas when our personal rules of conduct conflict, the real difficulties arise when we have to make decisions which affect the interests of others. We can work out what weighting to give to our own rules through trial and error. But business decisions require us to do the same for others by allocating weights to all the conflicting interests which may be involved. Frequently, for example, we must balance the interests of employees against those of shareholders. But even that sounds more straightforward than it really is, because there may well be differing views among the shareholders, and the interests of past, present, and future employees are unlikely to be identical.

Eliminating ethical considerations from business decisions would simplify the management task, and Milton Friedman has urged something of the kind in arguing that the interaction between business and society should be left to the political process. 'Few trends could so thoroughly undermine the very foundation of our free society,' he writes in *Capitalism and Freedom*, 'as the acceptance by corporate officials of a social responsibility other than to make as much money for their shareholders as possible.'

But the simplicity of this approach is deceptive. Business is part of the social system and we cannot isolate the economic elements of major decisions from their social consequences. So there are no simple rules. Those who make business decisions have to assess the economic and social consequences of their actions as well as they can and come to their conclusions on limited information and in a limited time.

We judge companies – and managers – by their actions, not their pious statements of intent

As will already be apparent, I use the word ethics to mean the guidelines or rules of conduct by which we aim to live. It is, of course, foolhardy to write about ethics at all, because you lay yourself open to the charge of taking up a position of moral superiority, of failing to practice what you preach, or both. I am not in a position to preach nor am I promoting a specific code of conduct. I believe, however, that it is useful to all of us who are responsible for business decisions to acknowledge the part which ethics plays in those decisions and to encourage discussion of how best to combine commercial and ethical judgments. Most business decisions involve some degree of ethical judgment; few can be taken solely on the basis of arithmetic.

While we refer to a company as having a set of standards, that is a convenient shorthand. The people who make up the company are responsible for its conduct and it is their collective actions which determine the company's standards. The ethical standards of a company are judged by its actions, not by pious statements of intent put out in its name. This does not mean that those who head companies should not set down what they believe their companies stand for, hard though that is to do. The character of a company is a matter of importance to those in it, to those who do business with it, and to those who are considering joining it.

What matters most, however, is where we stand as individual managers and how we behave when faced with decisions which require us to combine ethical and commercial judgments. In approaching such decisions, I believe it is helpful to go through two steps. The first is to determine, as precisely as we can, what our personal rules of conduct are. This does not mean drawing up a list of virtuous notions, which will probably end up as a watered-down version of the Scriptures without their literary merit. It does mean looking back at decisions we have made and working out from there what our rules actually are. The aim is to avoid confusing ourselves and everyone else by declaring one set of principles and acting on another. Our ethics are expressed in our actions, which is why they are usually clearer to others than to ourselves.

Once we know where we stand personally we can move on to the second step, which is to think through who else will be affected by the decision and how we should weight their interests in it. Some interests will be represented by well-organized groups, others will have no one to put their case. If a factory manager is negotiating a wage claim with employee representatives, their remit is to look after the interest of those who are already employed. Yet the effect of the wage settlement on the factory's costs may well determine whether new employees are likely to be taken on. So the manager cannot ignore the interest of potential employees in the outcome of the negotiation, even though that interest is not represented at the bargaining table.

Black and white alternatives are a regrettable sign of the times

The rise of organized interest groups makes it doubly important that managers consider the arguments of everyone with a legitimate interest in a decision's outcome. Interest groups seek publicity to promote their causes and they have the advantage of being single-minded: they are against building an airport on a certain site, for example, but take no responsibility for finding a better alternative. This narrow focus gives pressure groups a debating advantage against managements, which cannot evade the responsibility for taking decisions in the same way.

In *The Hard Problems of Management*, Mark Pastin has perceptively referred to this phenomenon as the ethical superiority of the uninvolved, and there is a good deal of it about. Pressure groups are skilled at seizing the high moral ground and arguing that our judgments as managers is at best biased and at worst influenced solely by private gain because we have a direct commercial interest in the outcome of our decisions. But as managers we are also responsible for arriving at business decisions which take account of all the interests concerned; the uninvolved are not.

At times the campaign to persuade companies to divest themselves of their South African subsidiaries has exemplified this kind of ethical high-handedness. Apartheid is abhorrent politically, socially, and morally. Those who argue that they can exert some influence on the direction of change by staying put believe this as sincerely as those who favor divestment. Yet many anti-apartheid campaigners reject the proposition that both sides have the same end in view. From their perspective it is self-evident that the only ethical course of action is for companies to wash their hands of the problems of South Africa by selling out.

Managers cannot be so self-assured. In deciding what weight to give to the arguments for and against divestment, we must consider who has what at stake in the outcome of the decision. The employees of a South African subsidiary have the most direct stake, as the decision affects their future; they are also the group whose voice is least likely to be heard outside South Africa. The shareholders have at stake any loss on divestment, against which must be balanced any gain in the value of their shares through severing the South African connection. The divestment lobby is the one group for whom the decision is costless either way.

What is clear even from this limited analysis is that there is no general answer to the question of whether companies should sell their South African subsidiaries or not. Pressure to reduce complicated issues to straightforward alternatives, one of which is right and the other wrong, is a regrettable sign of the times. But boards are rarely presented with two clearly opposed alternatives. Companies faced with the same issues will therefore properly come to different conclusions and their decisions may alter over time.

A less contentious divestment decision faced my own company when we decided to sell our foods division. Because the division was mainly a UK business with regional brands, it did not fit the company's strategy, which called for concentrating resources behind our confectionery and soft drinks brands internationally. But it was an attractive business in its own right and the decision to sell prompted both a management bid and external offers.

Employees working in the division strongly supported the management bid and made their views felt. In this instance, they were the best organized interest group and they had more information available to them to back their case than any of the other parties involved. What they had at stake was also very clear.

From the shareholders' point of view, the premium over asset value offered by the various bidders was a key aspect of the decision. They also had an interest in seeing the deal completed without regulatory delays and without diverting too much management attention from the ongoing business. In addition, the way in which the successful bidder would guard the brand name had to be considered, since the division would take with it products carrying the parent company's name.

In weighing the advantages and disadvantages of the various offers, the board considered all the groups, consumers among them, who would be affected by the sale. But our main task was to reconcile the interests of the employees and of the shareholders. (The more, of course, we can encourage employees to become shareholders, the closer together the interests of these two stakeholders will be brought.) The division's management upped its bid in the face of outside competition, and after due deliberation we decided to sell to the management team, believing that this choice best balanced the diverse interests at stake.

Actions are unethical if they won't stand scrutiny

Companies whose activities are international face an additional complication in taking their decisions. They aim to work to the same standards of business conduct wherever they are and to behave as good corporate citizens of the countries in which they trade. But the two aims are not always compatible: promotion on merit may be the rule of the company and promotion by seniority the custom of the country. In addition, while the financial arithmetic on which companies base their decisions is generally accepted, what is considered ethical varies among cultures.

If what would be considered corruption in the company's home territory is an accepted business practice elsewhere, how are local managers expected to act? Companies could do business only in countries in which they feel ethically at home, provided always that their shareholders take the same view. But this approach could prove unduly restrictive, and there is also a certain arrogance in dismissing foreign codes of conduct without considering why they may be different. If companies find, for example, that they have to pay customs officers in another country just to do their job, it may be that the state is simply transferring its responsibilities to the private sector as an alternative to using taxation less efficiently to the same end.

Nevertheless, this example brings us to one of the most common ethical issues companies face – how far to go in buying business? What payments are legitimate for companies to make to win orders and, the reverse side of the coin, when do gifts to employees become bribes? I use two rules of thumb to test whether a payment is acceptable from the company's point of view: Is the payment on the face of the invoice? Would it embarrass the recipient to have the gift mentioned in the company's newsletter?

The first test ensures that all payments, however unusual they may seem, are recorded and go through the books. The second is aimed at distinguishing bribes from gifts, a definition which depends on the size of the gift and the influence it is likely to have on the recipient. The value of a case of whiskey to me would be limited, because I only take it as medicine. We know ourselves whether a gift is acceptable or not and we know that others will know if they are aware of the nature of the gift.

As for payment on the face of the invoice, I have found it a useful general rule precisely because codes of conduct do vary round the world. It has legitimized some otherwise unlikely company payments, to the police in one country, for example, and to the official planning authorities in another, but all went through the books and were audited. Listing a payment on the face of the invoice may not be a sufficient ethical test, but it is a necessary one; payments outside the company's system are corrupt and corrupting.

The logic behind these rules of thumb is that openness and ethics go together and that actions are unethical if they will not stand scrutiny. Openness in arriving at decisions reflects the same logic. It gives those with an interest in a particular decision the chance to make their views known and opens to argument the basis on which the decision is finally taken. This in turn enables the decision-makers to learn from experience and to improve their powers of judgment.

Openness is also, I believe, the best way to disarm outside suspicion of companies' motives and actions. Disclosure is not a panacea for improving the relations between business and society, but the willingness to operate an open system is the foundation of those relations. Business needs to be open to the views of society and open in return about its own activities; this is essential for the establishment of trust.

For the same reasons, as managers we need to be candid when making decisions about other people. Dr Johnson reminds us that when it comes to lapidary inscriptions, 'no man is upon oath.' But what should be disclosed in references, in fairness to those looking for work and to those who are considering employing them?

The simplest rule would seem to be that we should write the kind of reference we would wish to read. Yet 'do as you would be done by' says nothing about ethics. The actions which result from applying it could be ethical or unethical, depending on the standards of the initiator. The rule could be adapted to help managers determine their ethical standards, however, by reframing it as a question: If you did business with yourself, how ethical would you think you were?

Anonymous letters accusing an employee of doing something discreditable create another context in which candor is the wisest course.

Such letters cannot by definition be answered, but they convey a message to those who receive them, however warped or unfair the message may be. I normally destroy these letters, but tell the person concerned what has been said. This conveys the disregard I attach to nameless allegation, but preserves the rule of openness. From a practical point of view, it serves as a warning if there is anything in the allegations; from an ethical point of view, the degree to which my judgment of the person may now be prejudiced is known between us.

Shelving hard decisions is the least ethical course

The last aspect of ethics in business decisions I want to discuss concerns our responsibility for the level of employment; what can or should companies do about the provision of jobs? This issue is of immediate concern to European managers because unemployment is higher in Europe than it is in the United States and the net number of new jobs created has been much lower. It comes to the fore whenever companies face decisions which require a trade-off between increasing efficiency and reducing numbers employed.

If you believe, as I do, that the primary purpose of a company is to satisfy the needs of its customers and to do so profitably, the creation of jobs cannot be the company's goal as well. Satisfying customers requires companies to compete in the marketplace, and so we cannot opt out of introducing new technology, for example, to preserve jobs. To do so would be to deny consumers the benefits of progress, to short-change the shareholders, and in the longer run to put the jobs of everyone in the company at risk. What destroys jobs certainly and permanently is the failure to be competitive.

Experience says that the introduction of new technology creates more jobs than it eliminates, in ways which cannot be forecast. It may do so, however, only after a time lag, and those displaced may not, through lack of skills, be able to take advantage of the new opportunities when they arise. Nevertheless, the company's prime responsibility to everyone who has a stake in it is to retain its competitive edge, even if this means a loss of jobs in the short run.

Where companies do have a social responsibility, however, is in how we manage that situation, how we smooth the path of technological change. Companies are responsible for the timing of such changes and we are in a position to involve those who will be affected by the way in which those changes are introduced. We also have a vital resource in our capacity to provide training, so that continuing employees can take advantage of change and those who may lose their jobs can more readily find new ones.

In the United Kingdom, an organization called Business in the Community has been established to encourage the formation of new enterprises. Companies have backed it with cash and with secondments.

The secondment of able managers to worthwhile institutions is a particularly effective expression of concern, because the ability to manage is such a scarce resource. Through Business in the Community we can create jobs collectively, even if we cannot do so individually, and it is clearly in our interest to improve the economic and social climate in this way.

Throughout, I have been writing about the responsibilities of those who head companies and my emphasis has been on taking decisions, because that is what directors and managers are appointed to do. What concerns me is that too often the public pressures which are put on companies in the name of ethics encourage their boards to put off decisions or to wash their hands of problems. There may well be commercial reasons for those choices, but there are rarely ethical ones. The ethical bases on which decisions are arrived at will vary among companies, but shelving those decisions is likely to be the least ethical course.

The company which takes drastic action in order to survive is more likely to be criticized publicly than the one which fails to grasp the nettle and gradually but inexorably declines. There is always a temptation to postpone difficult decisions, but it is not in society's interests that hard choices should be evaded because of public clamor or the possibility of legal action. Companies need to be encouraged to take the decisions which face them; the responsibility for providing that encouragement rests with society as a whole.

Society sets the ethical framework within which those who run companies have to work out their own codes of conduct. Responsibility for decisions, therefore, runs both ways. Business has to take account of its responsibilities to society in coming to its decisions, but society has to accept its responsibilities for setting the standards against which those decisions are made.

Note

This chapter won *Harvard Business Review*'s 1986 Ethics in Business Prize for the best original article written and submitted by a corporate manager on the ethical problems business executives face.

References

Friedman, Milton (1963) *Capitalism and Freedom*. Chicago: University of Chicago Press.
Pastin, Mark (1986) *The Hard Problems of Management*. USA: Jossey-Bass.

Index

industry compared with Japan 198, *200*,
	220–1, 229–30
R & D expenditure 201, 202–3, *209*, 211

Vail, Theodore 120, 123, 125, 127
value, Marxist theory 168, 190
value activities, configuration 137–9
variables, key, in prospective approach 59
vision, strategic 125, 249, 256, 266, 275

Wack, Pierre 233, 235–54

Wallace, C.D. & Pahl, R. 178
Weber, Max 160
Whaley, Barton 250
Williams, Raymond 172, 191
Williamson, Oliver E. 74, 75–100
Wohlstetter, Roberta 250–1
work, informal, *see* economy, informal

Yamaha, war with Honda 221–2
Yanmar Diesel, flexible production 220
Young, Patricia 111